IMAGES
of America

LUDLOW

IMAGES
of America

LUDLOW

Karen E. Pilon

ARCADIA
PUBLISHING

Copyright © 1999 by Karen E. Pilon
ISBN 978-0-7385-0224-3

Published by Arcadia Publishing
Charleston, South Carolina

Printed in the United States of America

Library of Congress Catalog Card Number: 2008940652

For all general information contact Arcadia Publishing at:
Telephone 843-853-2070
Fax 843-853-0044
E-mail sales@arcadiapublishing.com
For customer service and orders:
Toll-Free 1-888-313-2665

Visit us on the Internet at www.arcadiapublishing.com

Contents

Acknowledgments

The decision to do this book came easily. There were, however, several times when I wondered what had I gotten myself into, but throughout the whole process, I believed that it was all worth it. Ludlow deserved to have its history in pictures where everyone could see it, and I was determined to get it done. This book is intended to coax a smile, spark some memories, and show the younger generations what our town means to all of us.

My deepest thanks go to my parents, Don and Betty Kibbe, because (obviously) I wouldn't be here without them. They instilled in me a deep love of the land and a great respect for history. My first taste of history was growing up in my parents old saltbox house with my sisters, Diane and Sarah. In the early 1970s, we were exposed to all sorts of noises, doors opening by themselves, and weird, unexplained occurrences. That always had me thinking, "what happened long ago?"

Many thanks to my husband, Kent, for his help with the computer logistics and to our children, Nathan and Audrey, who sometimes got impatient with me (and vice versa!). They're glad the book is done!

I would also like to thank my co-members on the Ludlow Historical Commission: Betty Kibbe (chairperson), Elsie Hiersche, Lillian Lewison, Edna White, Muriel Francisco, John Meyrick, Joe Kozaczka, and Al LeMay, all of whom supported this endeavor. To Elsie Hiersche and her husband, Tom, who passed away on July 18, 1999, many thanks. Without their bits of information and thoughts, I would have been lost. Thank you to my good friend Ruth Gilman, who so graciously loaned pictures, as did my parents. A note of gratitude also to the late Herbert McChesney, former town historian, as much of the pictures in this book come from his old files. Thanks also go to my brother-in-law Kirk Pilon and his wife Dee (my "other sister"), not only for the use of their computer and printer but for their enthusiasm about my project. Thank you to Ludlow Printing and to the women in the town clerk's office who tolerated my odd comings and goings. To non-residents who pick up this book, enjoy a bit of our little town and come for a visit. To the people of Ludlow, past, present, and future, enjoy!

INTRODUCTION

The Ludlow of today is vastly different than the Ludlow of 225 years ago. When Ludlow broke away from Springfield and signed its charter on February 28, 1774, some 200 to 300 people called it home. There were no bridges over the Chicopee River, only fords, which were often impassable. The earliest references to a bridge were about 1781. Ludlow was largely an agricultural community with many sawmills and gristmills, as three major streams snaked through town in addition to the Chicopee River. Farms in 1800 averaged in size from 50 to 100 acres. Dairy, poultry, and sheep farms were in abundance, as farmers needed to sustain their own families as well as turn a profit.

About 1900, the mills started popping up along the Chicopee River, drawing much of the population to the downtown or village area; today, this area is comprised of East, Sewall, and State Streets. The Ludlow Manufacturing Associates were responsible for the migration; they provided schools, housing, a hospital, and recreational facilities for mill employees.

Even as the 20th century progressed, Ludlow remained small and quiet. When the baby boom hit after World War II, new housing developments sprang up. Much of Ludlow's farmland was lost to construction: the building of the Ludlow Reservoir in 1873; the building of the Westover Air Force Base (now Westover Air Reserve Base) in the late 1930s; and the building of the Massachusetts Turnpike in the 1950s.

Today, Ludlow has a population of about 19,000, and her people are a mix of all cultures. We are proud of our town; every 25 years brings a parade, town picnic, and celebrations of that nature. This year, 1999, marks the 225th anniversary of Ludlow's incorporation. Ludlow boasts no claims to fame, and no inns tout that "George Washington slept here." No revolutions were started here, and that is probably just as well. Ludlow's people lived quietly and comfortably, enjoying life. It sounds a bit like the Ludlow of today.

One

Early Ludlow

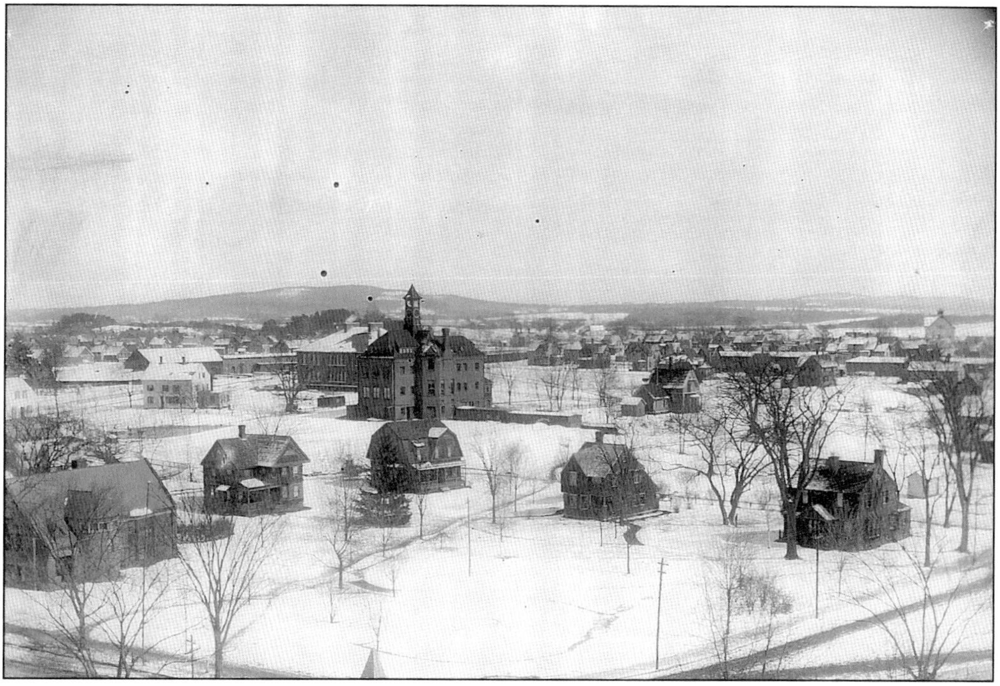

Ludlow Village, c. 1910. This overview shows Ludlow at the turn of the 20th century. Very much a mill town at this time, the housing, the library, and Union School (center) were all provided by the Ludlow Manufacturing Company. Sawmills and gristmills were abundant in the early 1800s, giving Ludlow a vast agricultural and rural area. In the 1870s, the Ludlow Manufacturing Company was formed, thus attracting residents and employees to the village or "downtown" area. The exact origin of the name Ludlow is not known; most likely, it was taken from a prominent resident by the name of Roger Ludlow (a contemporary of William Pynchon, the founder of Springfield, Massachusetts).

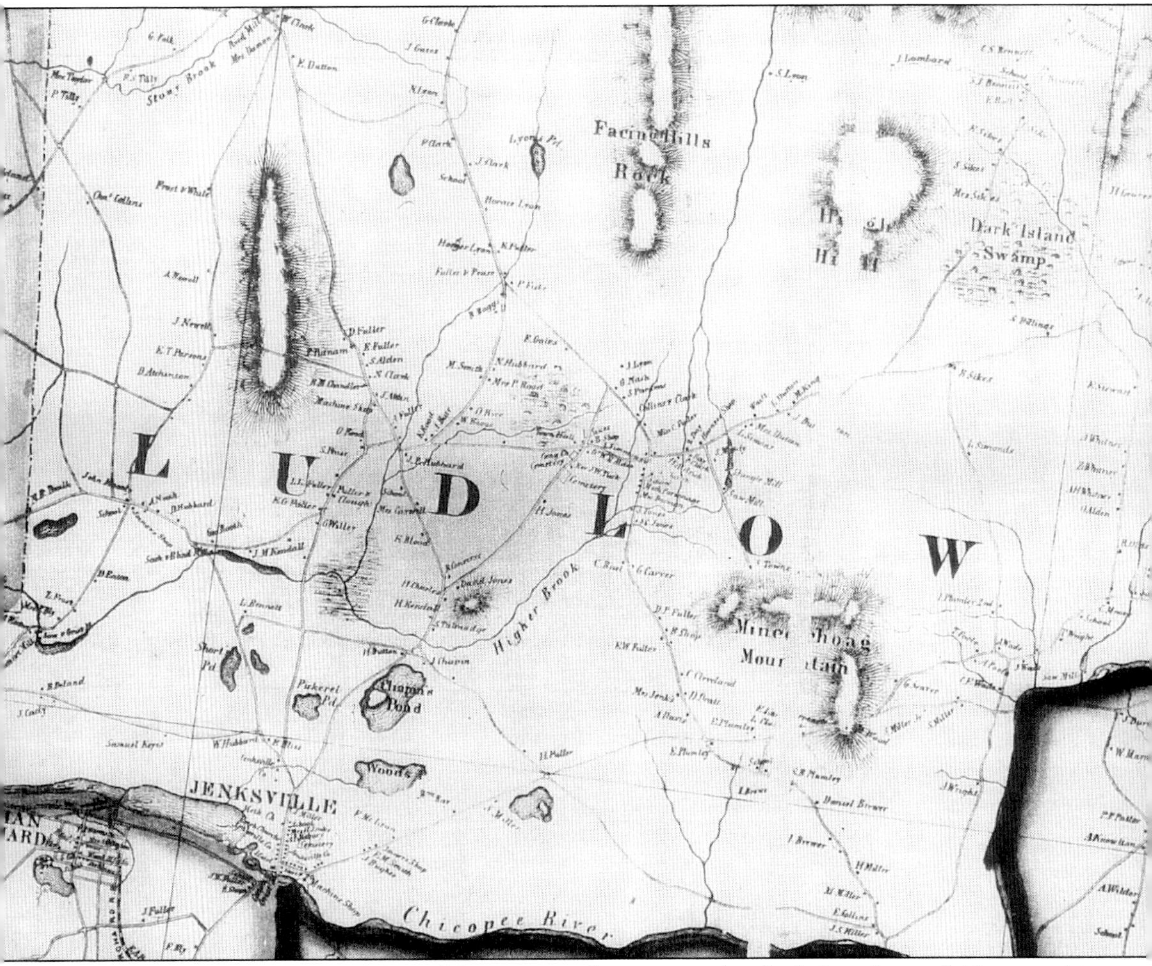

MAP OF LUDLOW, 1857. Most of the main roads remain today; little has changed. Note on this map, family names are listed along each road, denoting residences. Originally part of Springfield, Ludlow was incorporated on February 28, 1774. Some early settlers included the families of Joseph Miller, Aaron Colton, Shem Chapin, Joshua Fuller, and James Miller. On Facing Hills Rock, high above the town, a bungalow belonging to Frederick Burr once stood. The stone foundation still remains, although time and vandals have taken their toll.

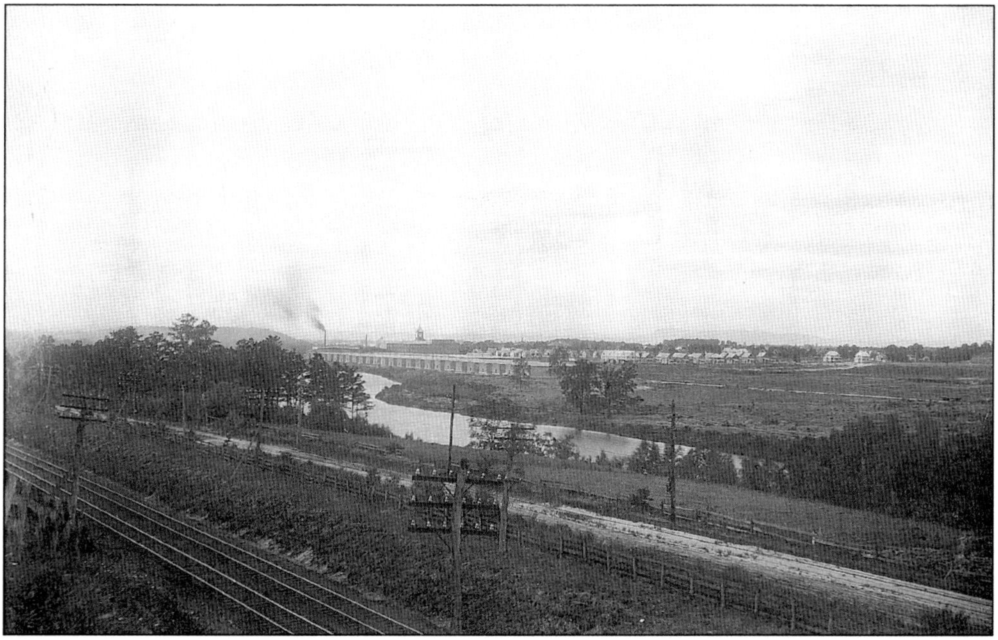

Ludlow Manufacturing Company, View from North Wilbraham. This view shows the rows of mills on the north side of the Chicopee River. The clock tower is also visible above the other mills. Housing for the mill employees spreads out around the outskirts.

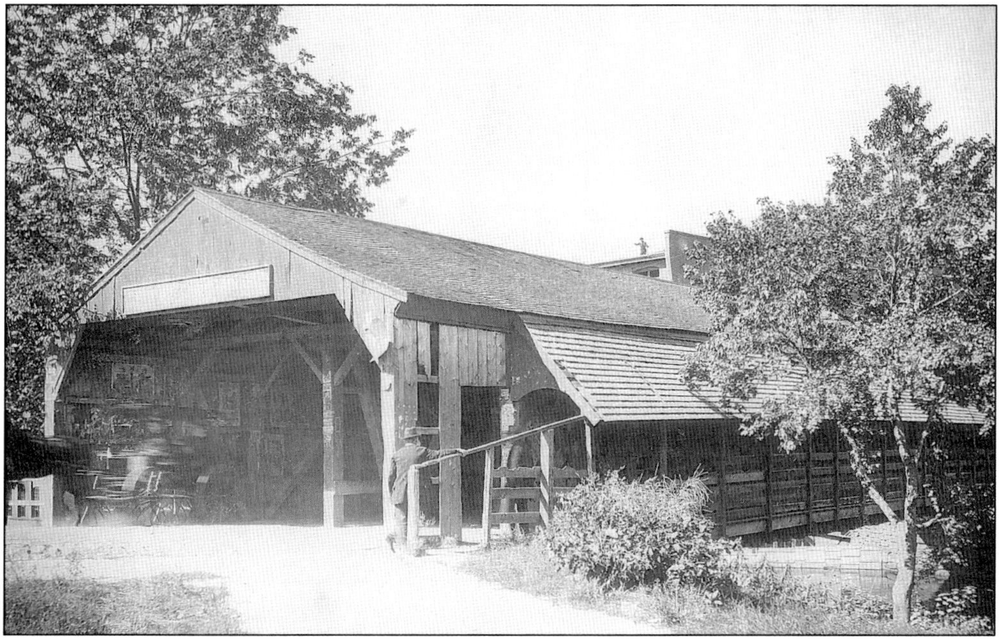

Put's Bridge, South Side, July 1897. This photograph was taken shortly before construction started on a new iron bridge. Many attempts were made to bridge the Chicopee River in several places, and these bridges often needed replacing. The new iron bridge, which was built to replace this one, was needed to accommodate the ever-increasing traffic, and the present one was built in 1931. The one shown was built in 1822 and replaced with a deck-type iron bridge in 1898.

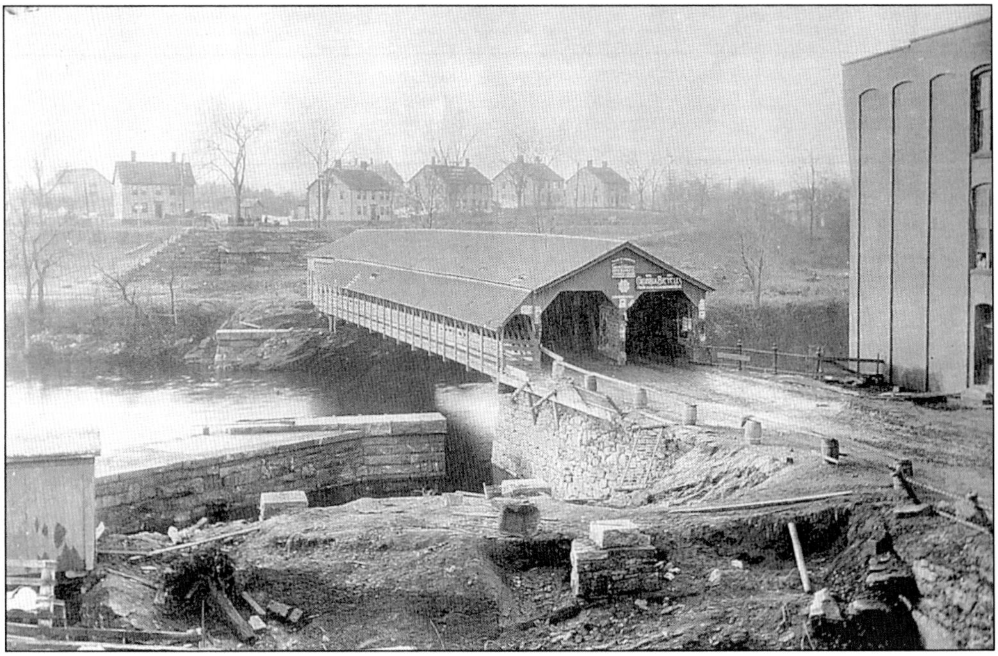

PUT'S BRIDGE, DECEMBER 1897. This view is from the Ludlow side, showing Indian Orchard across the river. Construction on the new iron bridge would begin soon. Its location is to the left in this picture.

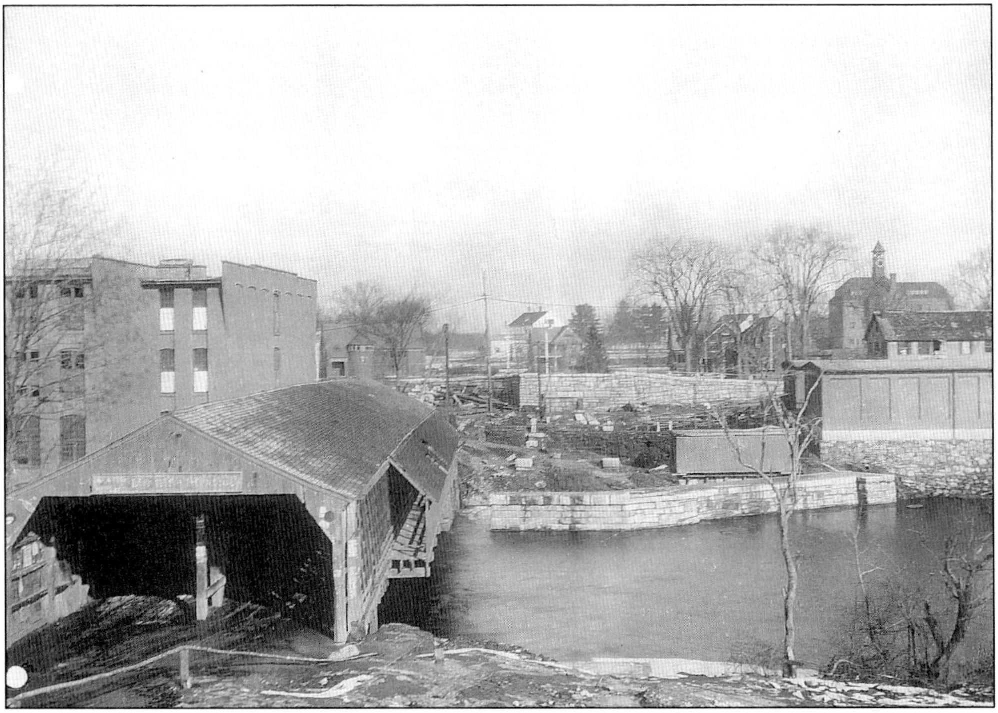

PUT'S BRIDGE, DECEMBER 1897. Here we see the old abutment from the Springfield or Indian Orchard side. Note the pedestrian walkway is partially torn away. Hubbard Memorial Library and the Union School are seen in the background.

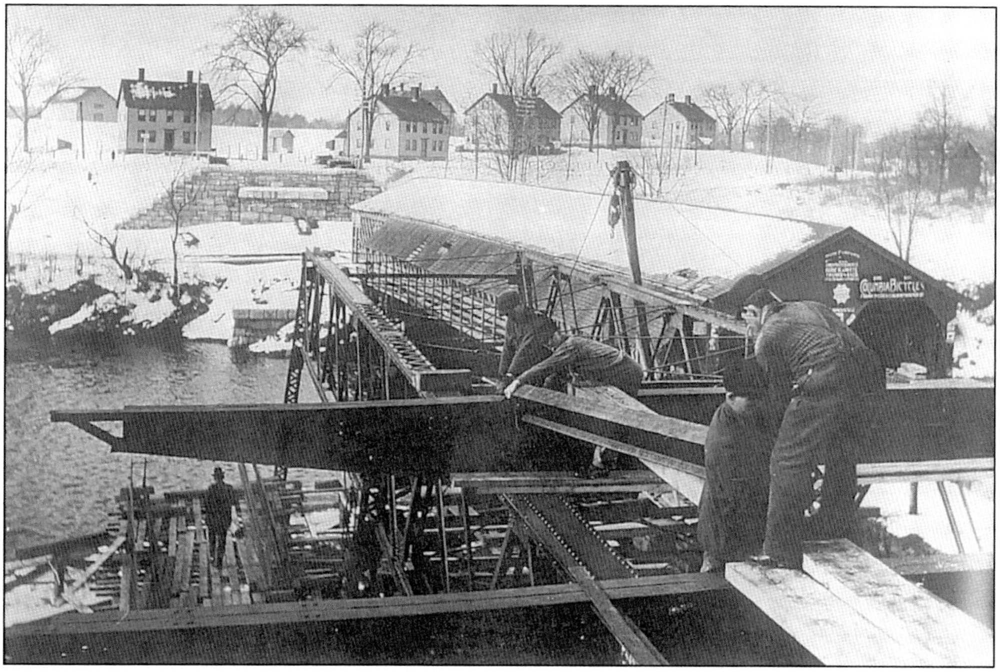

LAYING BEAMS, FEBRUARY 1898. Shown here in the midst of snow, the bridge was being completed. Formal opening ceremonies were held on April 16, 1898. The cost to build the bridge, $29,477, was shared by the Town of Ludlow, the Ludlow Manufacturing Company, and the City of Springfield. Over the next 30 years, increasing traffic weakened the bridge, and it was demolished in October 1930. The number of travelers across the river was limited until construction on the present-day bridge was completed in early 1931.

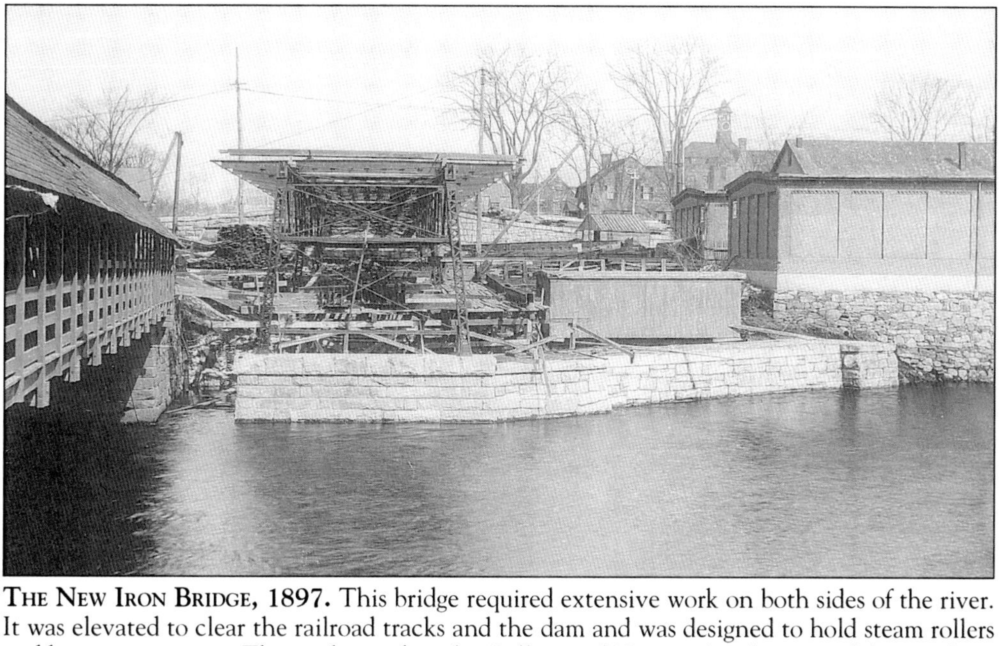

THE NEW IRON BRIDGE, 1897. This bridge required extensive work on both sides of the river. It was elevated to clear the railroad tracks and the dam and was designed to hold steam rollers and heavy equipment. The work was done by Collins and Norton, local agents of the Pittsburg Bridge Company.

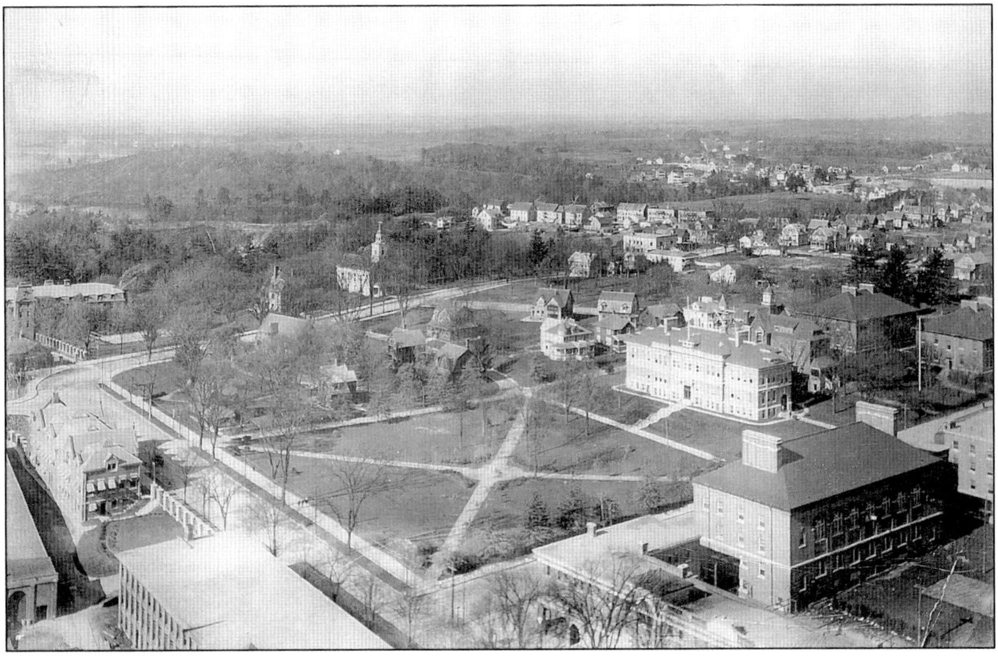

EAST STREET PARK. This photo, taken c. 1911, shows Ludlow Village at its peak. Shown at the bottom, left-hand corner are the mill offices: (counter clockwise) the business block on East Street, the Stevens Memorial Building, and the new Ludlow High School. Mill employee houses are seen on the outskirts of the village.

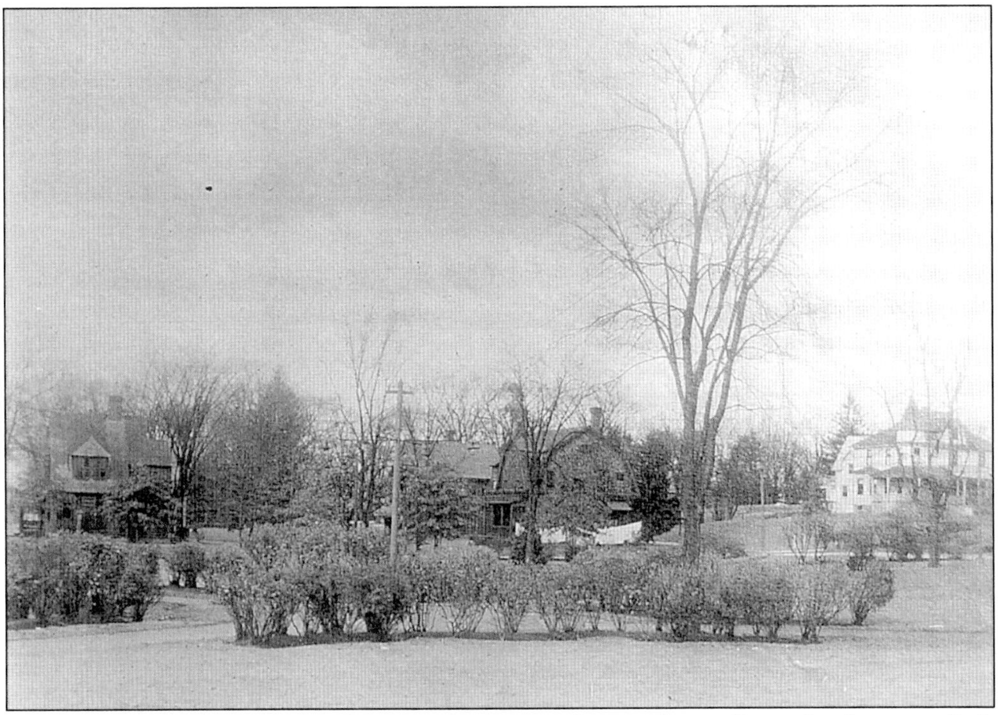

EAST STREET PARK, C. 1910. This view shows some houses that still stand today, near Park Street.

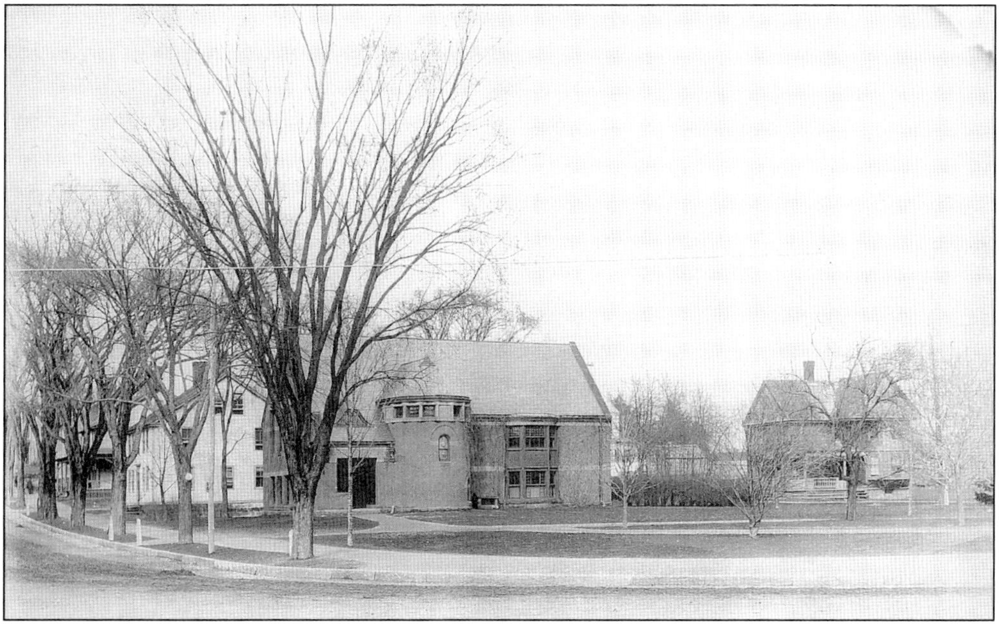

HUBBARD MEMORIAL LIBRARY, c. 1910. Charles Townsend Hubbard, founder of the Ludlow Manufacturing Company, had a dream of a library for his employees and the townspeople to use, free of charge. Mr. Hubbard died in January of 1887, and his widow and children proposed a building to be given to the town as a public library. The library was built in 1889, and in the spring of 1890, it was presented to the town. One hundred years later, in 1989, the library was expanded, and in 1990, it reopened to the public.

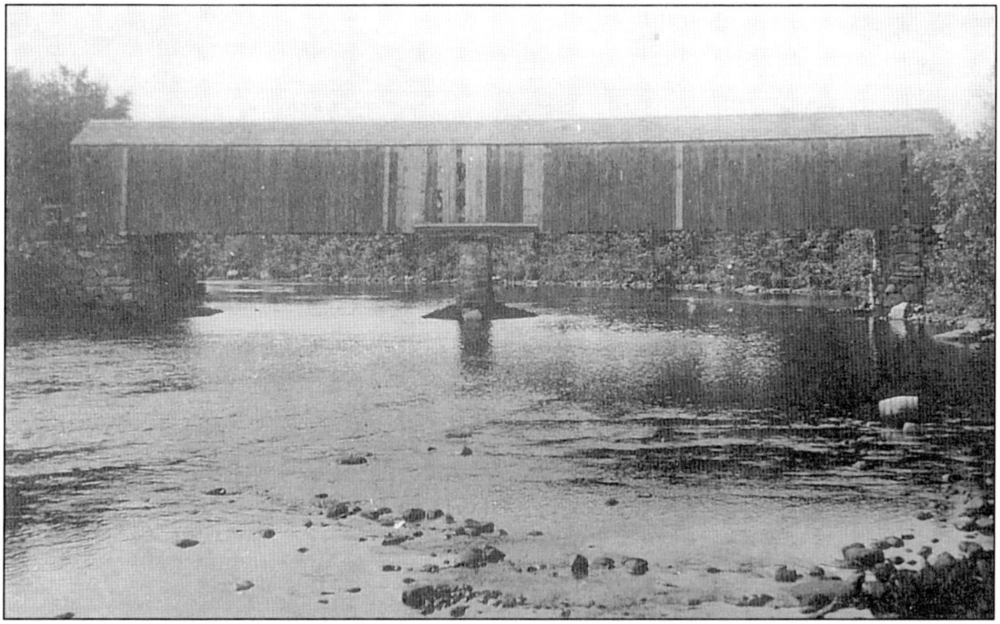

RED BRIDGE, c. 1900. This bridge over the Chicopee River, farther upstream from the Falls at Wallamanumps, was planned in 1836 and built in 1837. An overhaul was done in 1873, and then, the bridge was torn down in 1900 to build a heavier one, necessary for the hauling of machinery for construction of the Red Bridge Dam and Power Plant.

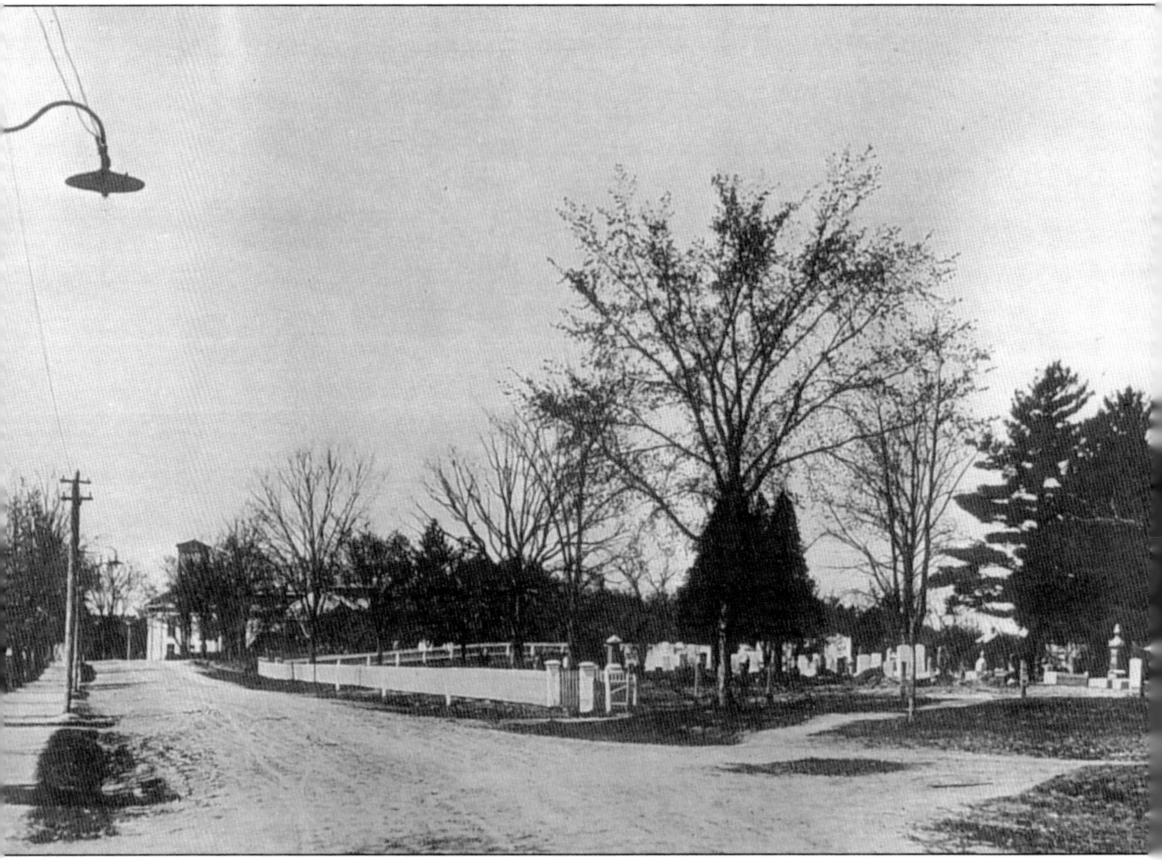

WINSOR STREET CEMETERY, MAY 1902. Located on the site of the present-day Masonic Temple and several residences, this cemetery was used in the early to mid-1800s and was known as the Jenksville or Village Cemetery. In 1902, the town voted to close the cemetery; the remains of the deceased were removed and reinterred at Island Pond Cemetery on Center Street.

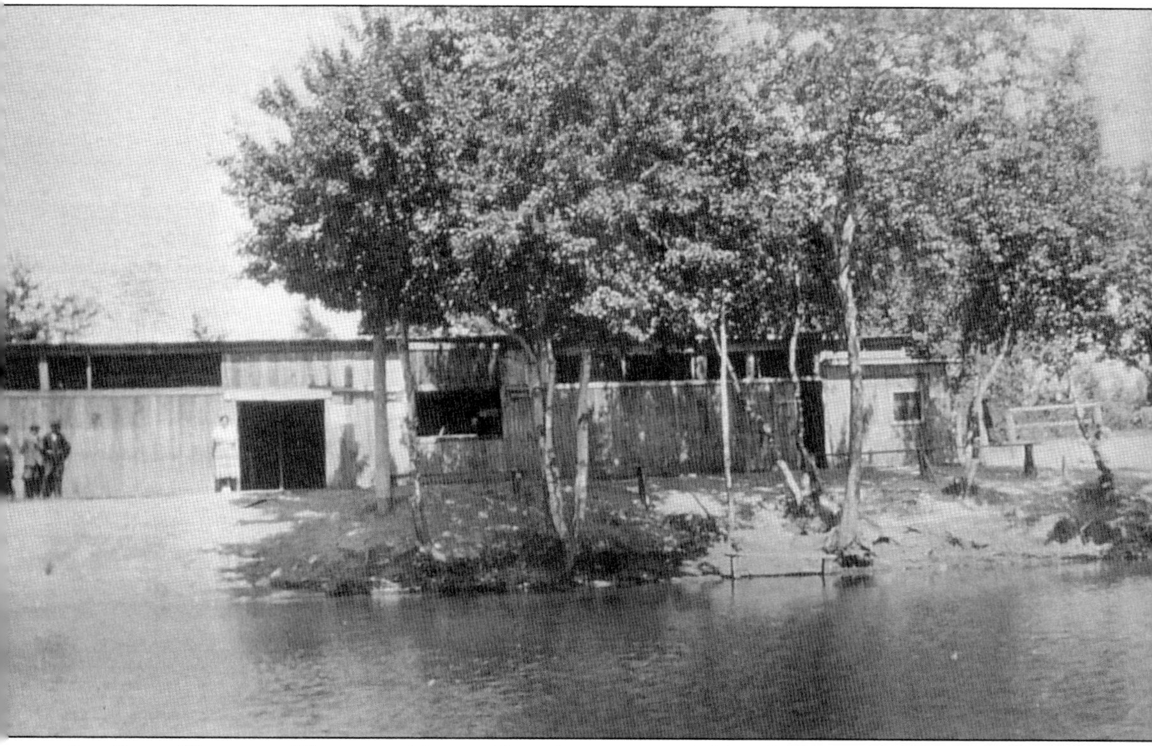

OLD BATH HOUSE AT HAVILAND POND. This photo was probably taken around 1900. Haviland Pond, with its own island and large, sandy beach, was a favorite place to gather. This bathhouse was destroyed by fire in 1925, and the present structure was built in its place.

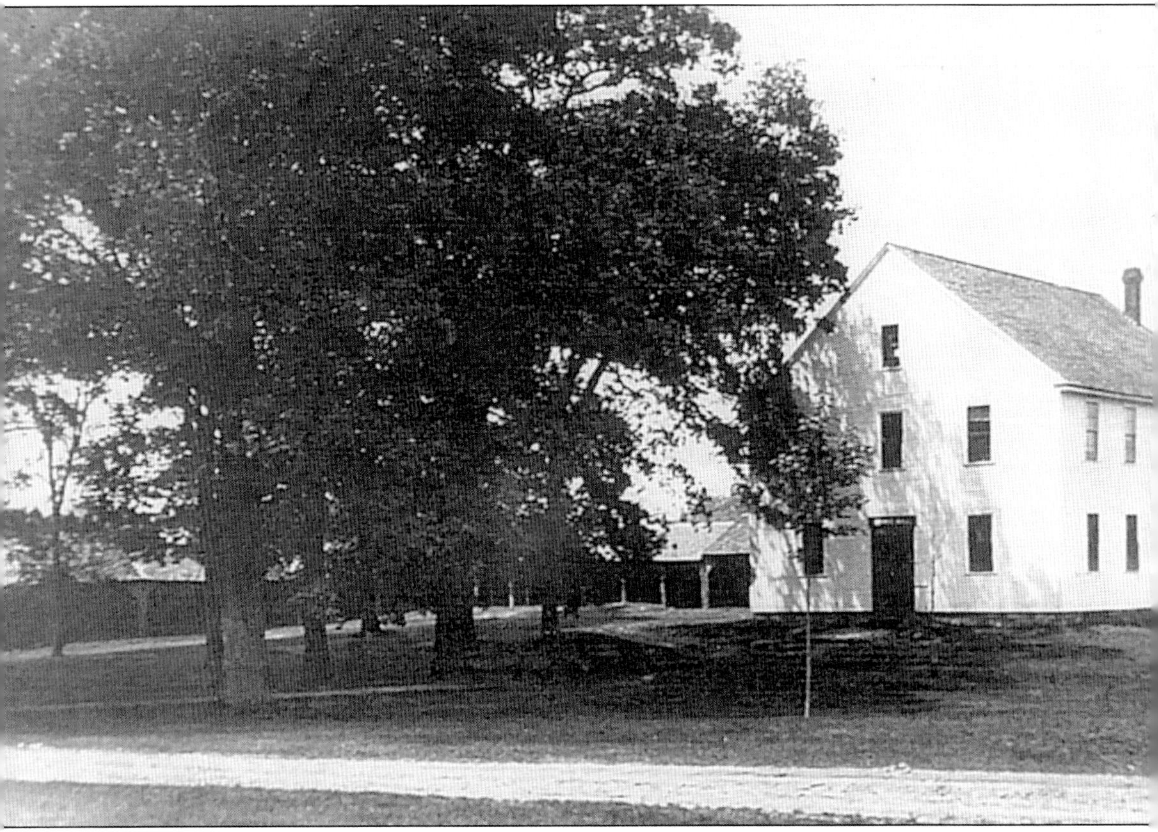

First Meetinghouse, August 8, 1908. Constructed very slowly in the 1780s, this meetinghouse was first used for a town meeting on August 3, 1784. Although suffering from various stages of disrepair over the years, First Meetinghouse stands tall and grand and still hosts meetings, lectures, and other events.

Two

BUSINESS, INDUSTRY, AND PUBLIC SERVICE

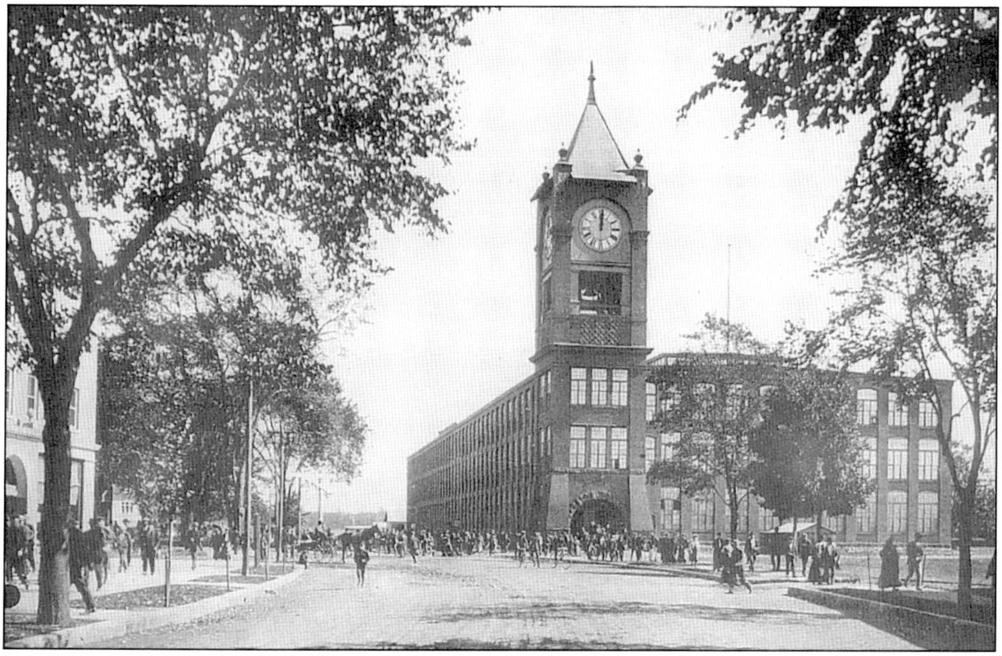

MILL #8 AND THE CLOCK TOWER, 1901. The Ludlow Manufacturing Company formally organized in 1868 under the direction of Charles Townsend Hubbard. About ten years later, he moved all business and machinery to Ludlow from East Braintree, Massachusetts, and began building more mills. Shown here is mill #8 and the now-famous clock tower. Six warehouses (to the left of the mill) were torn down to make room for State Street.

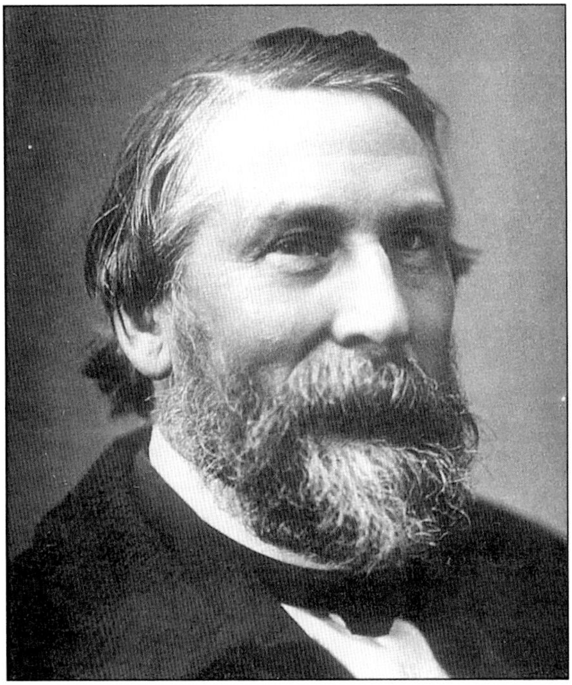

CHARLES TOWNSEND HUBBARD. The founder of the Ludlow Manufacturing Company, Charles T. Hubbard, also had a vision of a public library. The town's only public library is named in his honor and has served the town for well over 100 years. His son, Charles W. Hubbard, succeeded him when he died suddenly in January 1887.

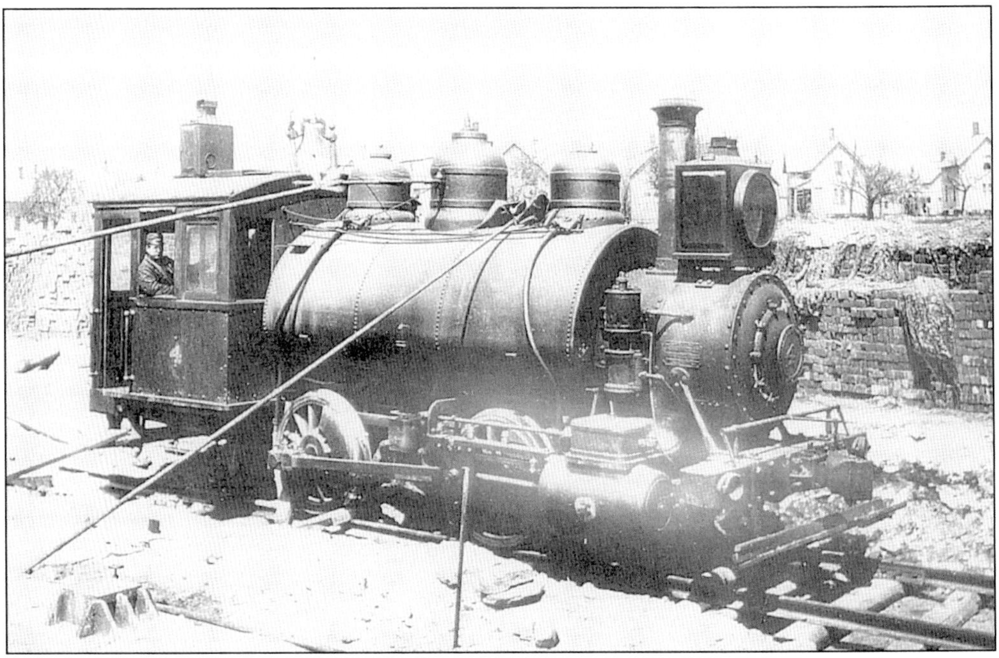

SCHENECTADY LOCOMOTIVE, NOVEMBER 1913. In the first half of the 19th century, Ludlow was bypassed when it came to railroads. A proposition was made in 1872 by Willis Phelps, a railroad promoter from Springfield, to begin construction of a Springfield extension railroad through Ludlow. Passenger trains stopped at Sewall Street, Collins Bridge, and Red Bridge. Ludlow was the busiest station on the line, and shipments included coal, grain, lumber, and other merchandise. The station at Sewall Street was torn down in 1960, and Ludlow's railroading days came to an end.

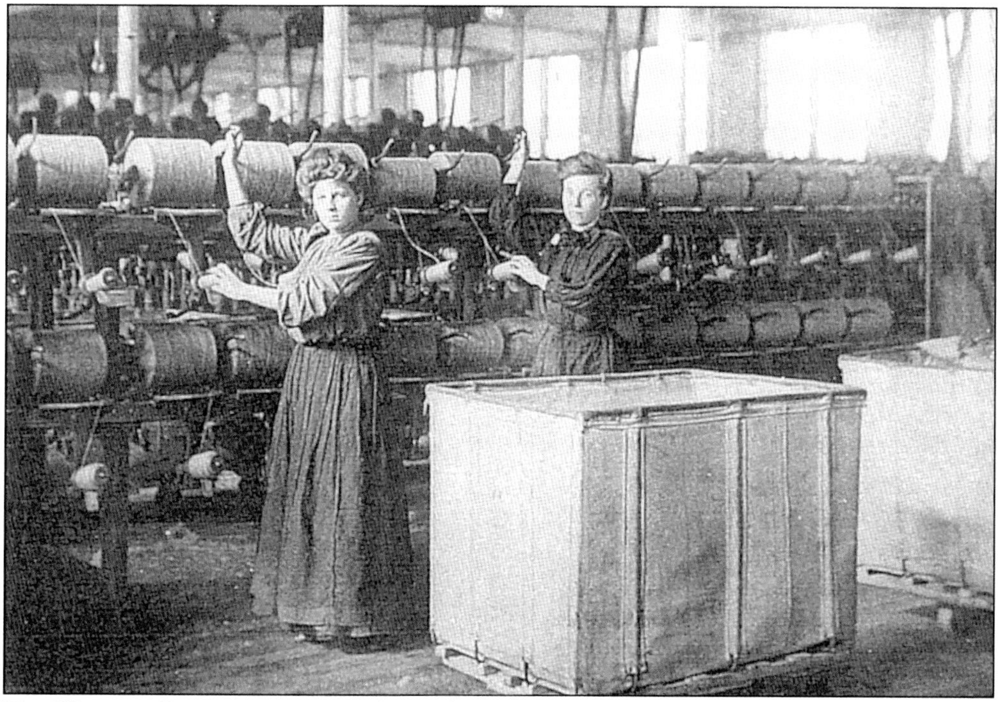

The Winding Room. Women textile employees are shown here working in the winding room. Ludlow Manufacturing produced wet and dry spun-cotton yarn, jute twine, webbing, gunny bagging, and "crash," a plain-weave fabric made from linen or mixed yarns.

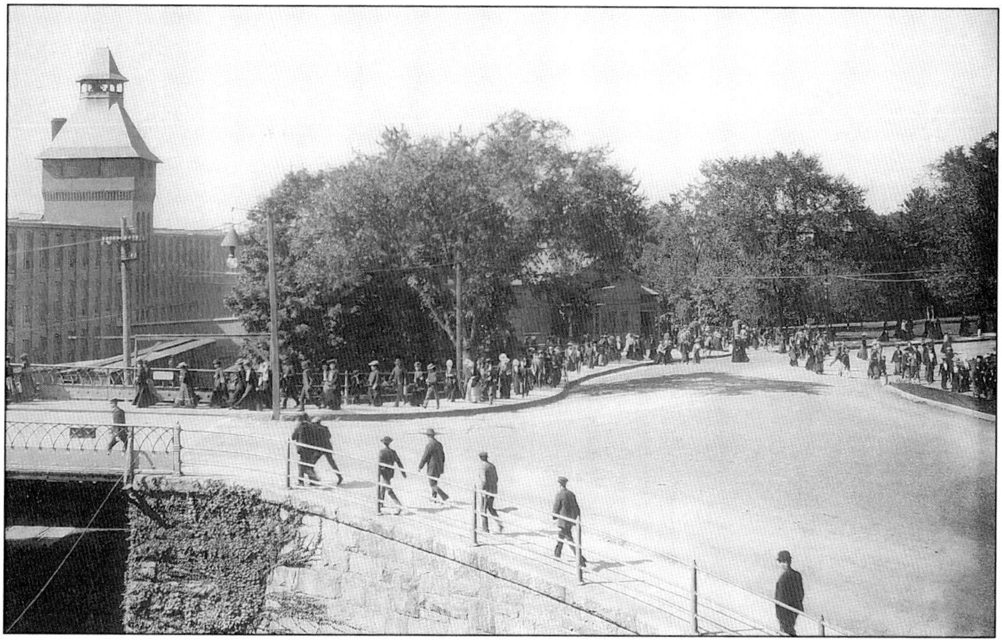

Headed to Work, c. 1900. Mill workers from the Indian Orchard section of Springfield are on their way to work. Bridges spanning the Chicopee River opened all sorts of opportunities for Ludlow and her people. Shown here is the iron bridge built in 1898; it was designed for heavier, more frequent traffic.

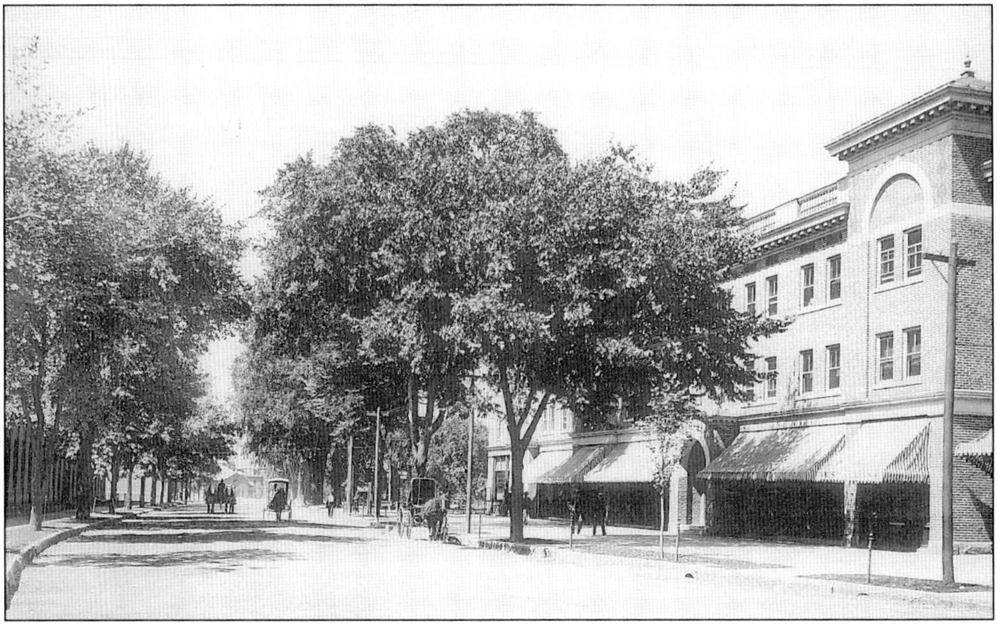

THE BUSINESS BLOCK, EAST STREET, 1903. Built in 1901, the three-story building provided business space as well as apartments for the fast-growing business district. Located on East Street between Chestnut and Sewall Streets, the block was, and still is, home to a variety of retail establishments, including (at that time) the post office. The offices of the Ludlow Manufacturing Company are to the left in this picture.

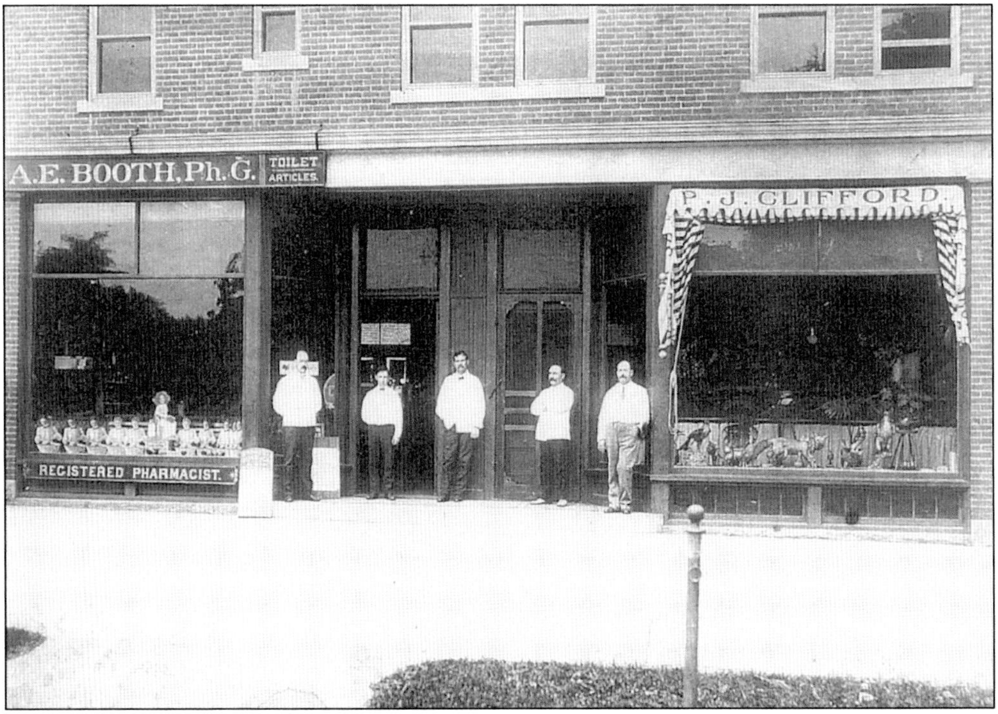

THE BUSINESS BLOCK, CHESTNUT STREET, 1903. Booth's Drug Store and Clifford's Barber Shop are two businesses that first occupied spots in the business block.

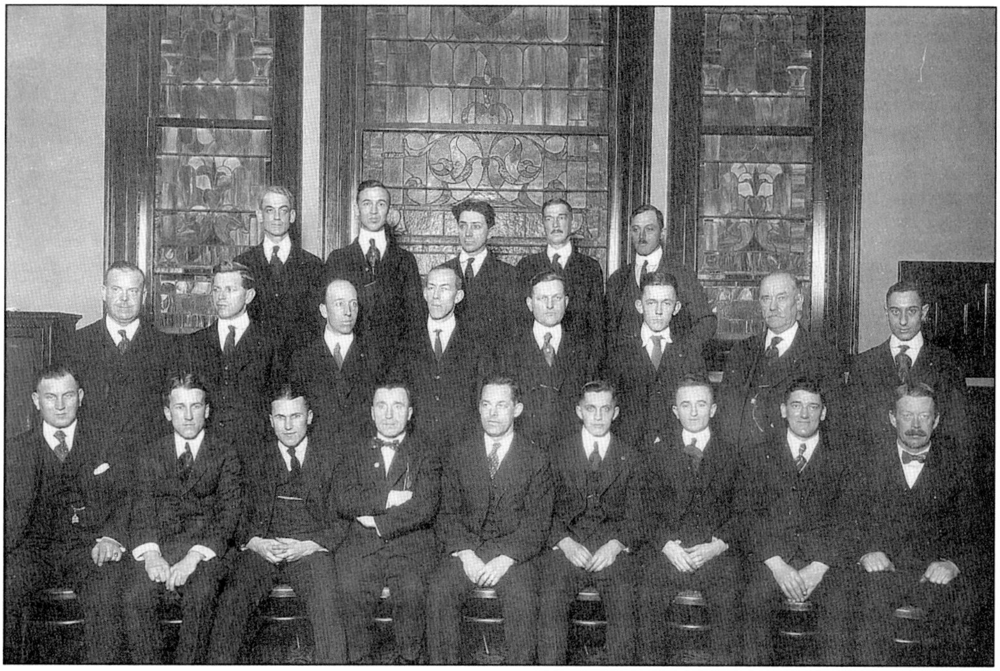

Ludlow Men's Choral Group, Early 1900s. In 1902, management of the Ludlow Manufacturing Company was transferred to a board of nine trustees known as the Ludlow Manufacturing Associates (LMA). A very civic-minded group, the LMA operated mills and owned employee housing and various real estate. Many sports teams and other groups (such as the one pictured) were sponsored by the LMA.

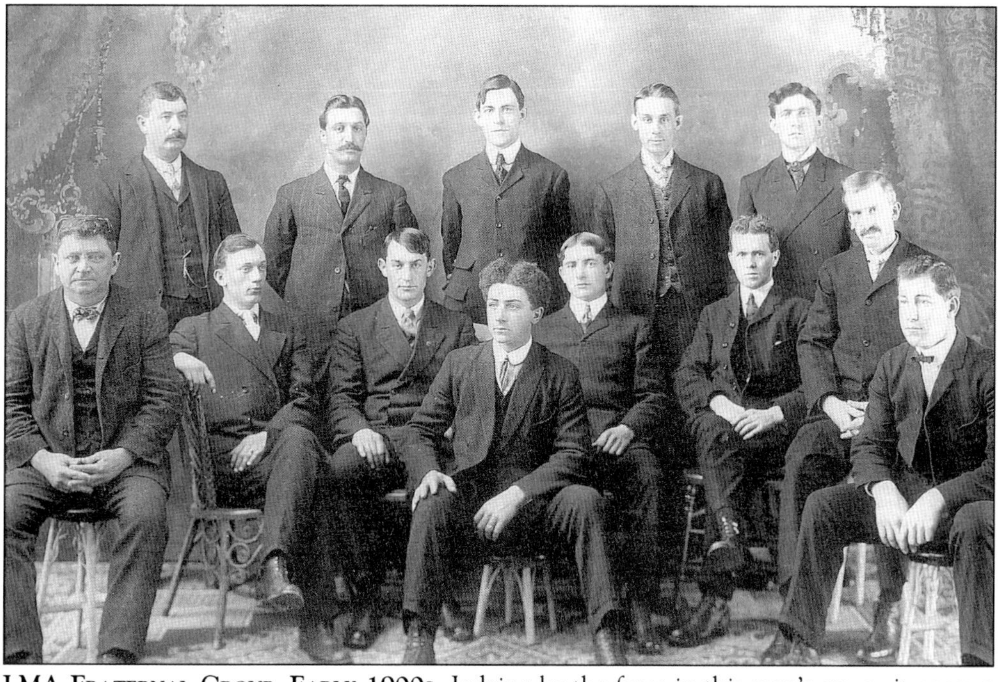

LMA Fraternal Group, Early 1900s. Judging by the faces in this men's group, it appears that many of these men belonged to more than one organization.

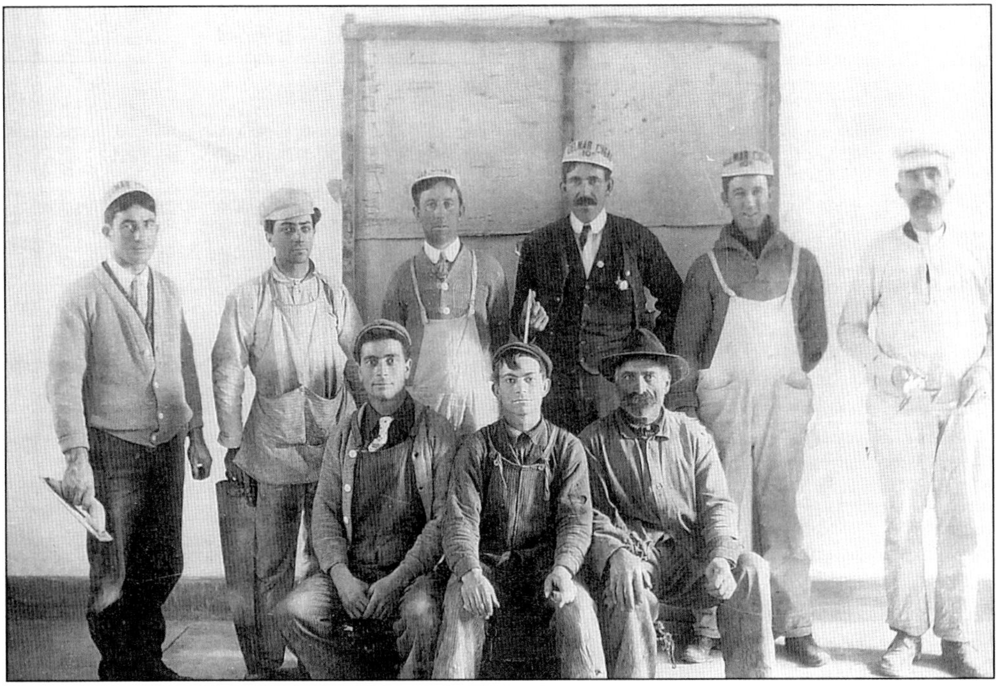

Ludlow Manufacturing Carpenters, Early 1900s.

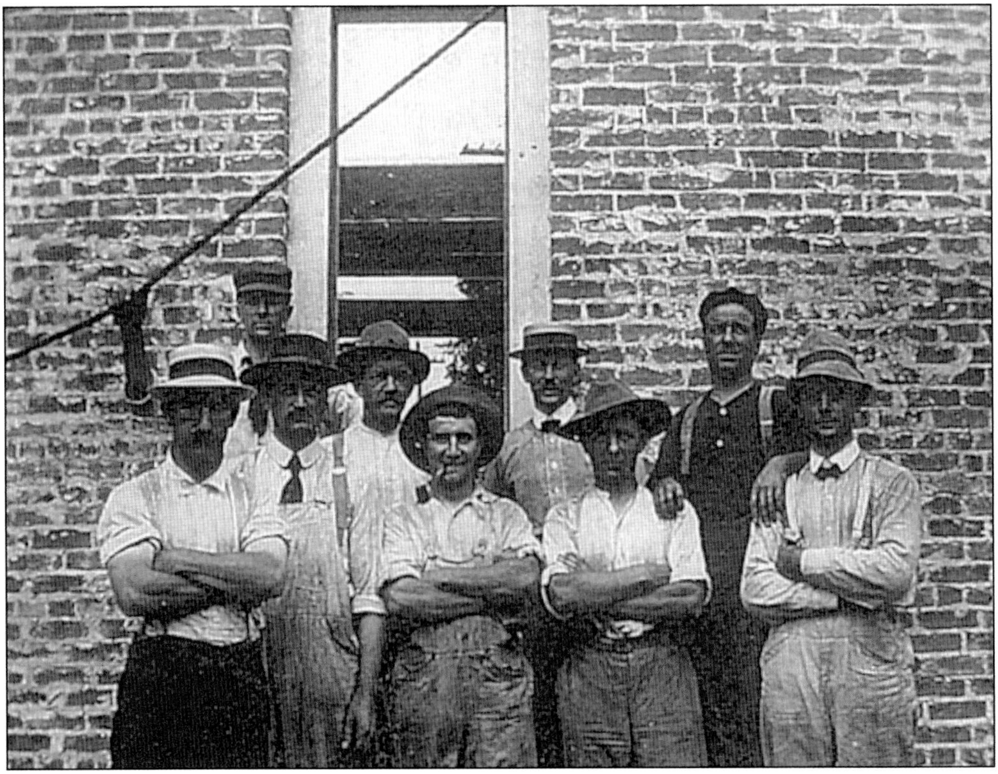

LMA Employees. This group of mill workers is probably manufacturing jute twine, a Ludlow staple for many years.

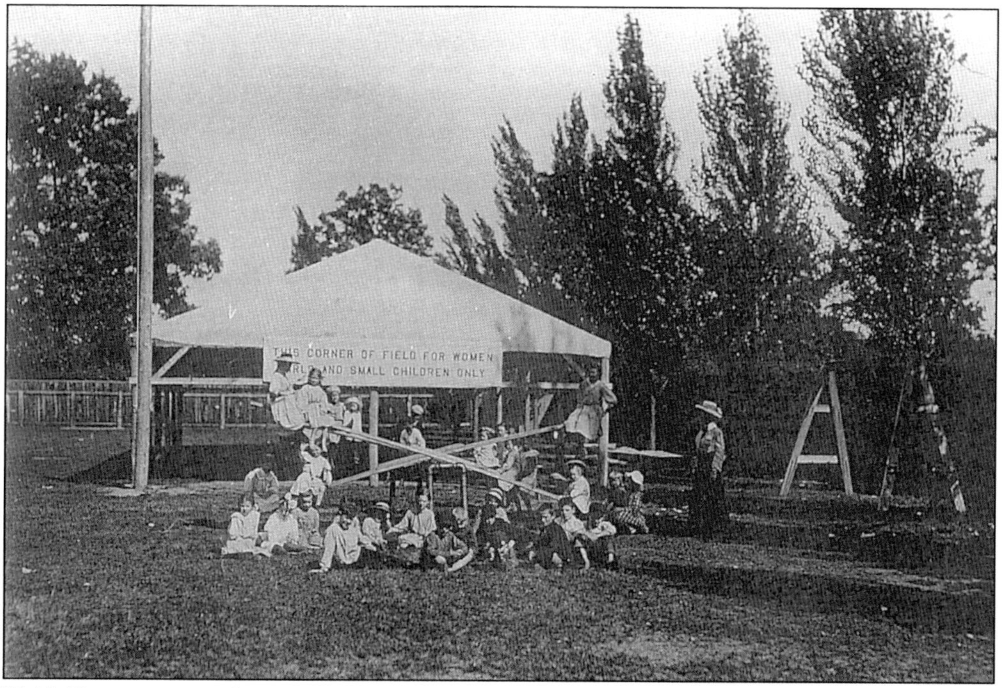

LMA Playground, September 1909. Segregation is evident in this sign, which reads, "This corner of field for woman, girls, and small children only."

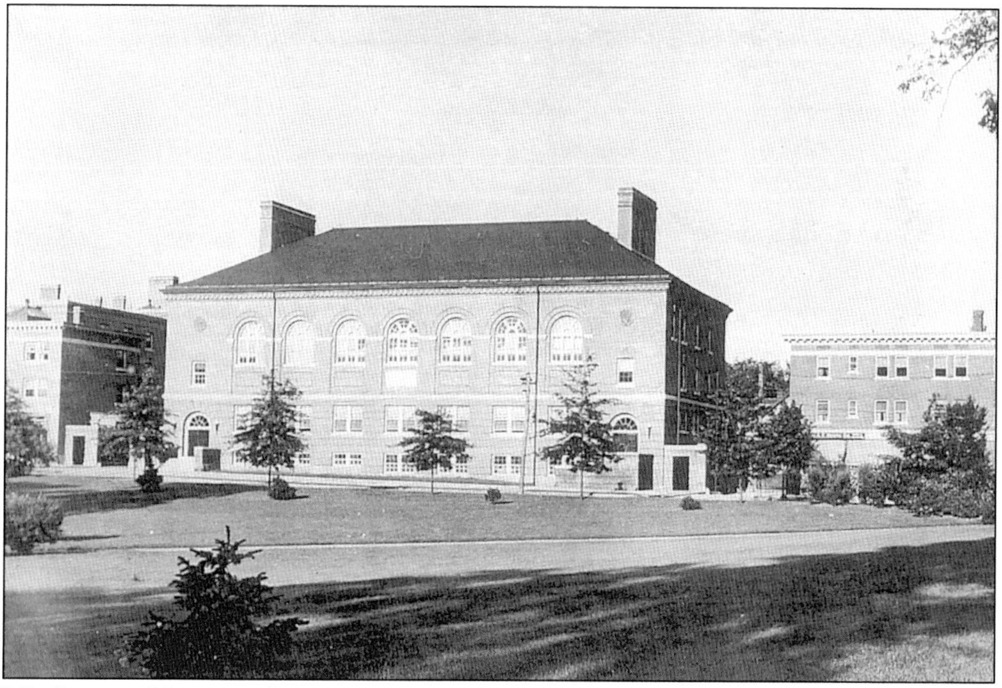

J.E. Stevens Memorial Building, 1907. John E. Stevens was a board member and agent for the LMA. He was so revered by townspeople that after his death in 1905, a building named in his honor provided recreational facilities for townspeople. Known as the "rec" for many years, it is now home (for a little while longer, at least) to the Ludlow Boys and Girls Club.

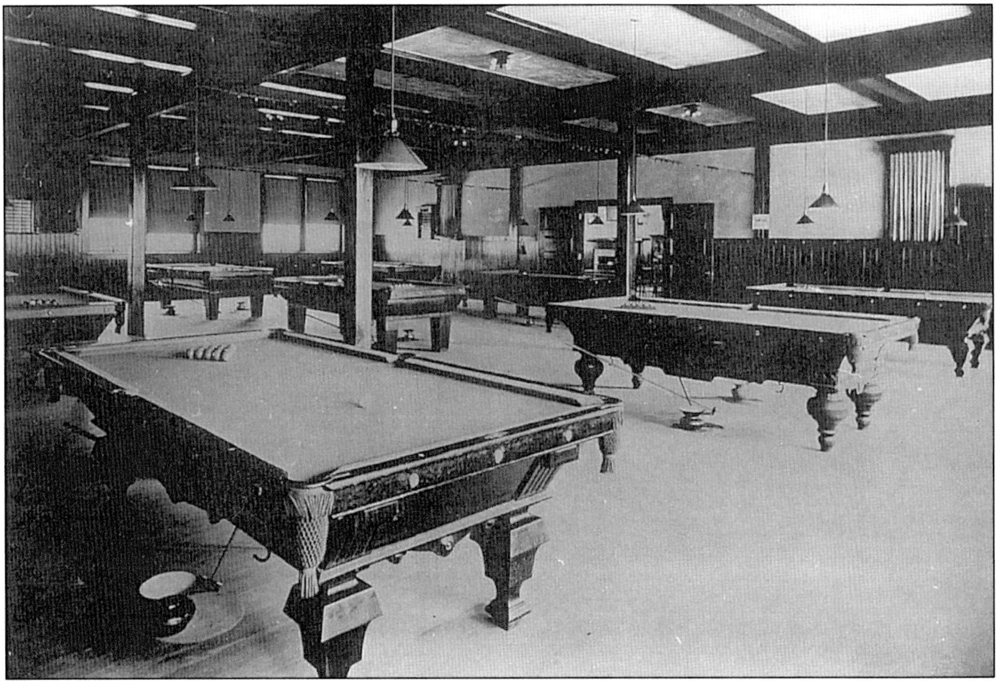

Pool Room or Billiards Room at the Stevens Memorial Building. The building also housed an auditorium, indoor pool, bowling alleys, reading and game rooms, library, and rooms for sewing and cooking.

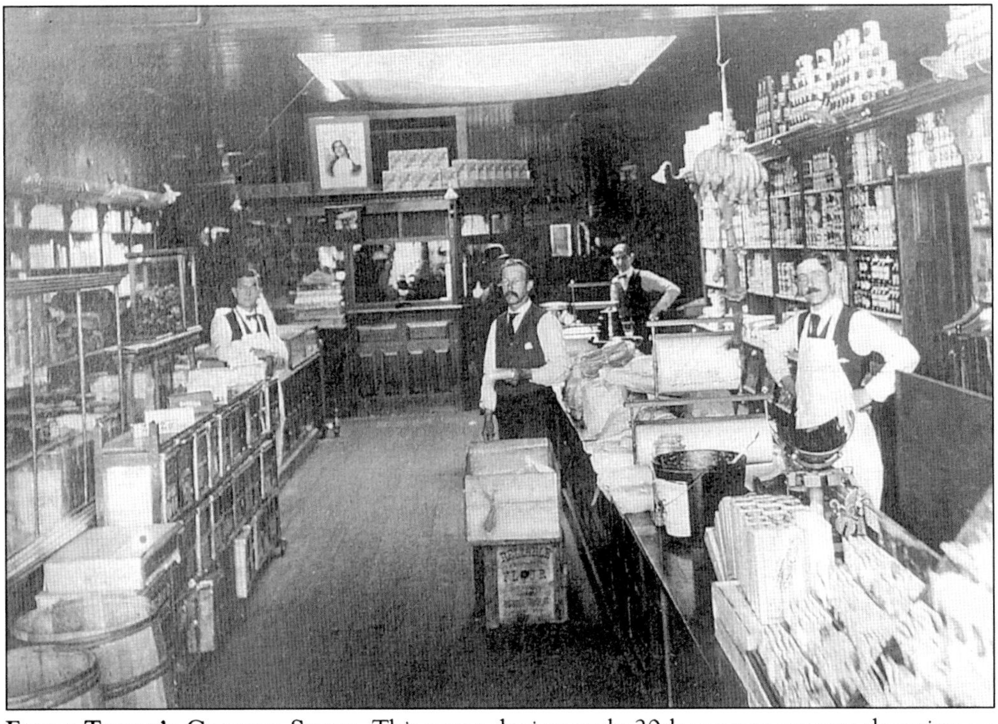

Frank Towne's Grocery Store. This scene depicts early-20th-century grocery shopping on East Street, in the business block.

LUDLOW BOTTLE, LUDLOW GLASS WORKS. For a few short years after the War of 1812, John Sikes operated a glass-making shop on Lyon Street. His company, called Ludlow Manufacturing Company (no relation to the company of later years), made olive-green and amber bottles and other glassware. Either mismanagement or the financial depression of 1819 took its toll on the fledgling company.

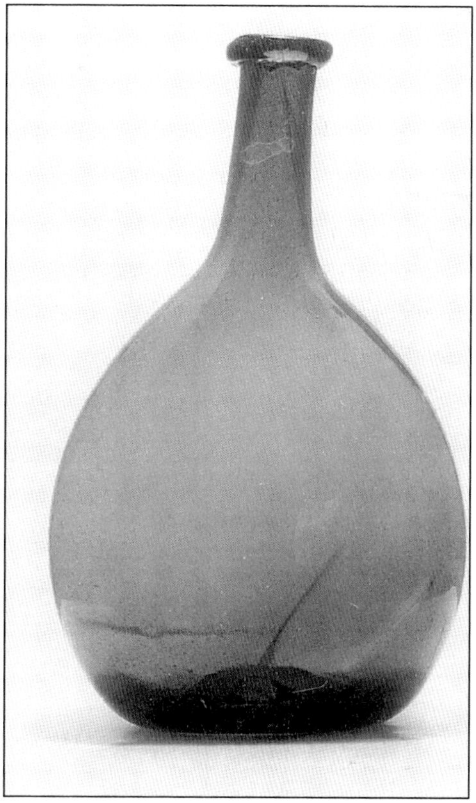

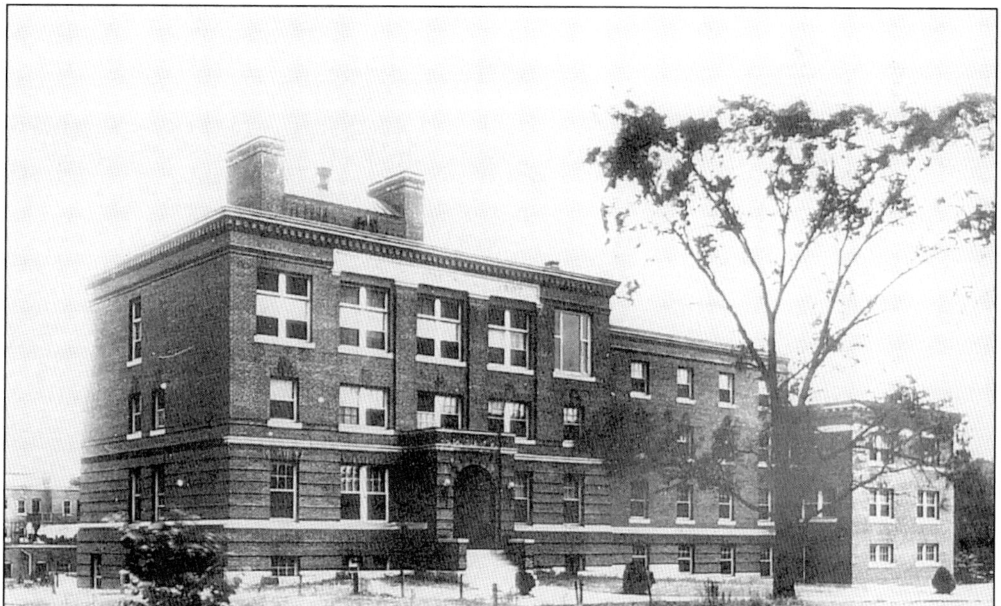

LUDLOW HOSPITAL, 1907. In order to care for their employees, the LMA constructed a 29-bed hospital in 1907. During the first year, there were 41 admissions. For an annual fee of $3 in 1909, members could receive free hospital care, physician's services, and surgery, if necessary.

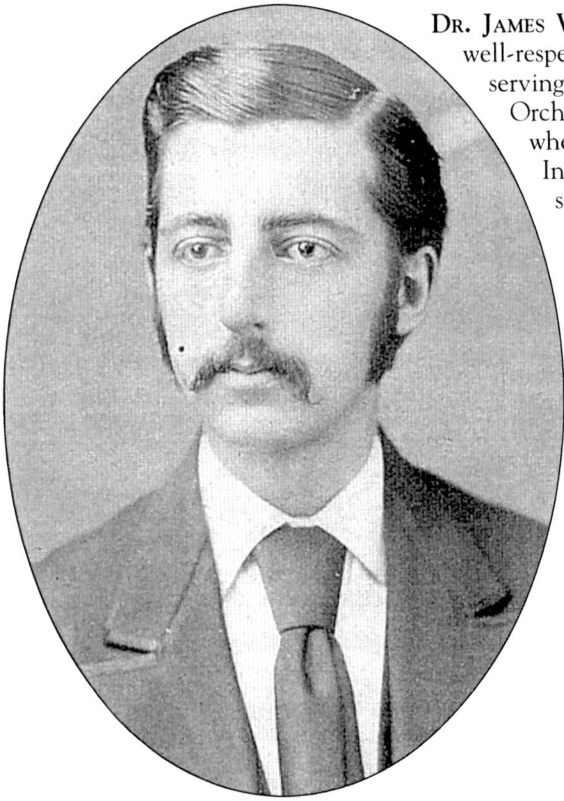

Dr. James W. Hannum, M.D. Dr. Hannum was a well-respected man and had his own practice serving residents of Ludlow as well as Indian Orchard. He also served as head physician when Ludlow Hospital was first opened. In the blizzard of 1888, a passenger train stalled between North Wilbraham and Indian Orchard. Dr. Hannum received a phone call regarding a sick child aboard the train, and he traveled to the train on foot to care for the child. Doc Hannum's home was one of five places in town with phone service at that time.

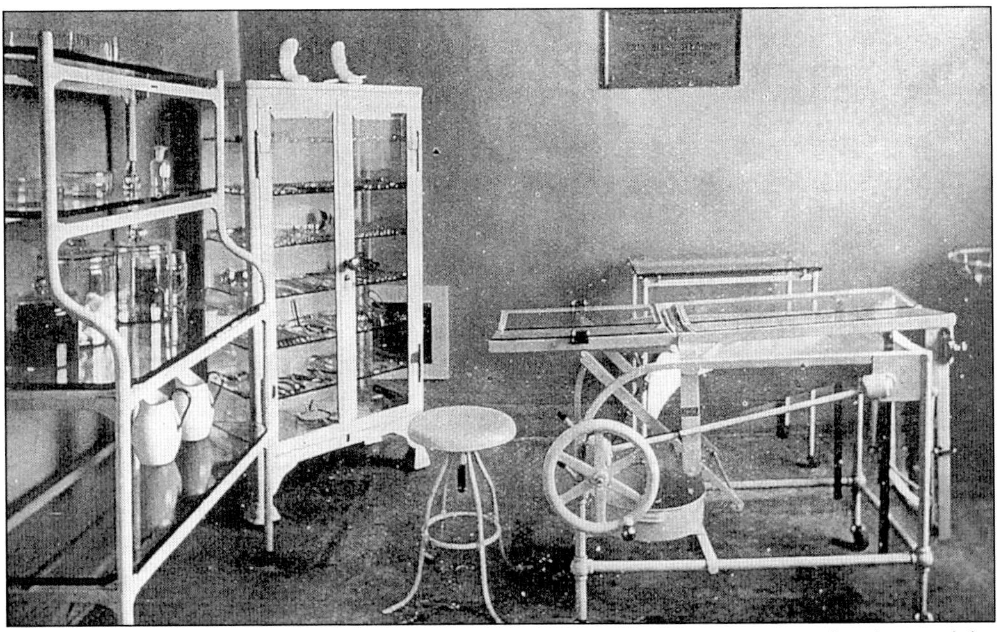

Ludlow Hospital Operating Room, 1909. Ludlow Hospital was then considered one of the best-equipped in western Massachusetts. Funds were donated to purchase equipment for the operating room, including an X-ray machine.

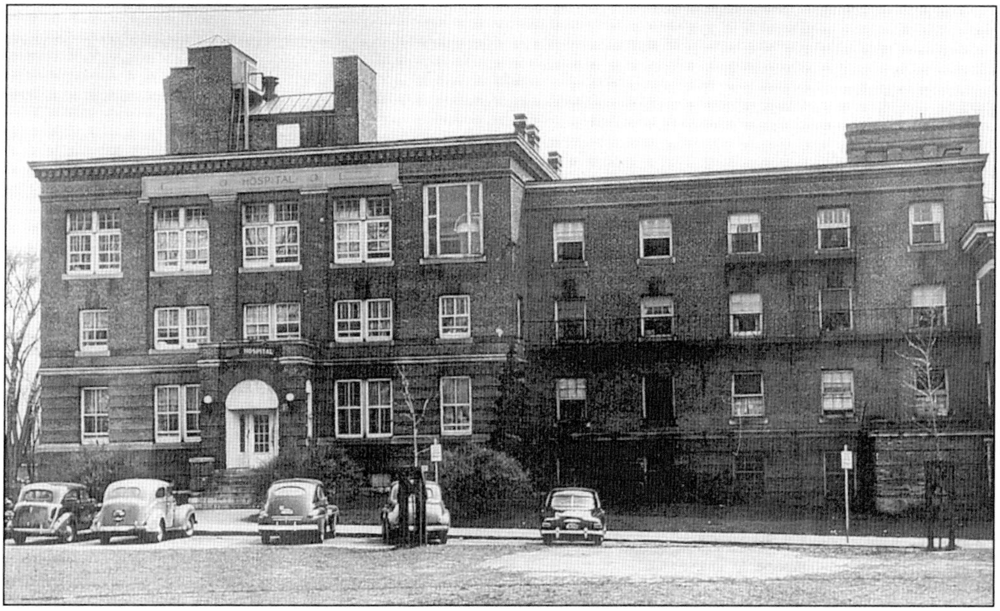

LUDLOW HOSPITAL, APRIL 1949. Townspeople were already seeing signs that the hospital was too small and did not meet new state regulations for fire codes. In 1952, the facility was nearly closed by the Commonwealth of Massachusetts Department of Public Health. Nothing materialized until a controversial fight broke out over building a new hospital and where to build it. Trustees chose not to locate it in Ludlow, but the townspeople fought long, hard, and successfully to have it remain in town.

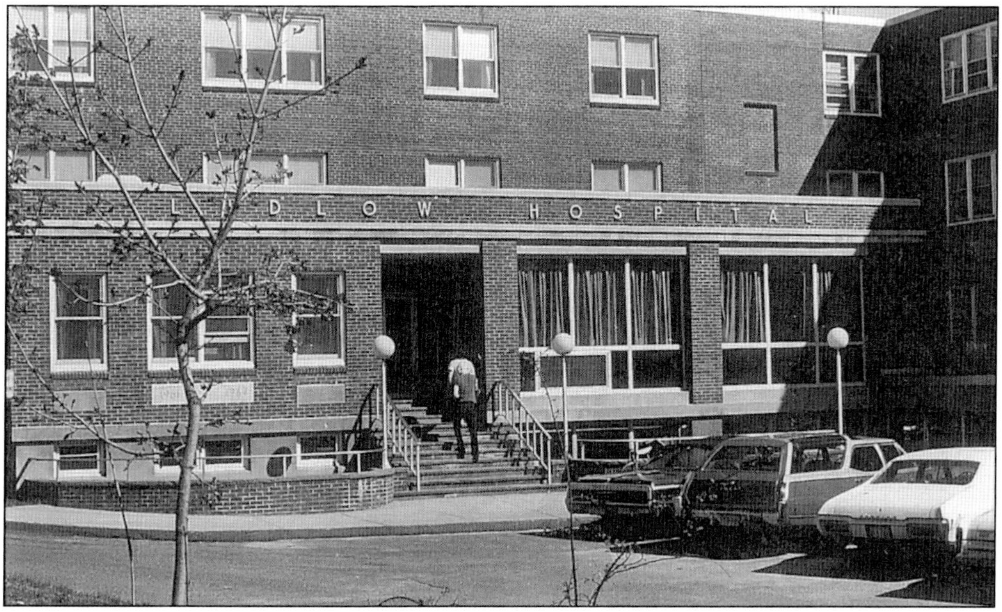

LUDLOW HOSPITAL, 1973. Adjacent to the old building, the new hospital was a modern, fire-proof, 75-bed facility with operating rooms, emergency rooms, an X-ray department, and a maternity suite (where the author was born in 1964). Dedicated in February 1962, the cost of the building was $871,000. Sadly, the hospital closed its doors forever in the mid-1990s; ambulatory services and rehabilitation are still located there.

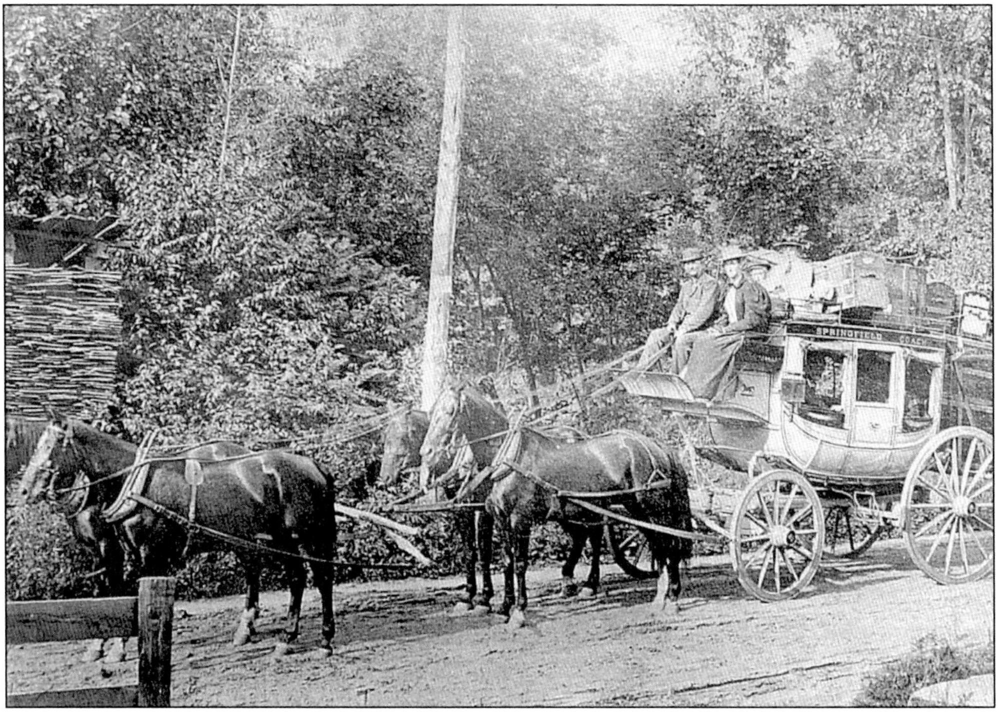

SPRINGFIELD STAGE COACH, 1880S. The presence of several taverns throughout Ludlow make it clear that stage coaches often passed through town, sometimes stopping for the night or for passengers to quench their thirst.

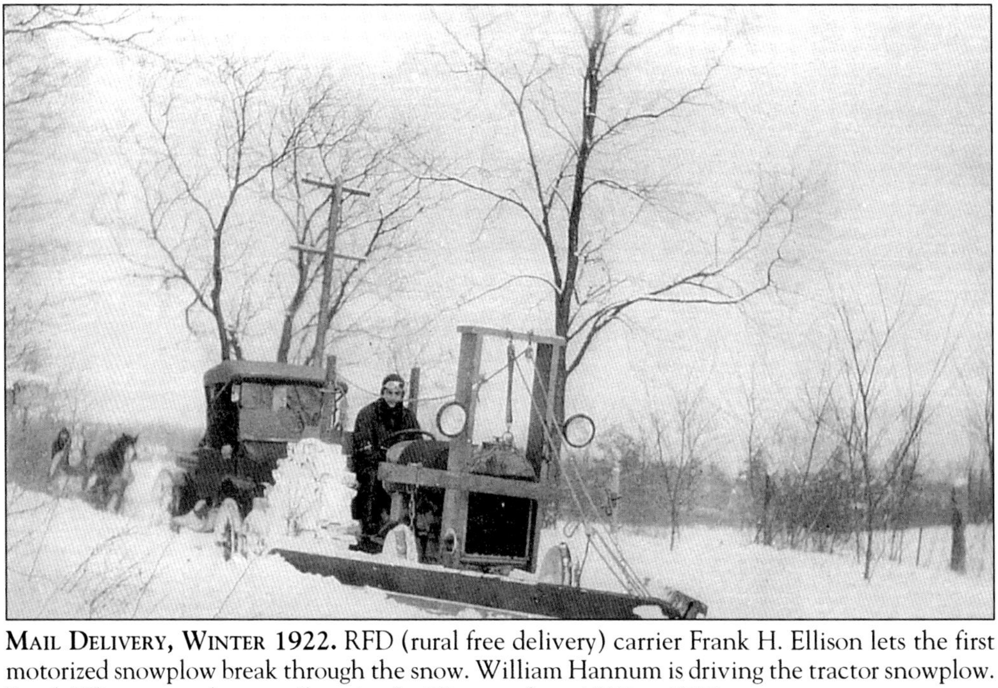

MAIL DELIVERY, WINTER 1922. RFD (rural free delivery) carrier Frank H. Ellison lets the first motorized snowplow break through the snow. William Hannum is driving the tractor snowplow. Frank Ellison served as a mail carrier for 39 years, from 1918 to 1957.

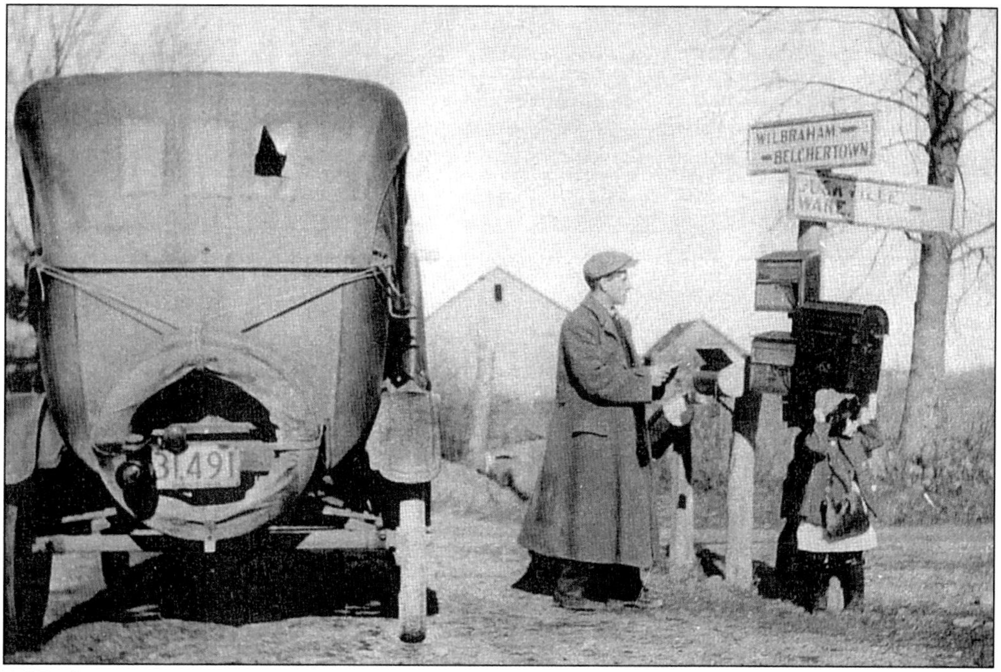

RFD Carrier Frank Ellison, 1918. RFD Route #1 included Lyon, Munsing, Rood, Alden, and upper East Streets as well as Belchertown Road. In 1918, there were 175 mailboxes along the route; that number increased to 547 during the next 25 years.

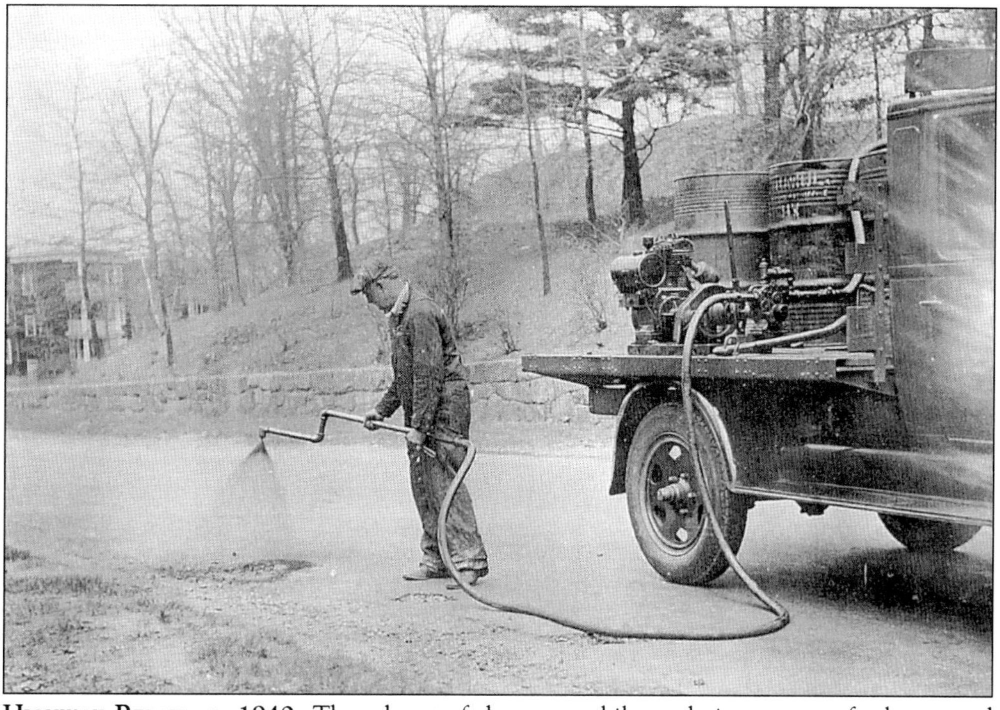

Highway Repair, c. 1940. The advent of the automobile made it necessary for better and more frequent road care. In 1940, there were approximately 2,000 cars registered in Ludlow, making it a must for gravel roads to be paved.

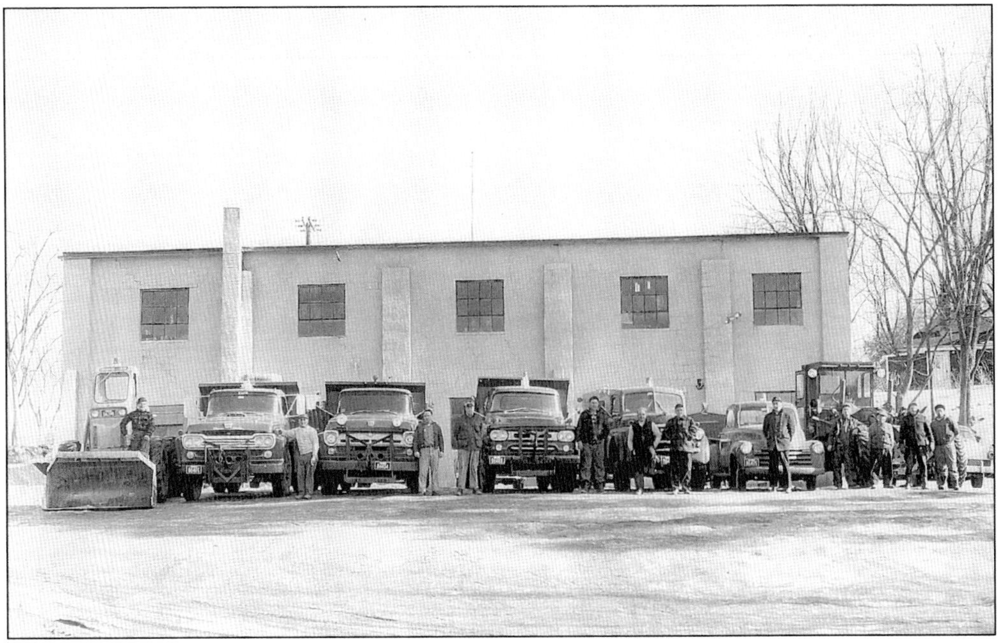

Ludlow Highway Department, 1960. This building on Center Street was formerly home to the highway department. It is now housed on Sportmen's Road.

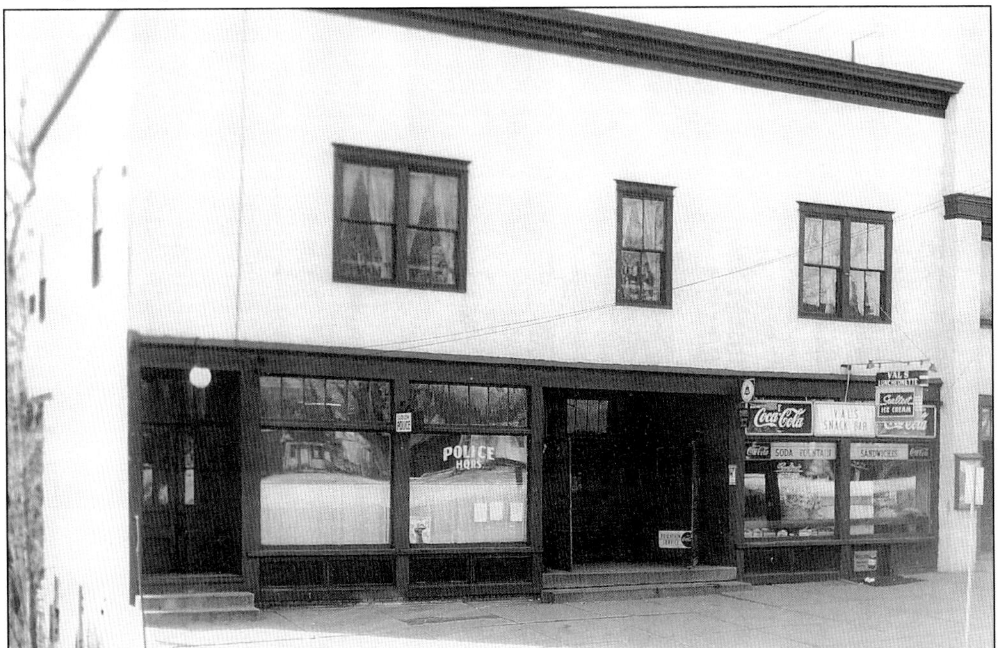

Old Police Station, Center Street, c. 1956. The old police headquarters, having been outgrown, was moved in 1967 to its new building on Center and Chapin Streets. Early Ludlow needed only a constable to oversee the town and, in following years, special police officers were appointed. As the population grew, permanent officers were appointed and began around-the-clock patrols.

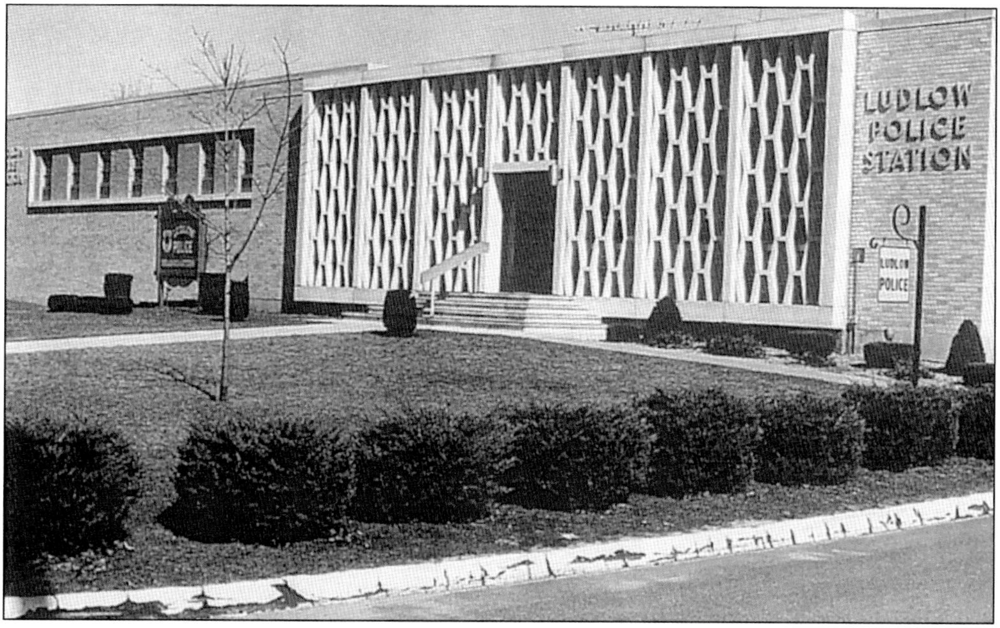

LUDLOW POLICE STATION, 1973. The new complex, built in 1967, combined both the police and fire departments in one building. The new space allowed for updated equipment, including a fingerprint and photo laboratory. Also available were a two-man detective bureau, a safety officer, and a juvenile officer. Radar equipment was added in 1970, and in 1971, the department began using a Breathalyzer. In the mid-1990s, the entire complex was revamped and updated. It is now called the Ludlow Police/Fire Safety Complex.

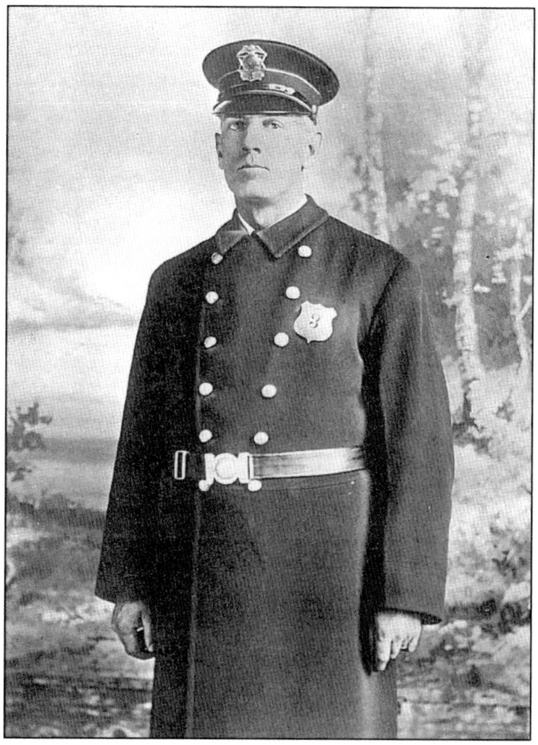

HENRY BENWAY, C. 1920S. Sgt. Henry Benway was acting police chief on two separate occasions, one in 1928 and the other in 1935. The first, in 1928, was under rather scandalous conditions, involving alleged prohibition, bootlegging, and bribery by Police Chief Joseph Fouche. Chief Fouche was acquitted of all charges against him, but public outcry forced his discharge.

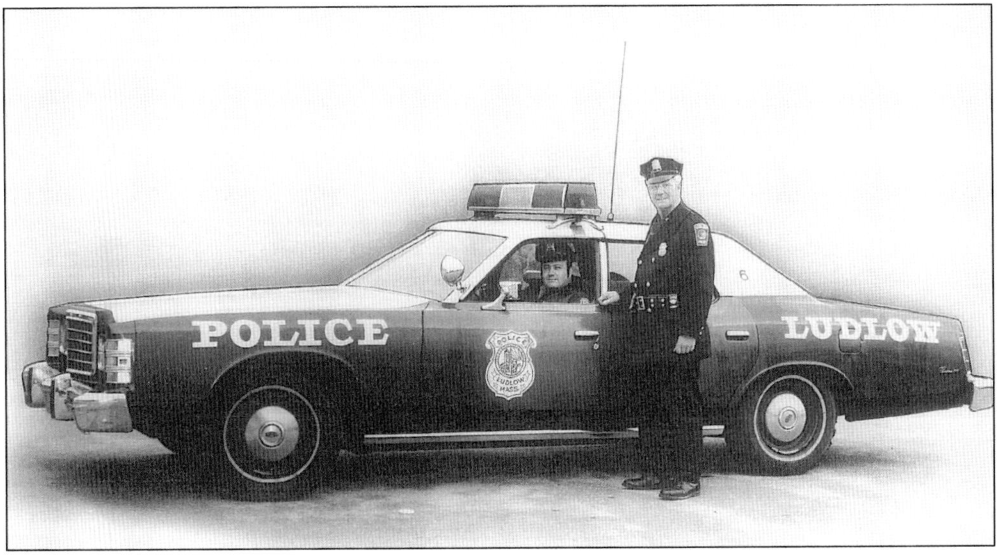

New Police Car, Early 1970s. In the 1920s, motorcycles were used to patrol Ludlow. Now, cars do most of the work, with bicycle patrols on duty in the downtown area.

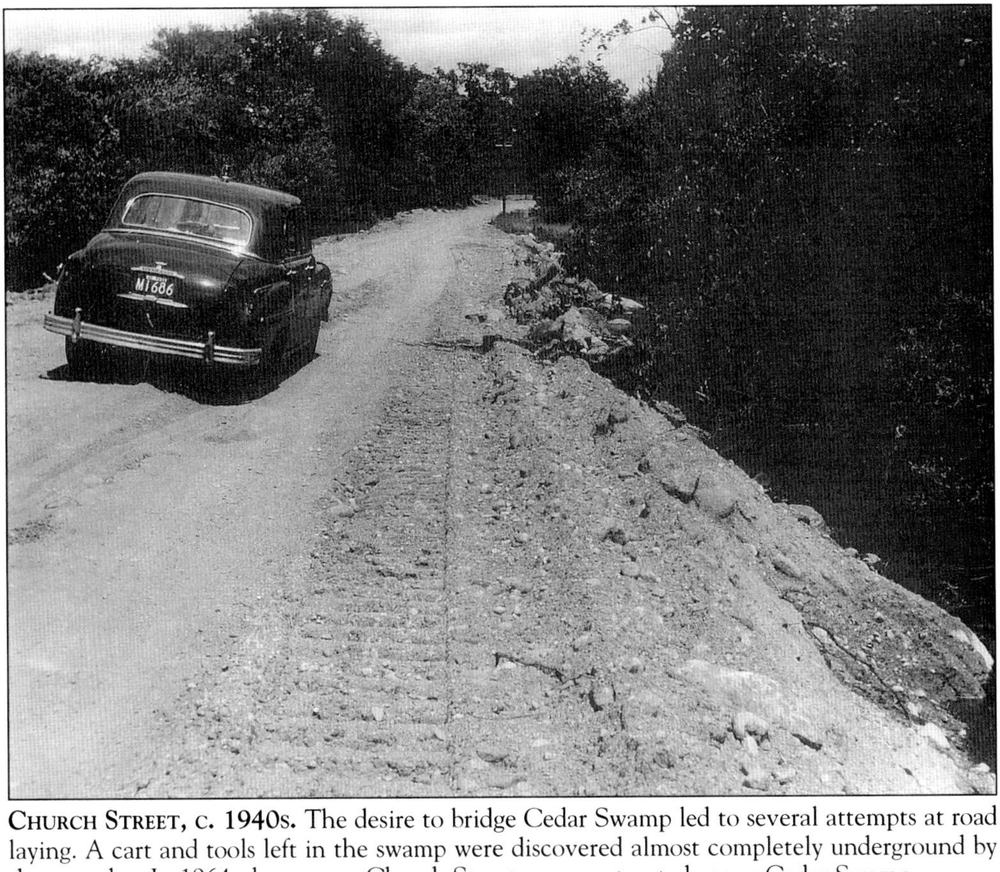

Church Street, c. 1940s. The desire to bridge Cedar Swamp led to several attempts at road laying. A cart and tools left in the swamp were discovered almost completely underground by the next day. In 1964, the present Church Street was constructed across Cedar Swamp.

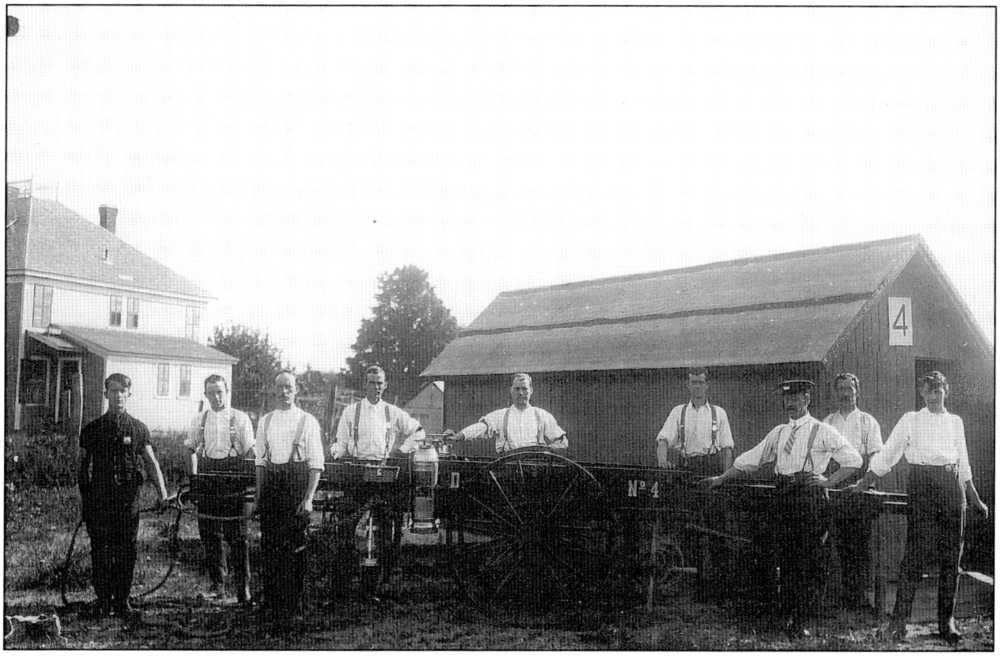

LMA's Hose Company #4, 1908. Early firefighters on Winsor Street, opposite Hampshire Street, were primarily organized to protect company property. The men worked with hand-drawn hose carts and formed bucket brigades.

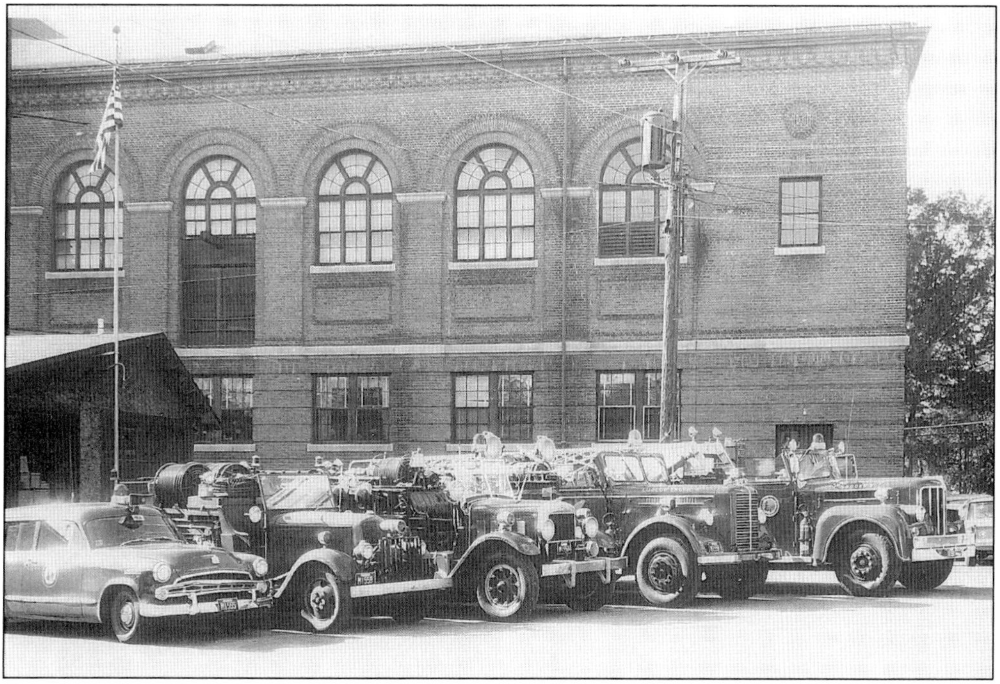

Old Fire Station behind Ludlow Hospital, Late 1950s. Pictured from left to right are the following: a 1950s Dodge, a 1933 Dodge, a 1932 Buffalo, a 1949 Oren, and a 1958 Maxim. The addition of the Oren and the Maxim, along with increased population, led to the need for a larger building for the Ludlow Fire Department.

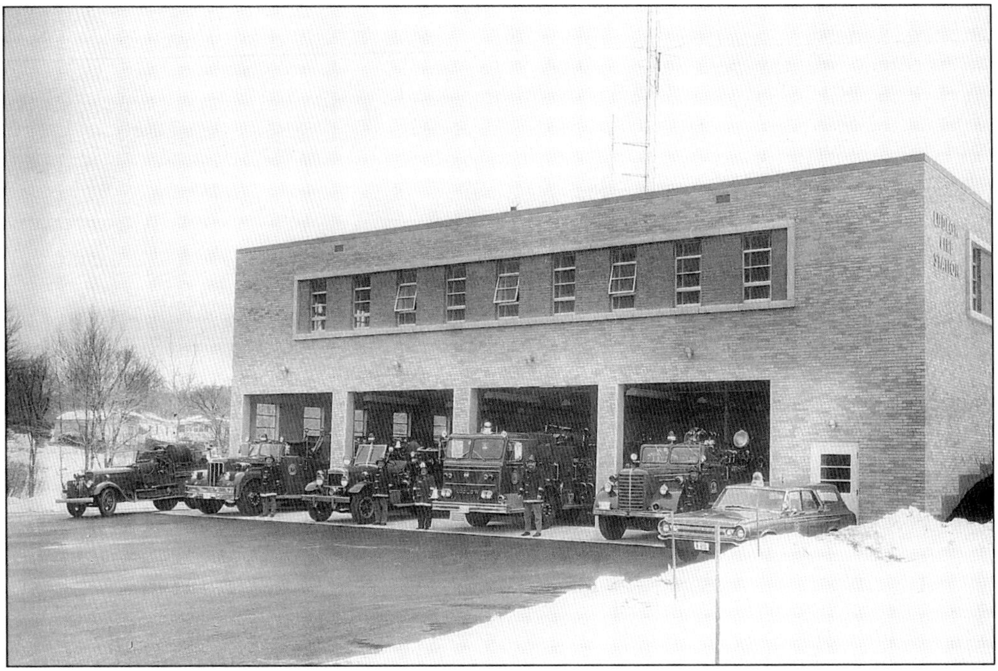

New Fire Station, c. 1968. The completion of the Ludlow Police and Fire Station at Center and Chapin Streets allowed garaging for all the engines. Firefighters are on duty 24 hours a day, with aid available from other towns if the need arises.

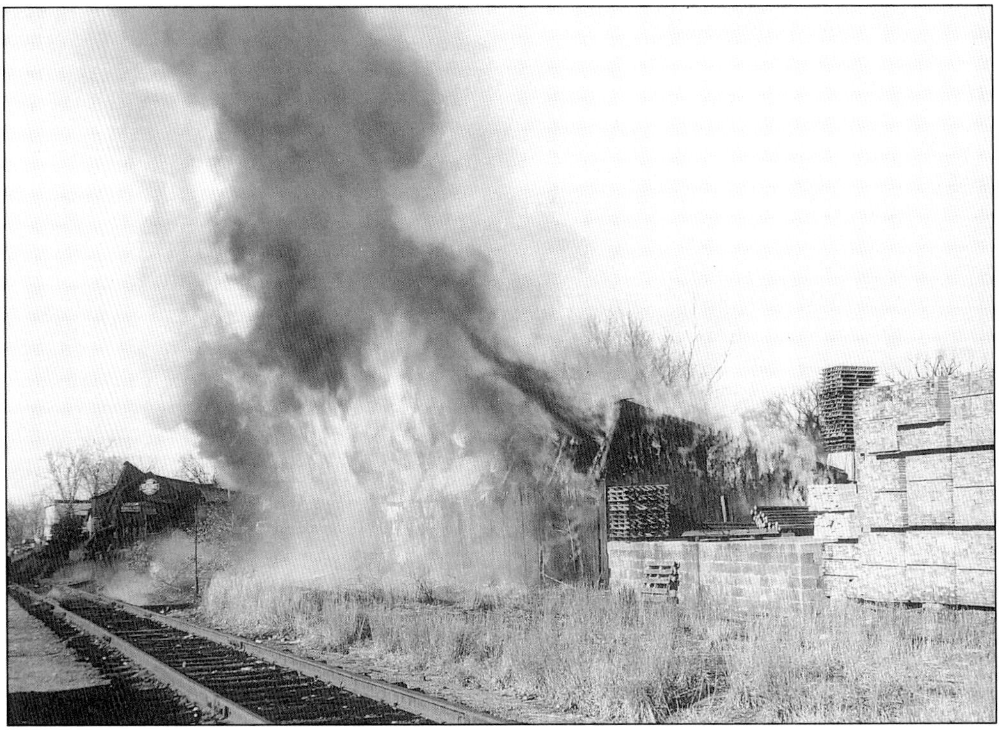

C.A. Smith Lumber and Feed. A fire at the lumber company on Hubbard Street burned old coal storage sheds on November 21, 1966.

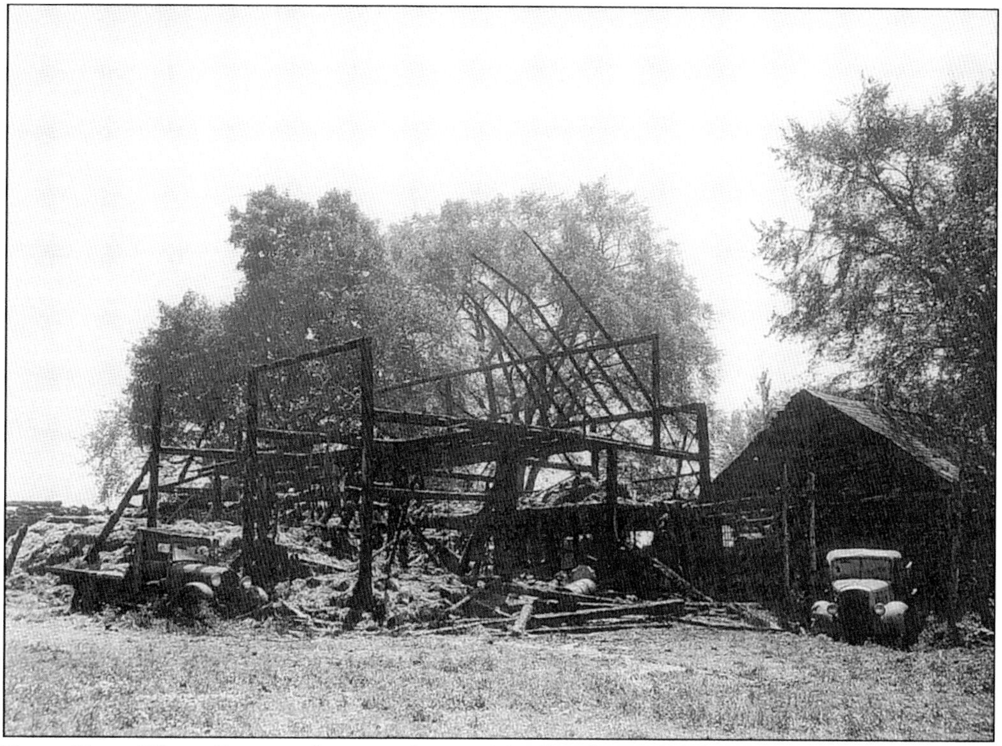

Barn Fire, West Street, August 20, 1955. This barn, filled with hay, may have been partially demolished due to Hurricane Diane, as evidenced from the date.

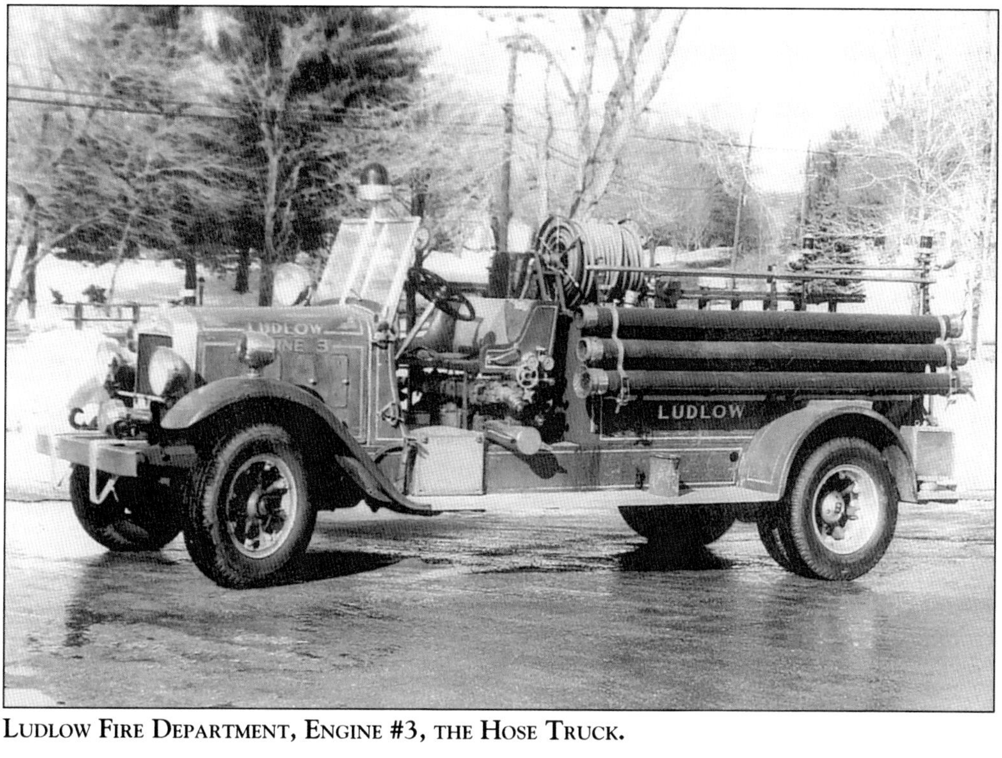

Ludlow Fire Department, Engine #3, the Hose Truck.

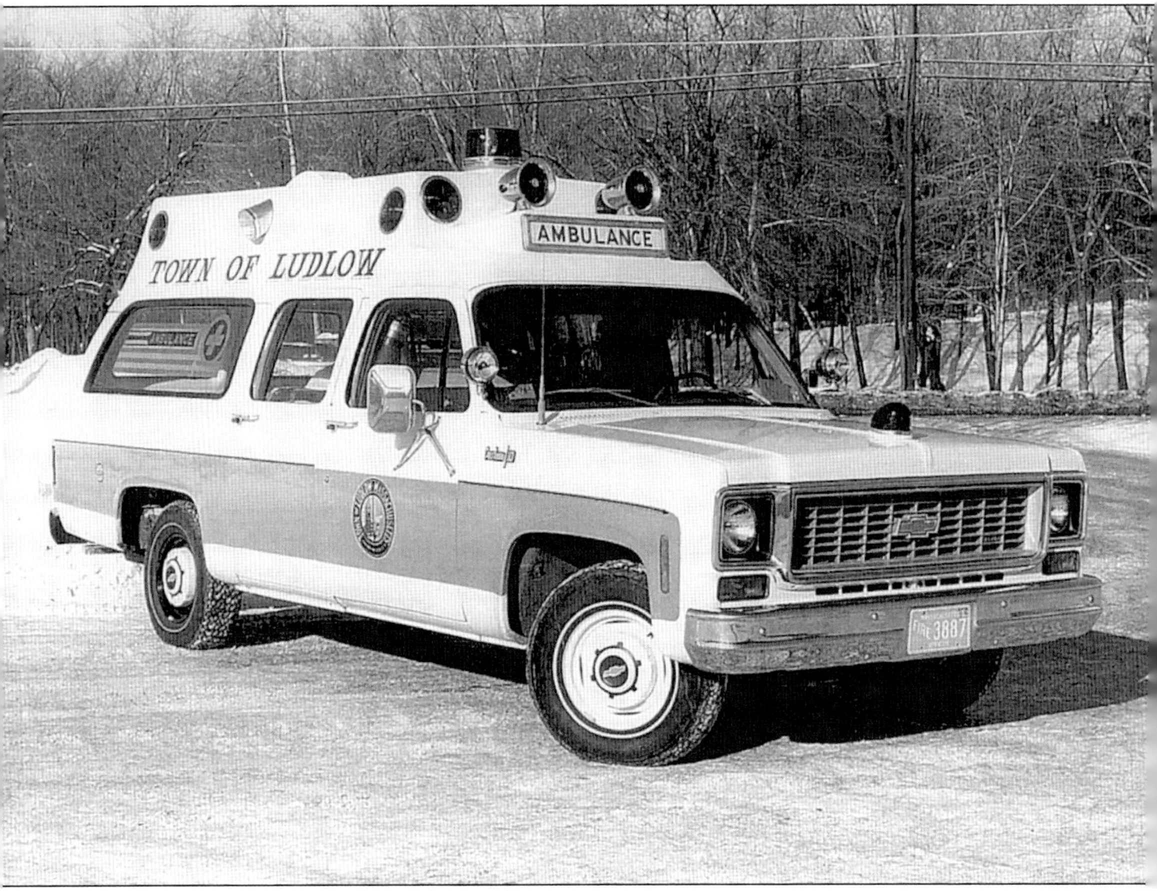

FIRST TOWN-OWNED AMBULANCE, FEBRUARY 1, 1977. Ludlow kept up with the changing times by adding emergency life-saving equipment, paramedics, and EMTs.

Three
Schools and Churches

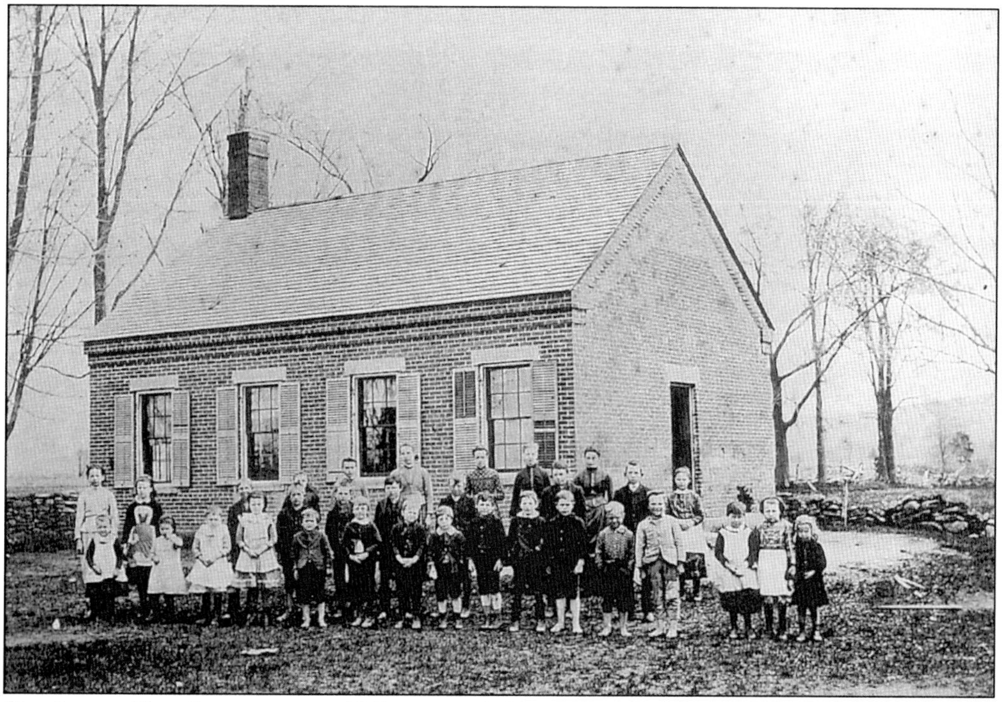

The Little Red Schoolhouse (#6), c. 1885. Located on Brook Street near the Granby line, the building is today a private residence. The town was divided into ten school districts in 1822, and half of those schoolhouses are still standing today. By the late 1930s, all rural schools were closed due to a decrease in pupils; this was probably the only time there was a decrease in student population.

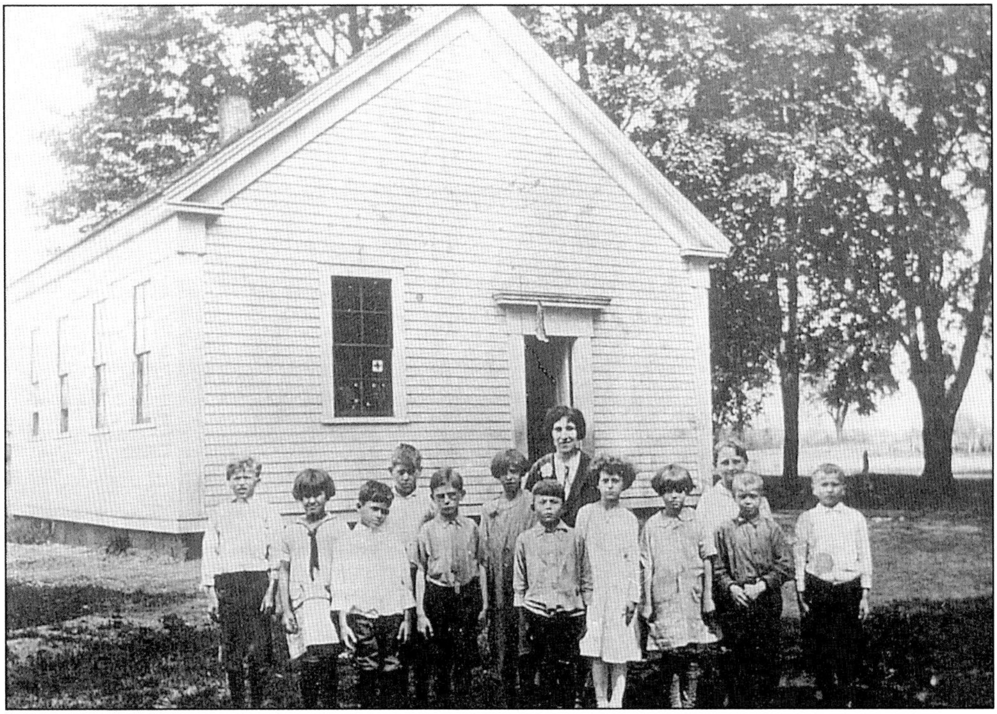

DISTRICT SCHOOL #3, 1927, WEST AND HOLYOKE STREETS. The school was formerly located across the street; in later years, it became a private residence. In 1994, against much opposition from the Ludlow Historical Commission, former students, and many townspeople, the school was torn down to make way for a car wash. As of 1999, however, the lot still stands vacant.

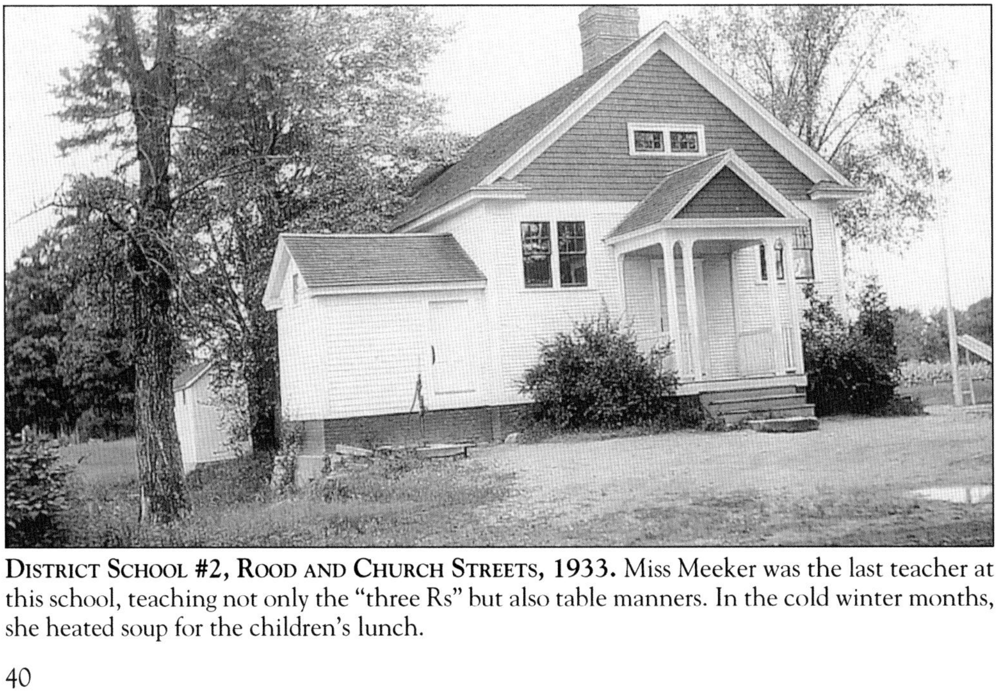

DISTRICT SCHOOL #2, ROOD AND CHURCH STREETS, 1933. Miss Meeker was the last teacher at this school, teaching not only the "three Rs" but also table manners. In the cold winter months, she heated soup for the children's lunch.

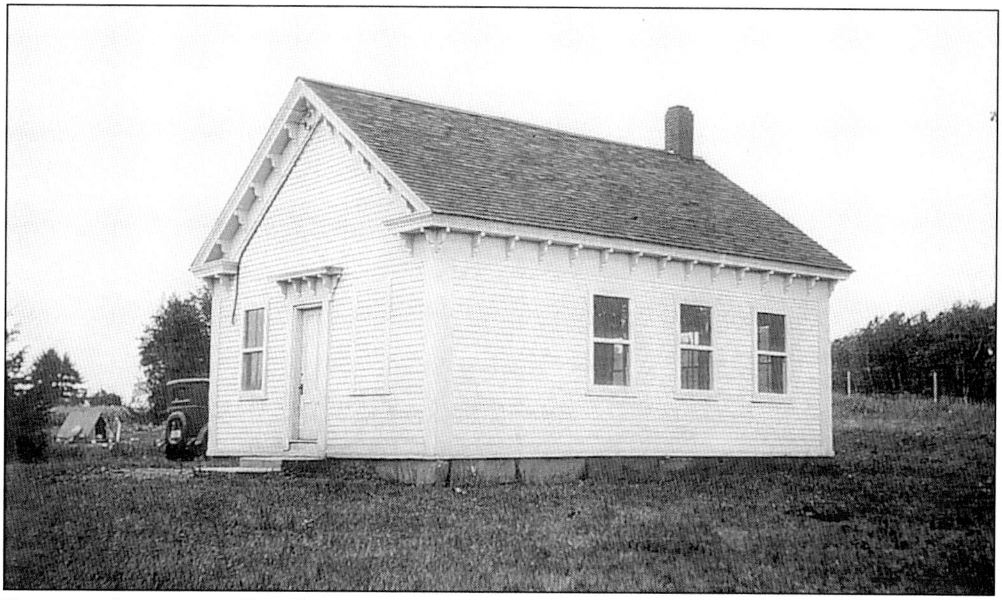

DISTRICT SCHOOL #9, RED BRIDGE, 1933. This school was on Poole Street, between Ventura and Alden Streets.

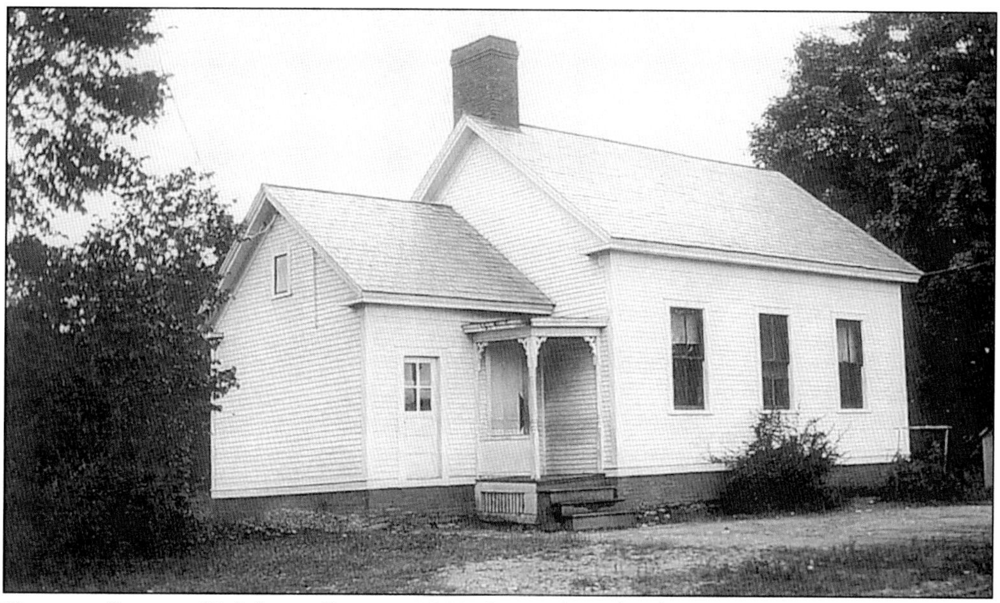

DISTRICT SCHOOL #5, MILLER STREET, 1933. Located south of East Street, this school is now a private residence.

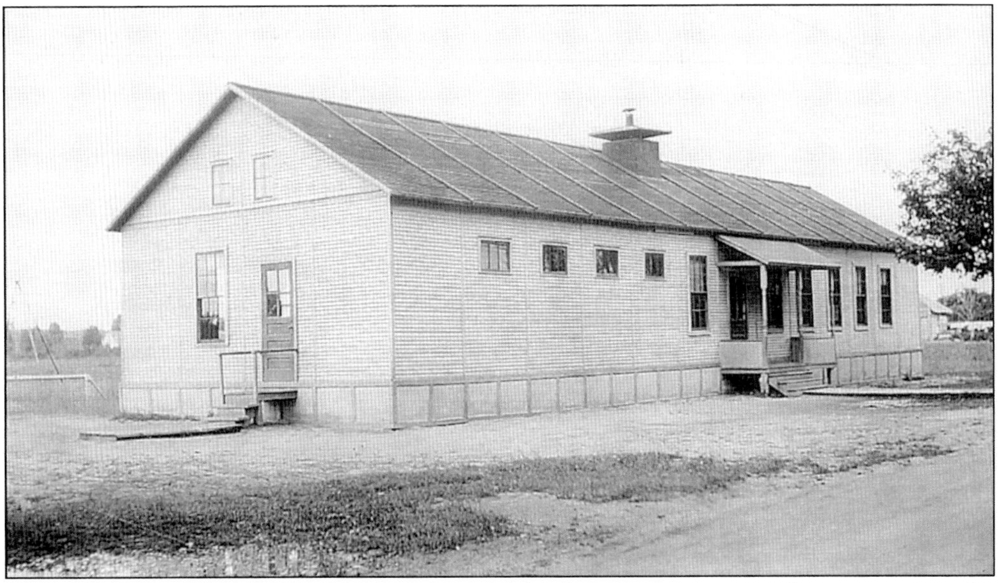

Portable School, Holyoke Street, 1933. School space was constantly outgrown in the early 1900s; two portable schools helped alleviate this problem. The opening of East Street Elementary School allowed the portable schools to be moved to the west end of town, providing those families with nearby schooling.

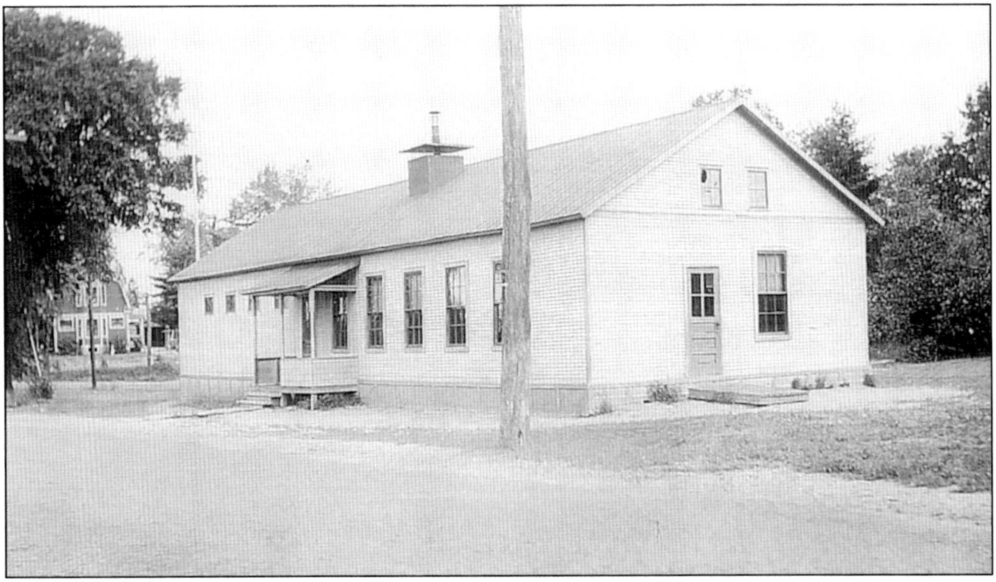

The Second Portable School, West and Cady Streets, 1933. Each portable school was expanded to four rooms.

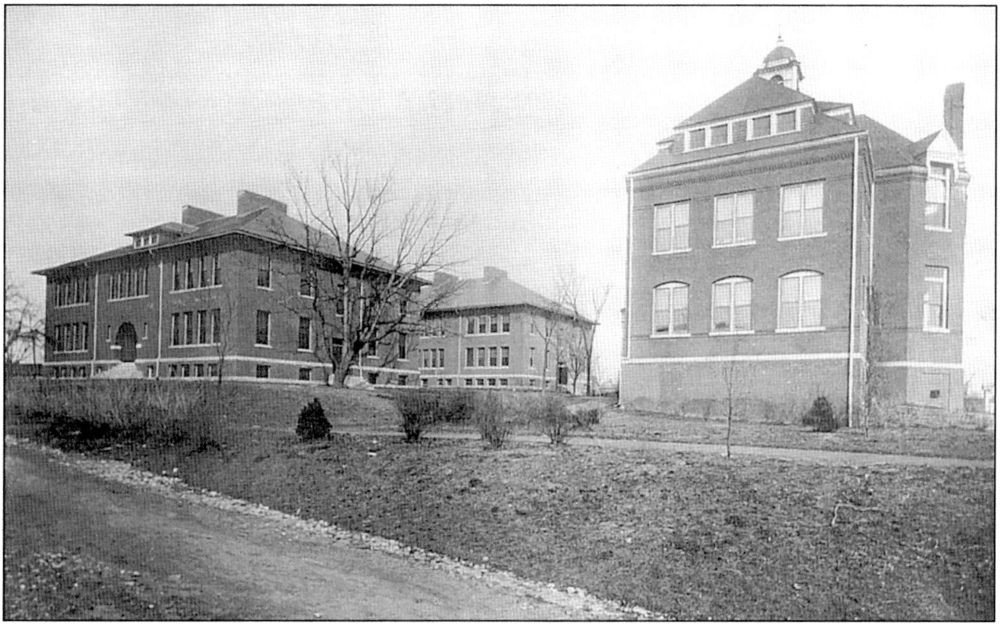

The Union School and the Primary and Cole Buildings, 1908. As the town's population grew, so did the number of students, often doubling in size in a matter of a few years. A six-room school was built by the LMA in 1884 and named the Union School. In 1900, the eight-room Cole Building was completed, with every room occupied at its opening. In 1907, the Primary Building was opened and quickly filled with students.

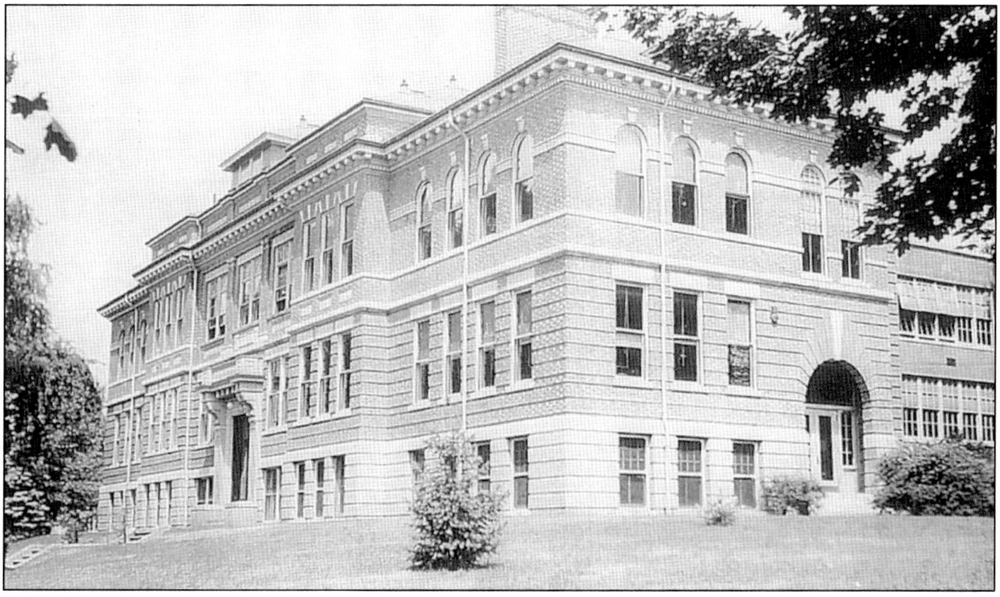

Ludlow High School, Chestnut Street, 1933. Built in 1910 on LMA-donated grounds, the new high school sat adjacent to the Union School. Ten years later, the two portable schools were erected to again alleviate overcrowding. In 1925, the high school was condemned for safety reasons. An addition was built in 1926, and in the 1960s, an entirely new high school was built on Chapin Street. The old high school is presently home to many senior citizens as well as the Ludlow Senior Center.

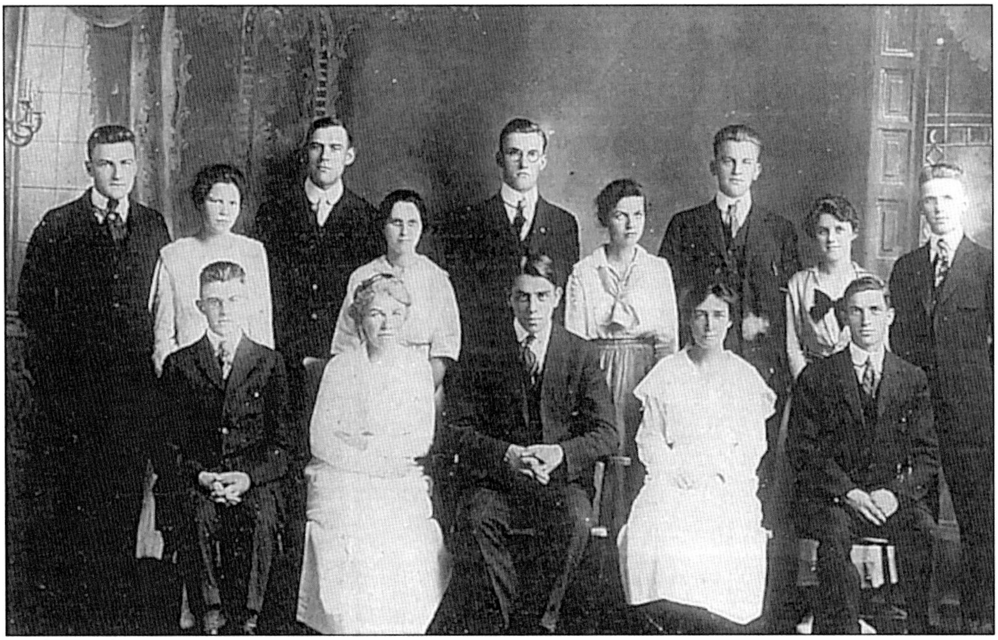

LUDLOW HIGH SCHOOL, CLASS OF 1918. Pictured from left to right in this view are as follows: (front row) Everett Goodall, Mrs. Gushee (principal), unidentified teacher, unidentified language teacher, and class president Walter Paine; (middle row) Marjorie Morris, unidentified, Lillian White, and Cora McClean; (back row) Paul Butler, ? Knight, ? Martin, and David Wilson.

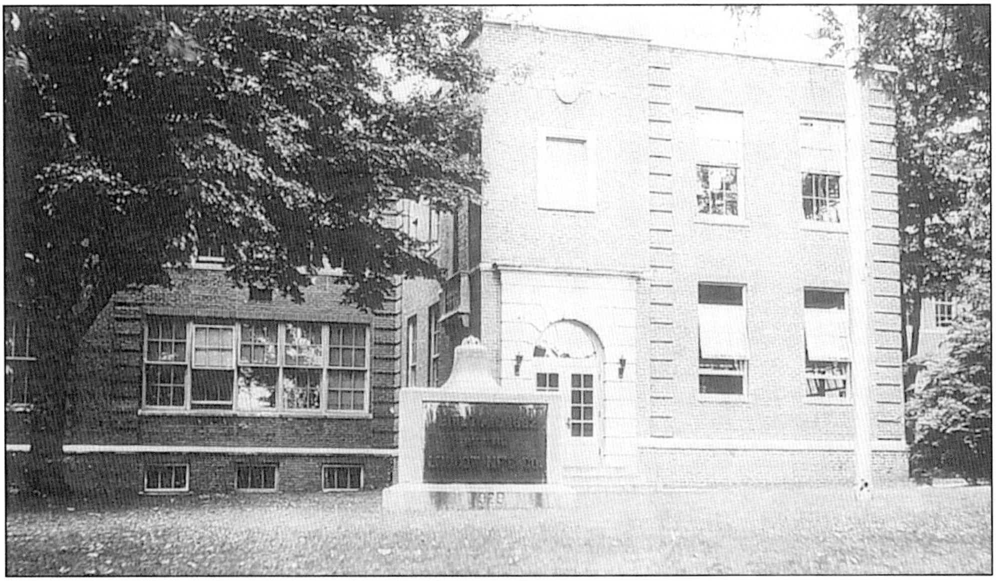

THE UNION SCHOOL BELL, 1930. The bell, which once sat atop the Union School, still sits on its concrete pad outside the old high school addition. The LMA presented it to the town when the bell was dismantled from the old school. The inscription on the redstone reads "Built A.D. 1882 by the Ludlow MFG. Co.," and the date on the pad reads 1929. Despite several attempts in recent years to remove the bell to the present high school, it will stay where it belongs, on the site of the old Union School.

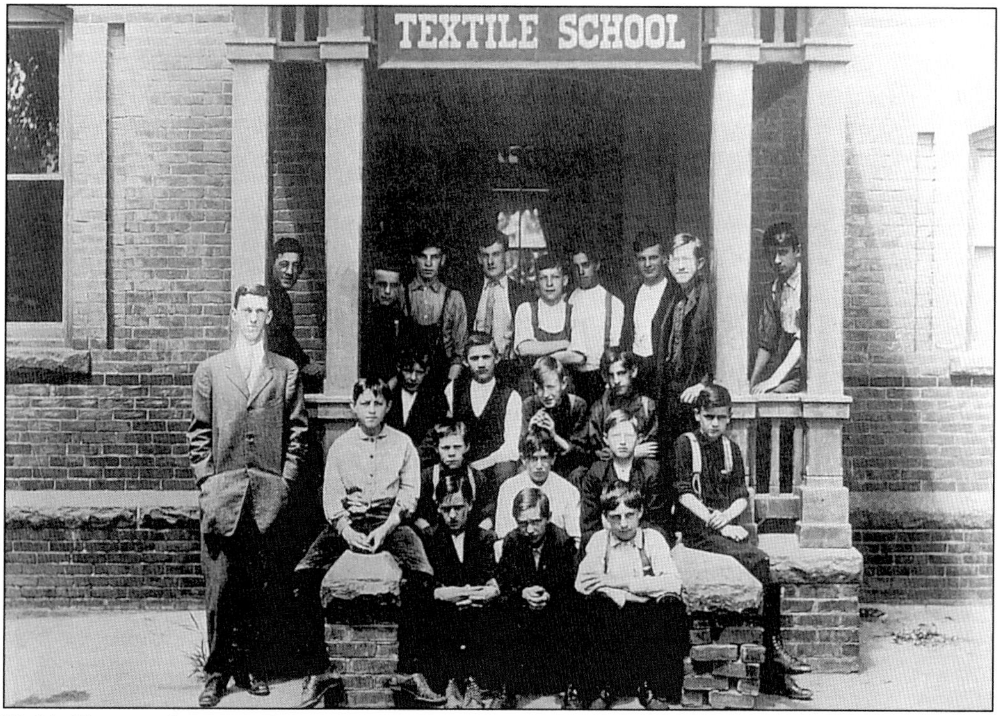

LMA Textile School, Class of 1909. Since many Ludlow residents were employed in the mills, it made sense to educate young boys not only in standard school fare but in the manufacture of jute and hemp products; they also learned the responsibilities of mill departments. Boys attended school for half days and worked in the mills for the other half, being paid for both school and work time. The school year ran 47 weeks, and the entire cost was covered by the LMA.

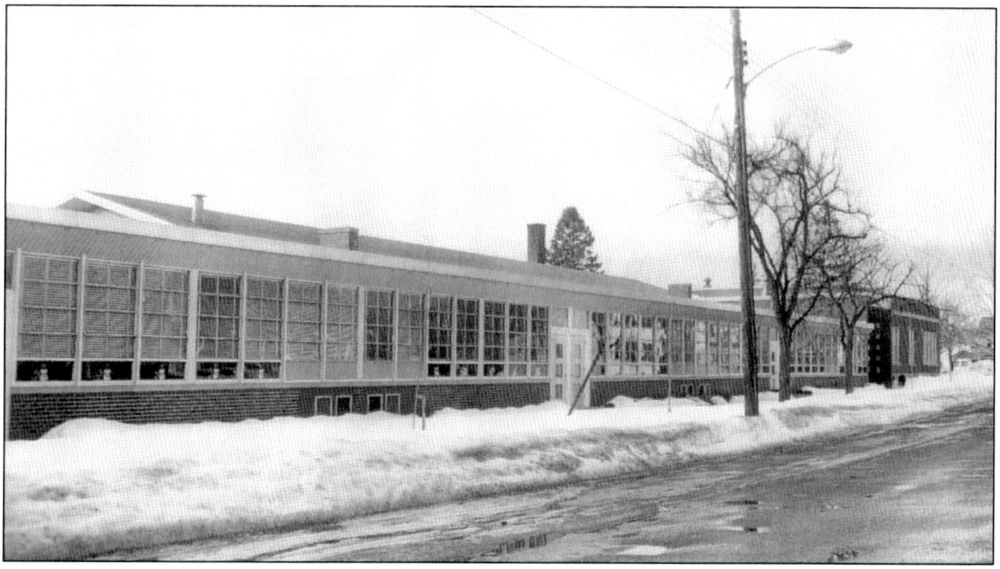

East Street Elementary School, c. 1960. Built in the 1920s, the East Street School had eight rooms and again only temporarily relieved overcrowding. An eight-room addition was built in 1960.

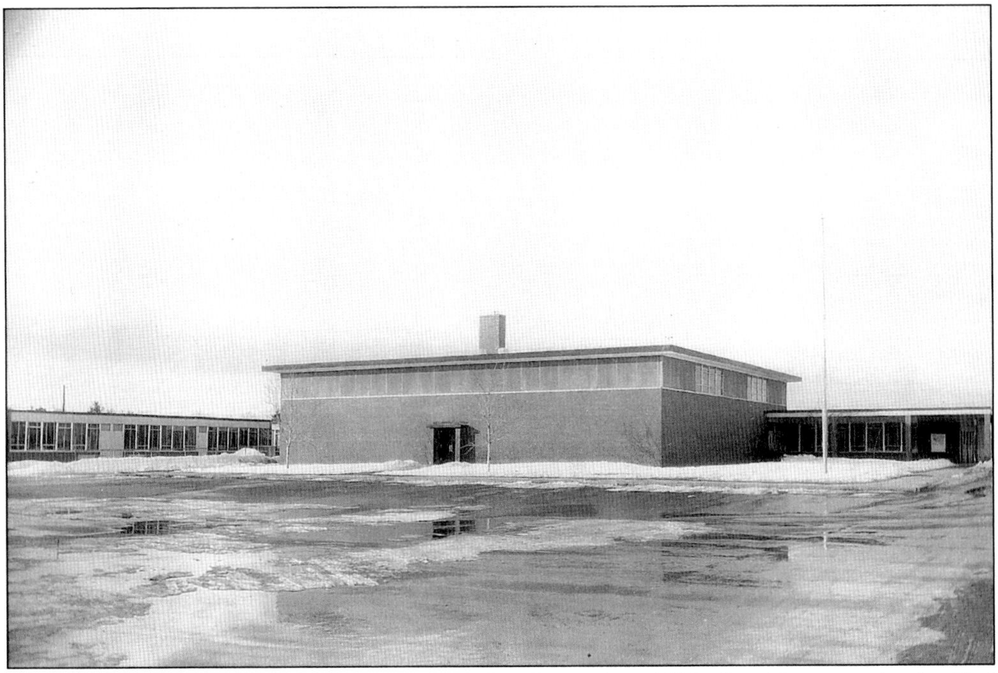

Chapin Street Elementary School, c. 1969. Opened in 1959, the 14-room school added 8 more rooms in 1964. The town continued to grow, needing more and bigger schools. At the time of this picture, grades one through six attended, with 550 students enrolled. Mr. Henry Casagrande was principal for many years, including the years this author attended (1970–1974).

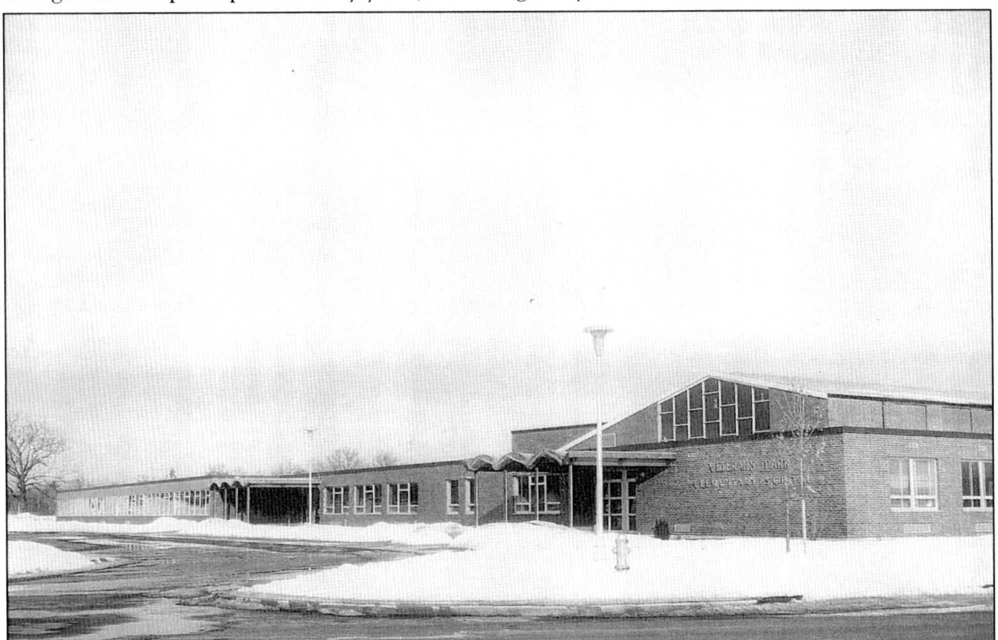

Veteran's Park Elementary School, Chapin Street, c. 1969. Built in 1967, Vet's Park had 18 rooms and was built behind the new high school. Grades one through six attended, with 575 pupils total. Mrs. Catherine Gauthier was principal at the time of this picture.

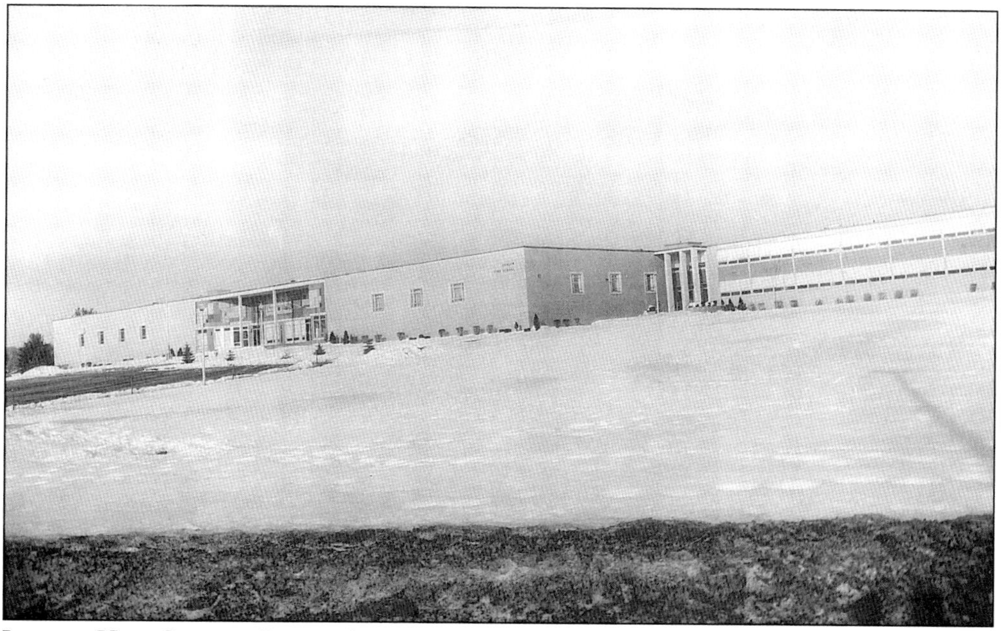

Ludlow High School, Chapin Street, c. 1969. The new LHS was built in 1962 and allowed for 1,000 students. Mr. John J. Hurley was principal when double sessions were implemented to accommodate the growing student body. Grades 10 through 12 attended school from 7:25 a.m. until 1:00 p.m., and grades 8 and 9 attended from 1:00 p.m. until 6:10 p.m. There had been seven separate periods of double sessions up to that point. An addition to the high school in 1972 increased its capacity to 1,600, and a new junior high school opened in 1974, behind the high school and Vet's Park School. Once again, work has begun in 1999 to renovate and update both the high school and middle school (junior high). This author witnessed first-hand some of the shuffling of students as the new junior high was constructed.

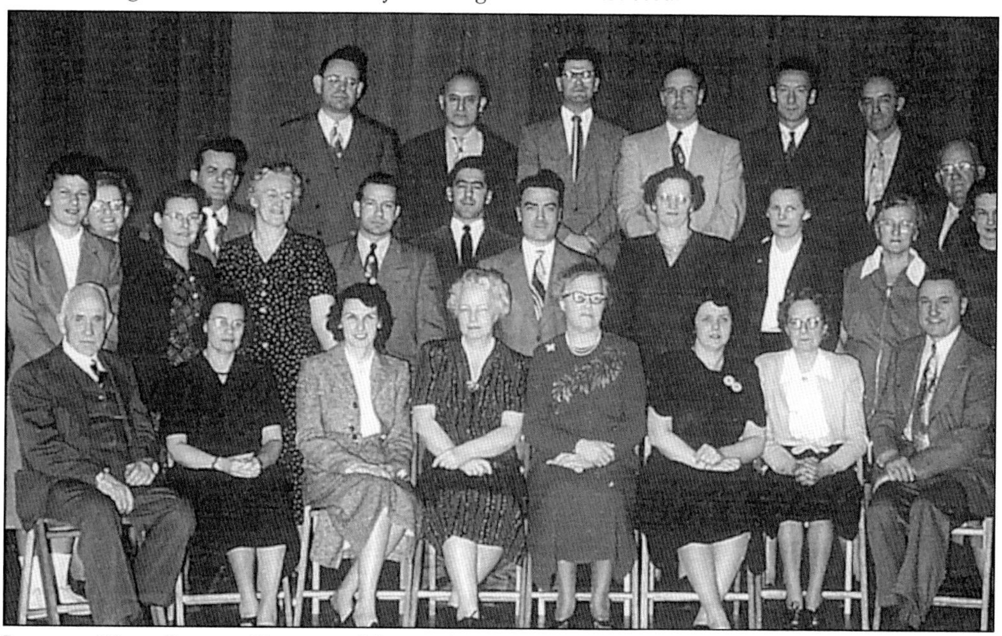

Ludlow High School Faculty, March 21, 1951.

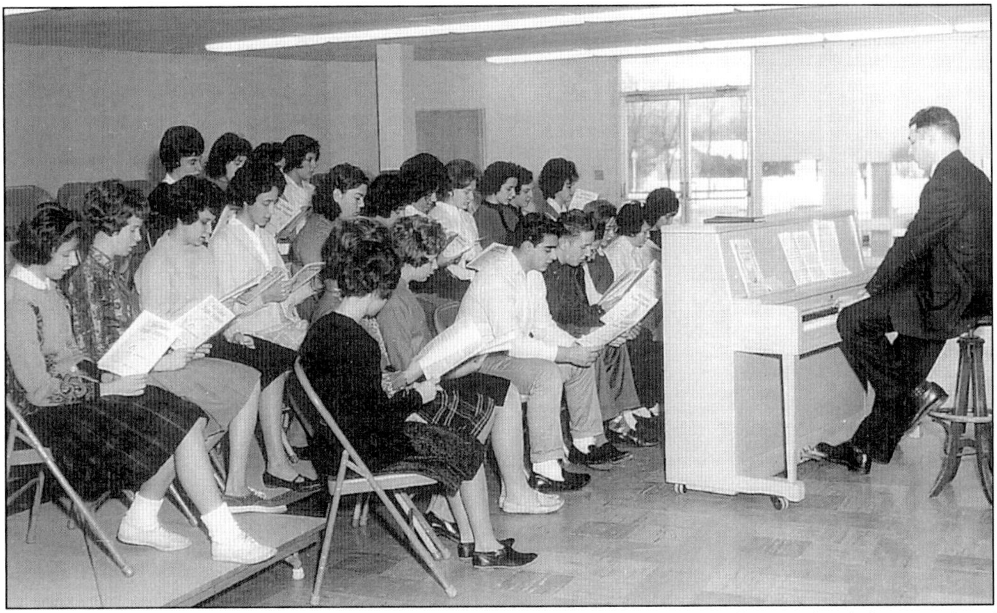

Choral Room, Ludlow High School. Mr. Gregory Wrinn musically touched thousands of students, many of whom went on to have careers in music. With, at times, nearly 100 students belonging to Concert Choir (cutting an album and putting on concerts and musical productions such as *The Sound of Music*, *Oklahoma*, and many others), "D block" was the best time of the school day.

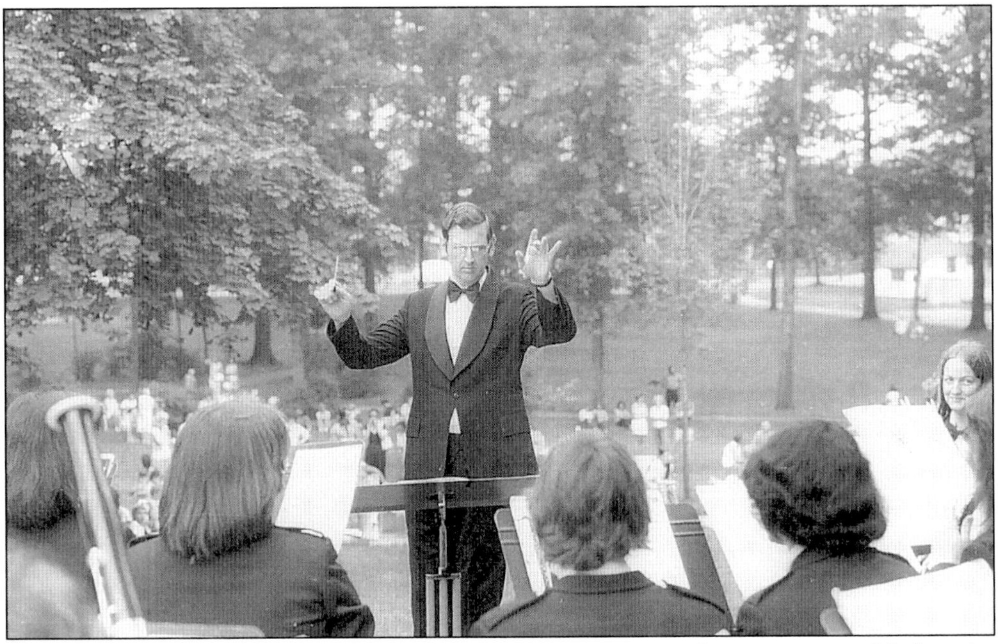

Ludlow High School Band, National Bicentennial Celebrations. Under the direction of Mr. Royce Layman, the Ludlow High Band was successful at many competitions, including being one of three bands chosen to represent the U.S. at the International Youth and Musical Festival in Vienna, Austria, in 1975. At that competition, they were awarded second place.

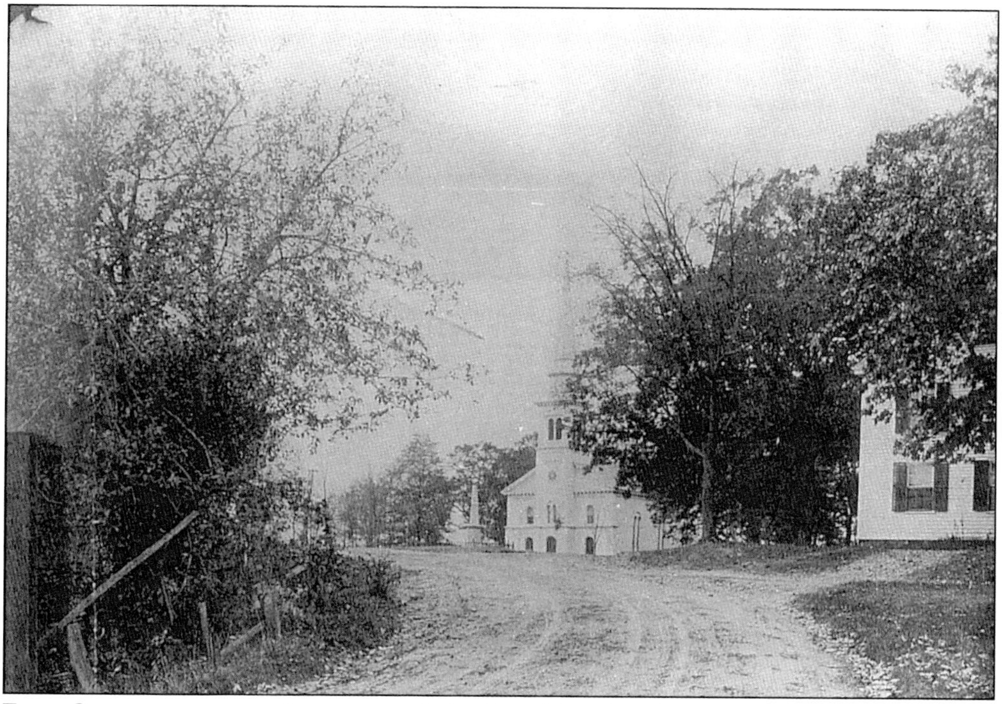

FIRST CHURCH, LUDLOW CENTER, C. 1890. The oldest church was constructed from 1840 to 1841. Located next to the First Meetinghouse in the town's historic Ludlow Center district, the church burned down twice, once in 1859 and again in the early 1980s. The landmark church was rebuilt both times and stands very close to the town's geographic center.

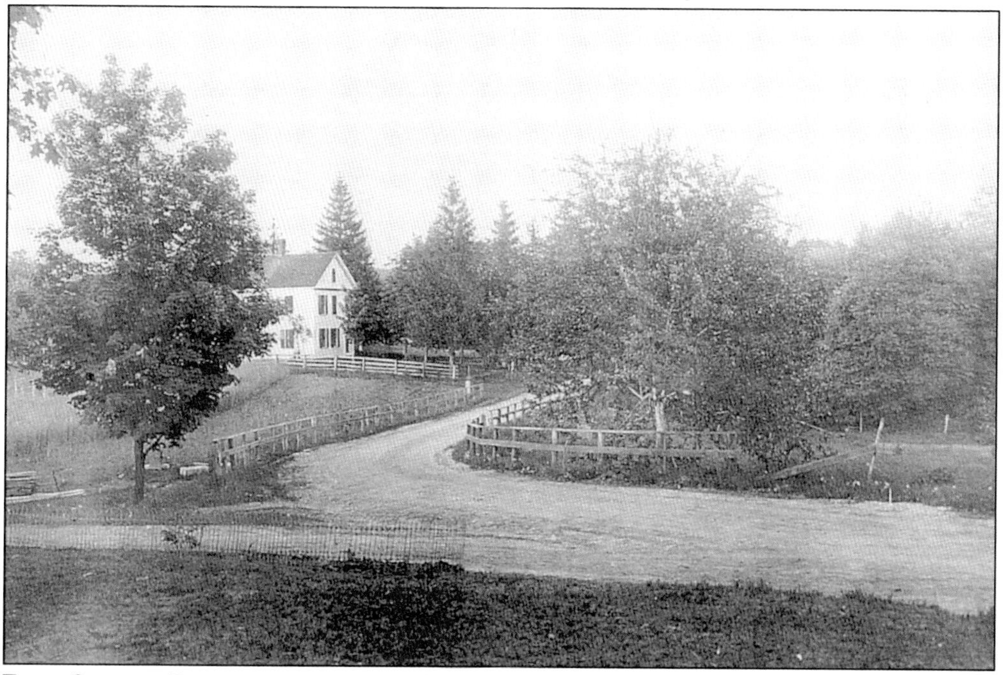

FIRST CHURCH PARSONAGE, C. 1890. The church parsonage is now a private residence at 877 Center Street, where Booth Street forks to the left.

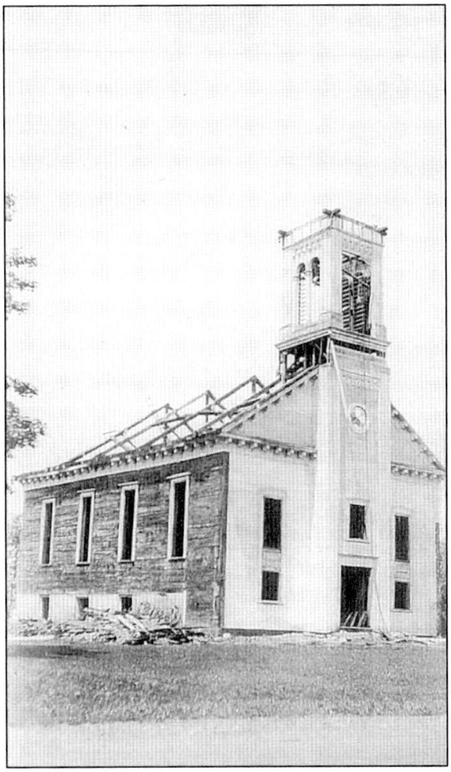

The Ludlow Center Methodist Church, Constructed in 1827 on Miller Street. As membership dwindled at the turn of the 20th century, a decision was made to relocate the congregation close to Ludlow Village, and in 1905, St. Paul's Methodist Church began services. Years later, the old Methodist church was sold and dismantled.

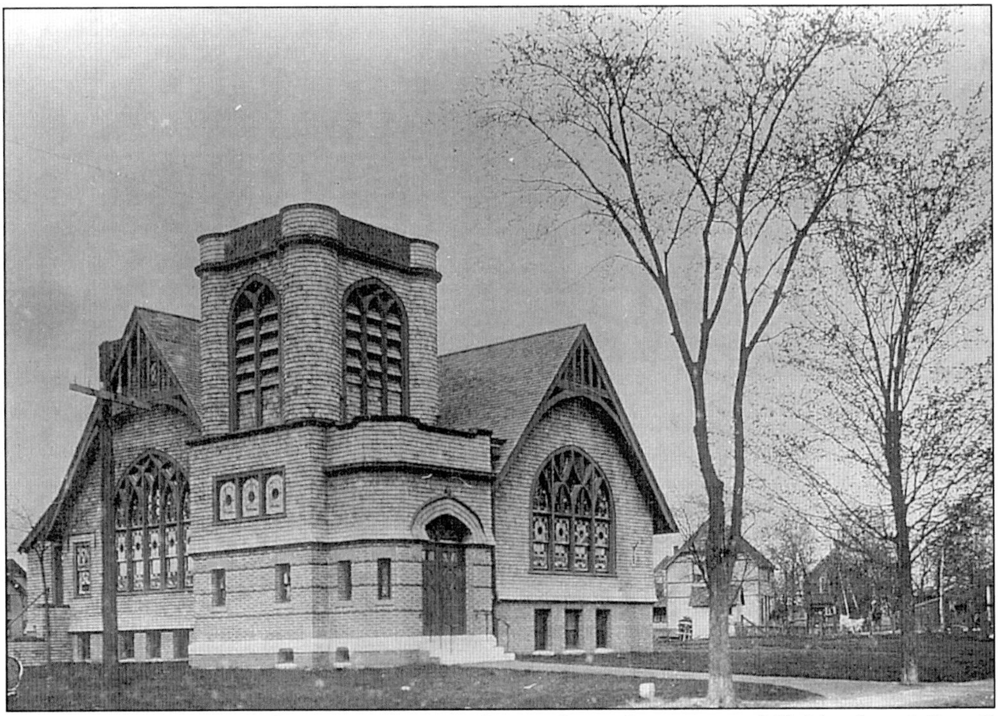

St. Paul's Methodist Church, c. 1910. Located on the corner of Hubbard and Sewall Streets, St. Paul's still serves the community.

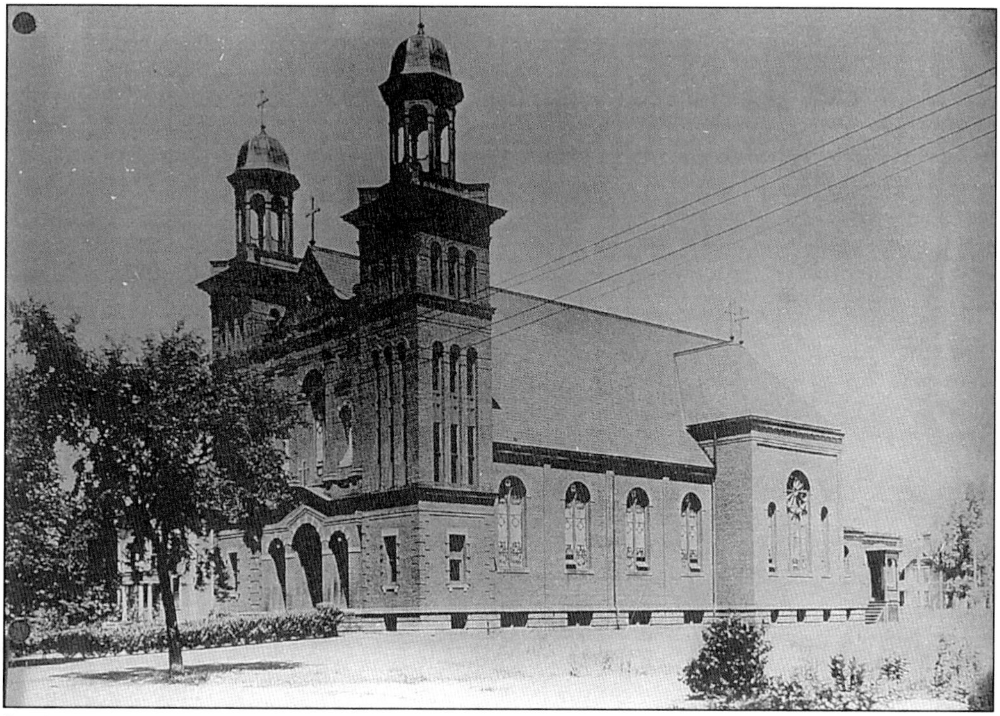

St. John the Baptist, July 1913. Built on Hubbard Street on land donated by the LMA, the church and rectory were completed in 1906. In 1926, both a school and convent were added to more fully serve the French-Canadian families in Ludlow.

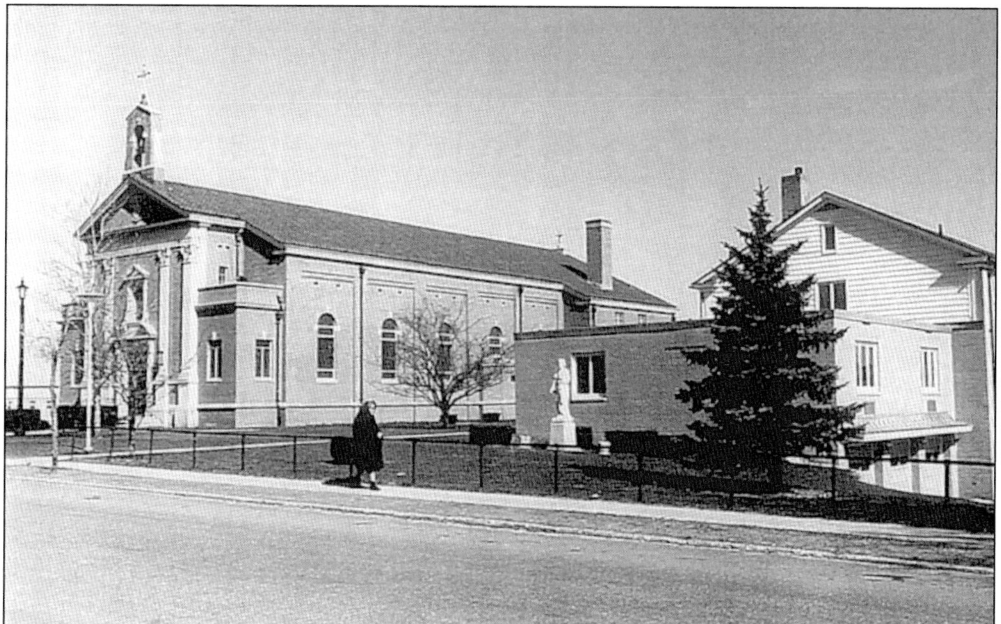

Christ the King Church and Rectory, Warsaw Avenue, 1973. Completed in May 1942, Christ the King served the Polish community. As land was acquired, a rectory and parish center were built. The dedication of these buildings was in September 1968.

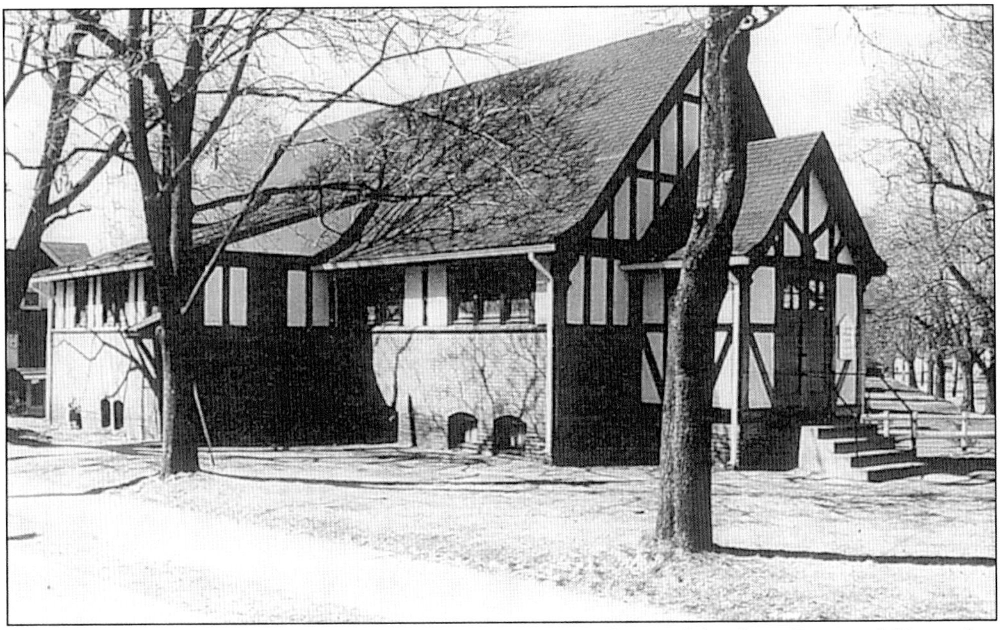

St. Andrew's Episcopal Church, 1973. LMA again donated land on East and Hampden Streets for construction in 1905. Despite valiant efforts to stay active, the congregation voted to disband in 1997. In digging out the cornerstone as a memento, parish members William and Linda Koss discovered a time capsule. Unknown to anyone and unrecorded in history books, the capsule contained old newspapers, church documents, an 1874 history of Ludlow, and a list of parishioners.

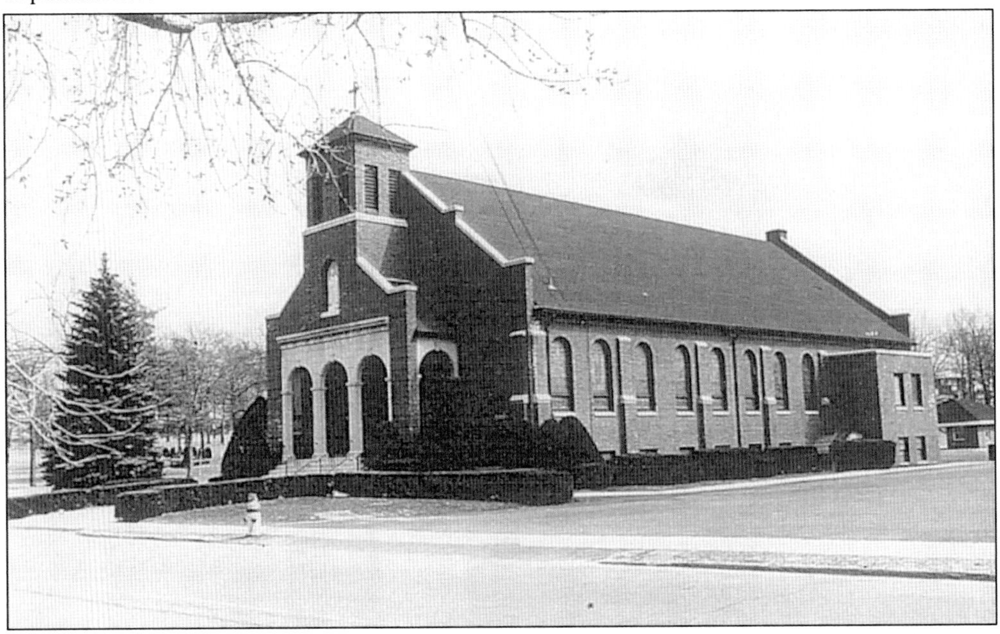

Our Lady of Fatima Church, 1973. As the Portuguese population grew, the need for their own church grew as well. LMA-donated property on Winsor Street allowed the groundbreaking in 1948, and a dedication was held in September 1949. The cornerstone of the church came from Fatima, Portugal.

Four

HOUSES

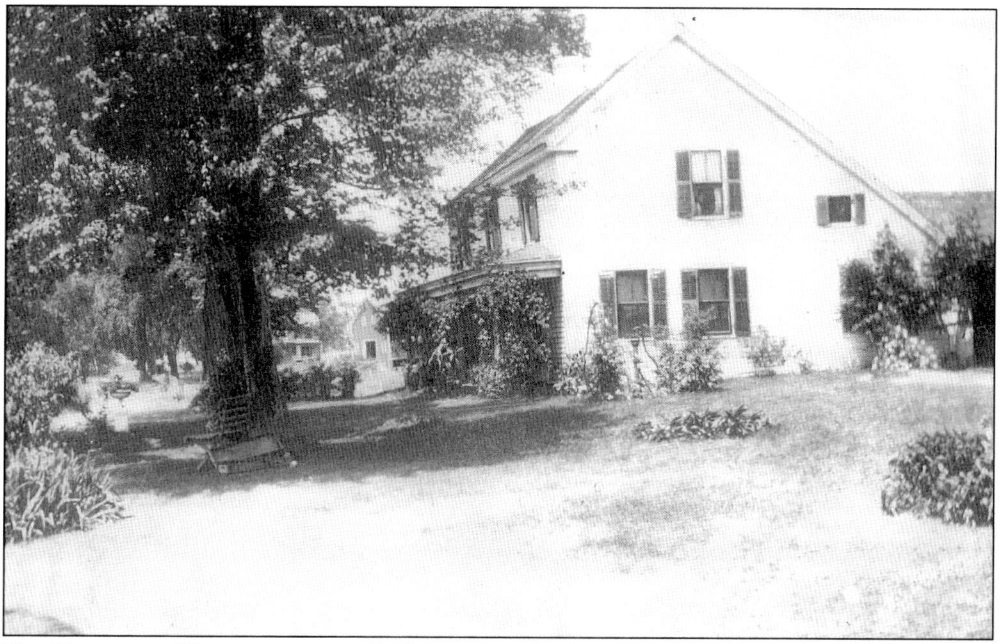

THE FAIRBANKS HOUSE, C. 1900. Built *c.* 1770, this house at 456 Holyoke Street is the only original, true saltbox-type house in Ludlow. The long, sloping roof faced north so cold winds would blow up and over the house. Now owned by Don and Betty Kibbe, the house and land are home to Windmill Farm and Garden Center, where this author grew up. Neighbor Arthur Guertin recalls that the barn seen in the background was owned by the Keefe brothers, and four full teams of horses with wagons could fit inside at the same time. (Photo courtesy Don and Betty Kibbe.)

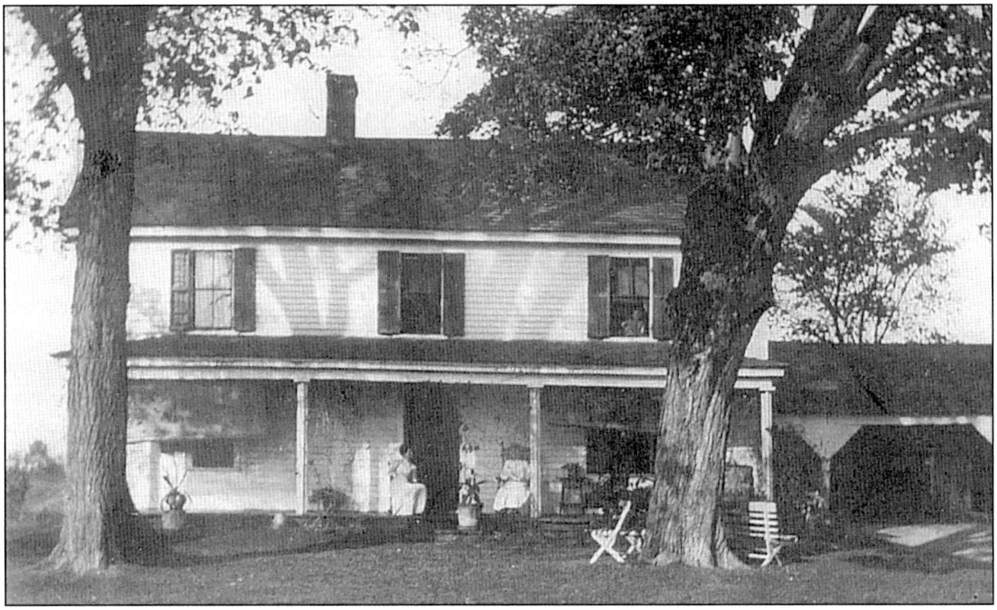

The Fairbanks House, 456 Holyoke Street. Note that Holyoke Street, then called Holyoke Road, seems like a dirt path in this view. Mrs. Charles Fairbanks purchased the house in 1874 and remodeled the house and barn. Former owners include John Paulk and Dan Hubbard. The house remained in the Fairbanks family until 1970, when present owners Don and Betty Kibbe bought it. (Photo courtesy Don and Betty Kibbe.)

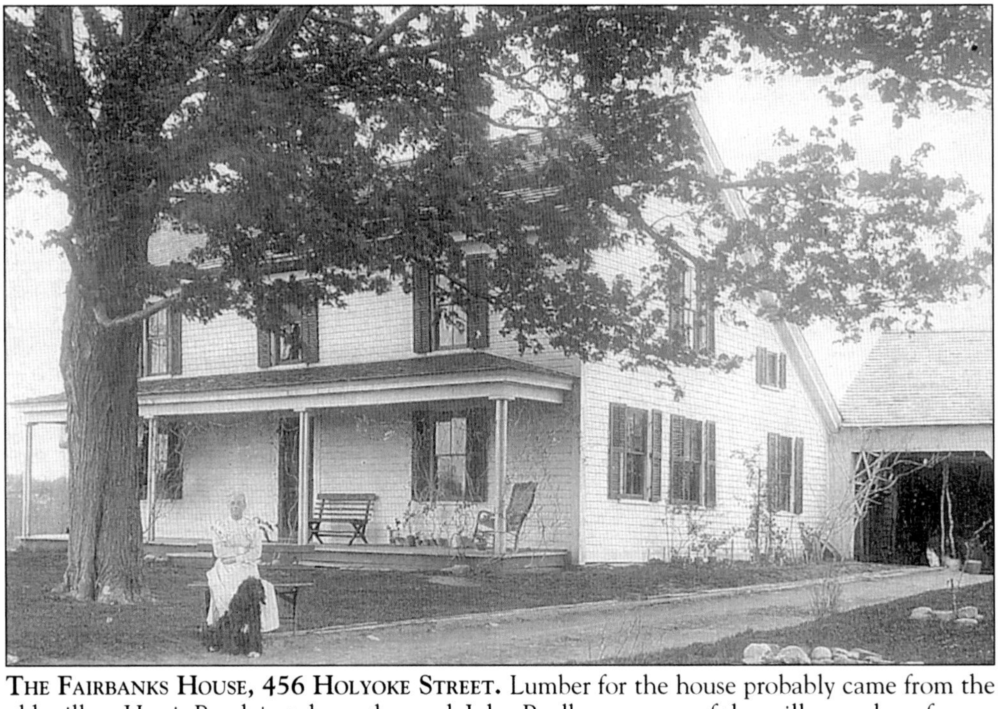

The Fairbanks House, 456 Holyoke Street. Lumber for the house probably came from the old mill on Harris Pond, just down the road. John Paulk, an owner of the mill, was also a former owner of this house and quite possibly was responsible for major renovations, which appear to have been done in the mid-1800s. (Photo courtesy Don and Betty Kibbe.)

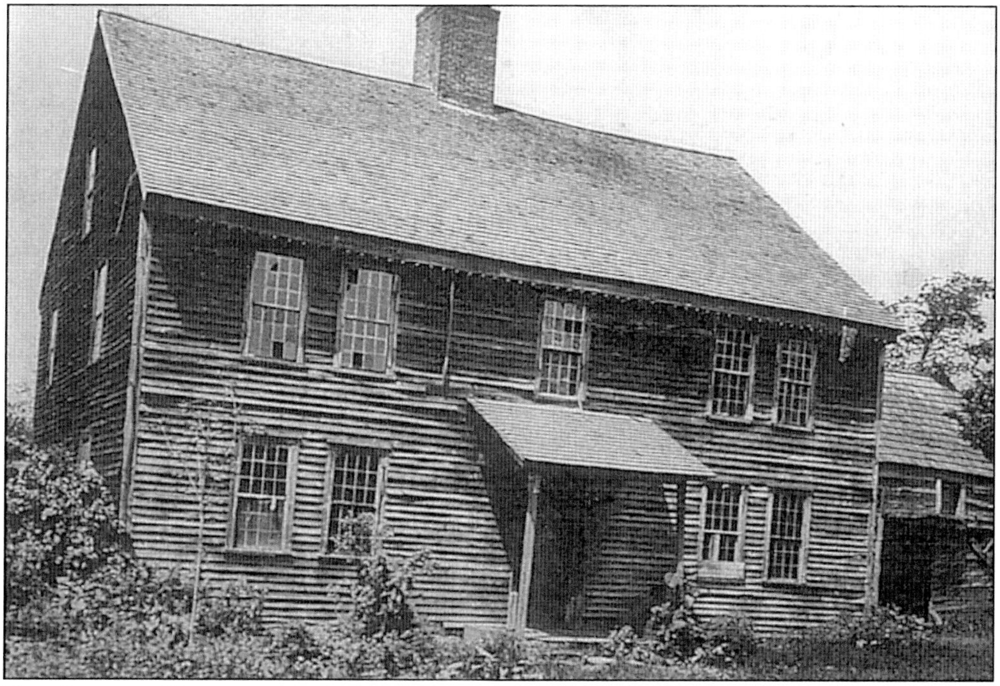

The Dorman House, near Ludlow Center. Probably built c. 1810, this was one of the places to post town meetings. In its early years, it was presumed to have been a tavern and dance house.

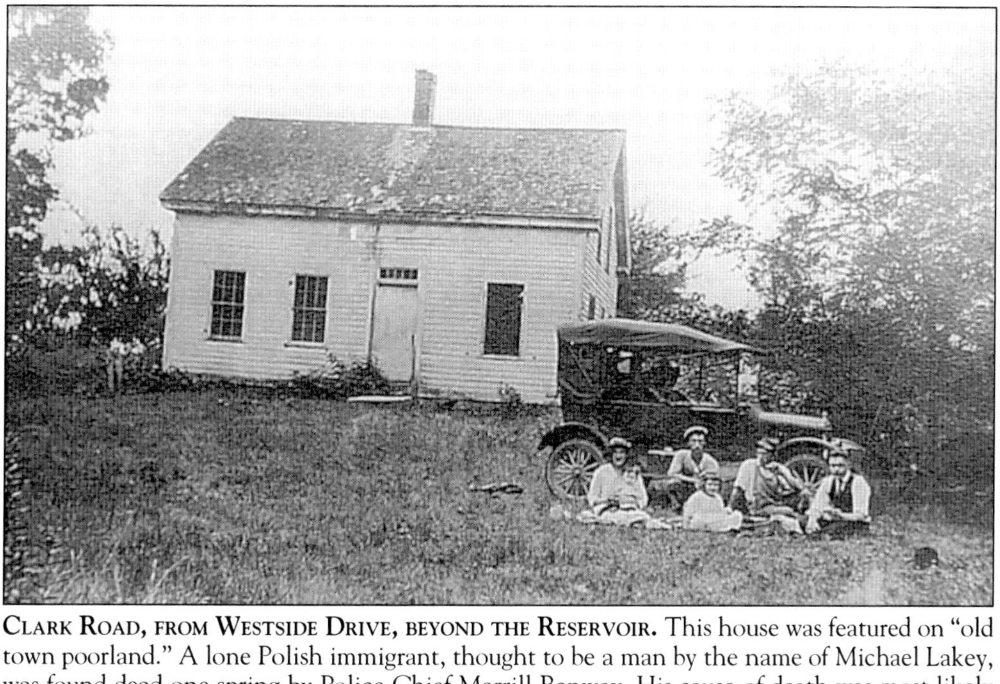

Clark Road, from Westside Drive, beyond the Reservoir. This house was featured on "old town poorland." A lone Polish immigrant, thought to be a man by the name of Michael Lakey, was found dead one spring by Police Chief Merrill Benway. His cause of death was most likely pneumonia.

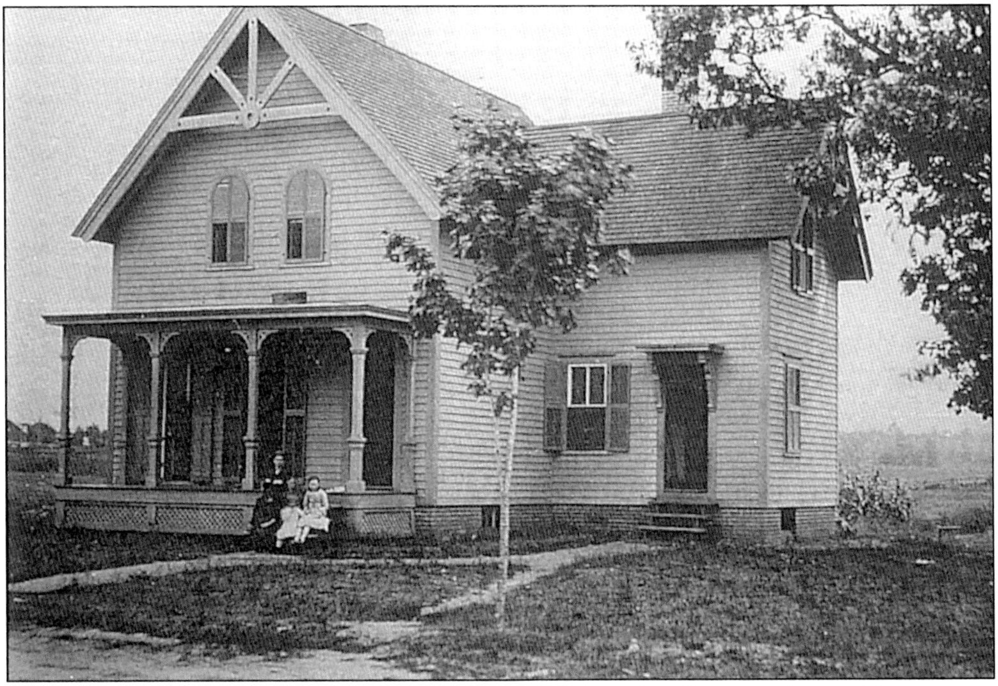

Winsor Street house, c. 1910. The LMA built housing for all its employees. Houses were allotted to employees based on their position in the mill. Rent was based on the size and style of the house.

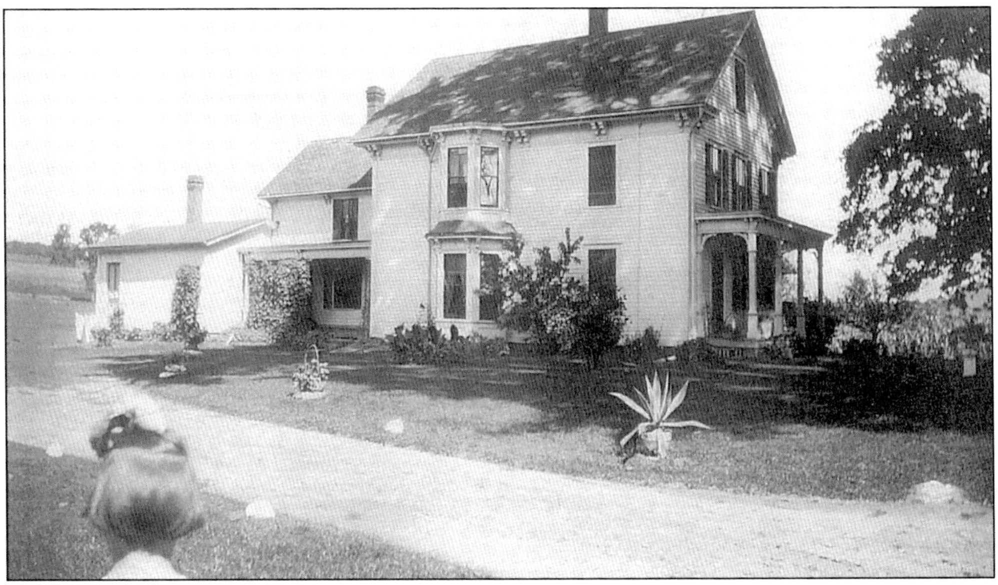

Fuller Street, c. 1910. The owners of this house were either relatives of the Fairbanks on Holyoke Street or good friends of theirs, as there are several pictures of this house and activities surrounding it in the Fairbanks album. (Photo courtesy Don and Betty Kibbe.)

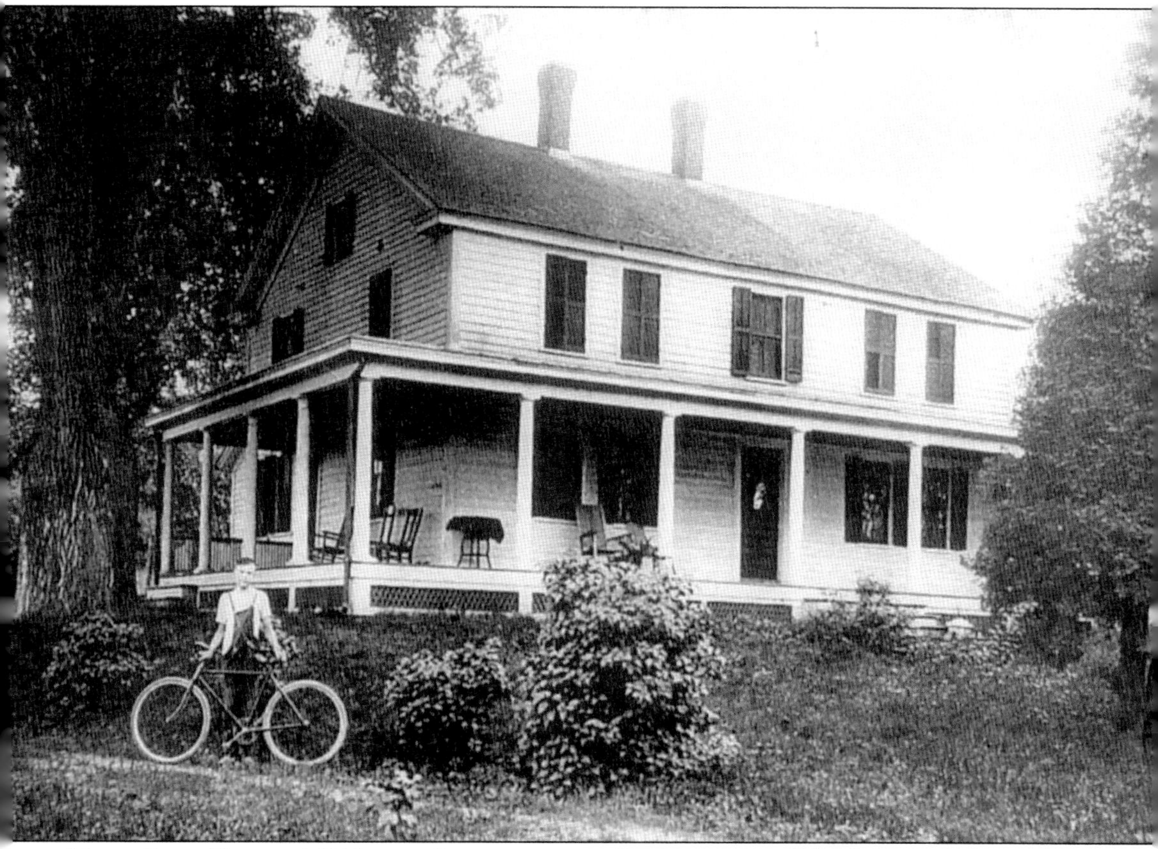

MOSES ROOD HOUSE, 467 FULLER STREET, C. 1910. Former owners of this house include Roger M. Chandler, John Knight, and Adelbert L. Bennett.

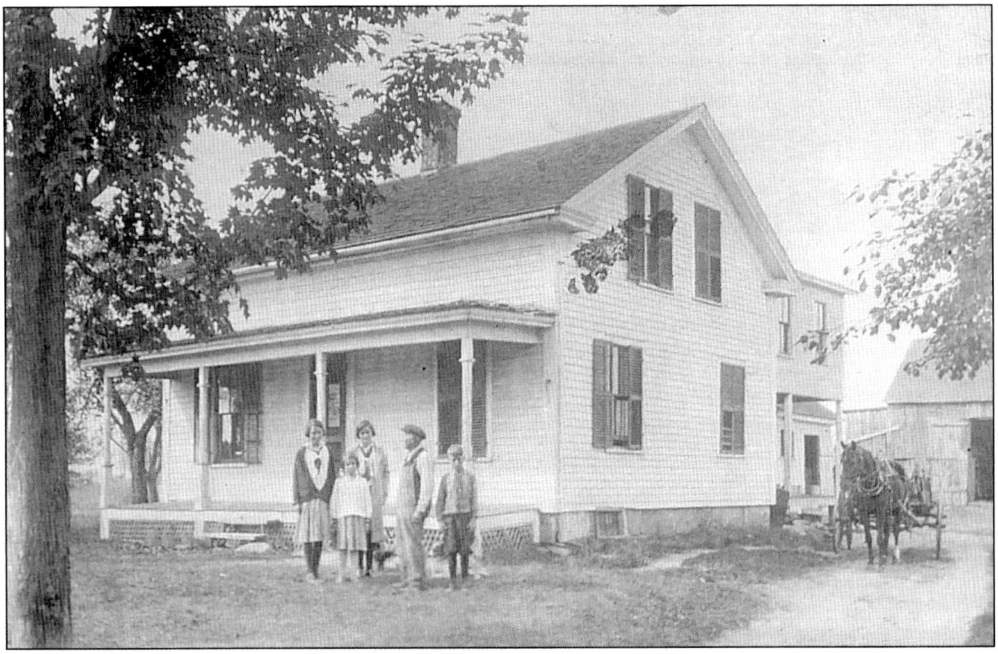

EDWARD MILLER HOUSE, 667 EAST STREET, C. 1924. The front part of the house was moved down from Cherry Valley when the reservoir was to be put in (1870–1873). Edward Miller had a livery stable on Chestnut Street, where the hospital building is now. Shown here, from left to right, are Priscilla Allen, Barbara Allen, Sylvia Gray, Edward Miller, and Harry Allen.

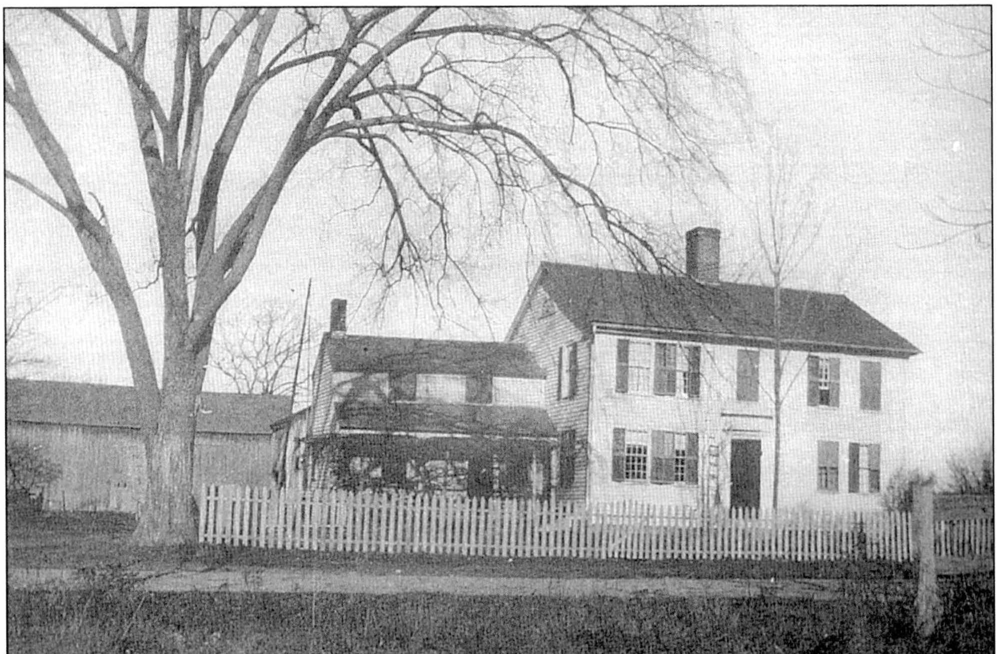

THE JOHN RAY HOMESTEAD, 519 EAST STREET, C. 1900. This home was built c. 1820 by William Ray, who used to forge bayonets for the U.S. Armory during the Civil War. His shop stood nearly opposite the house.

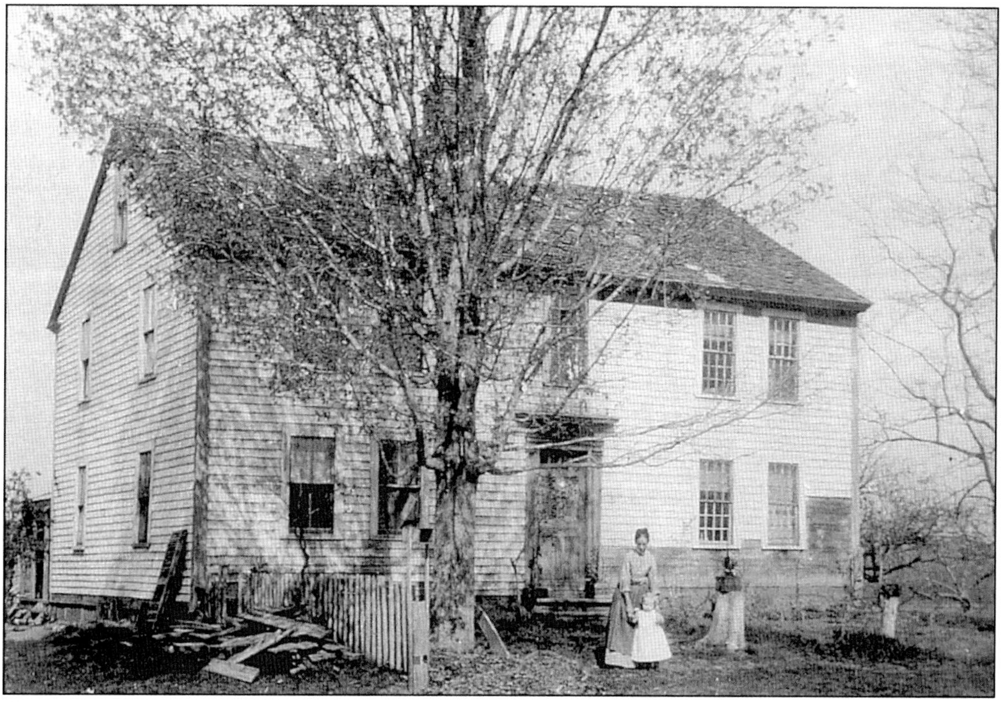

The Frank Ellison House, Miller Street, c. 1885. This was the home of RFD mail carrier Frank Ellison. Pictured are Cora Ellison and William D. Ellison.

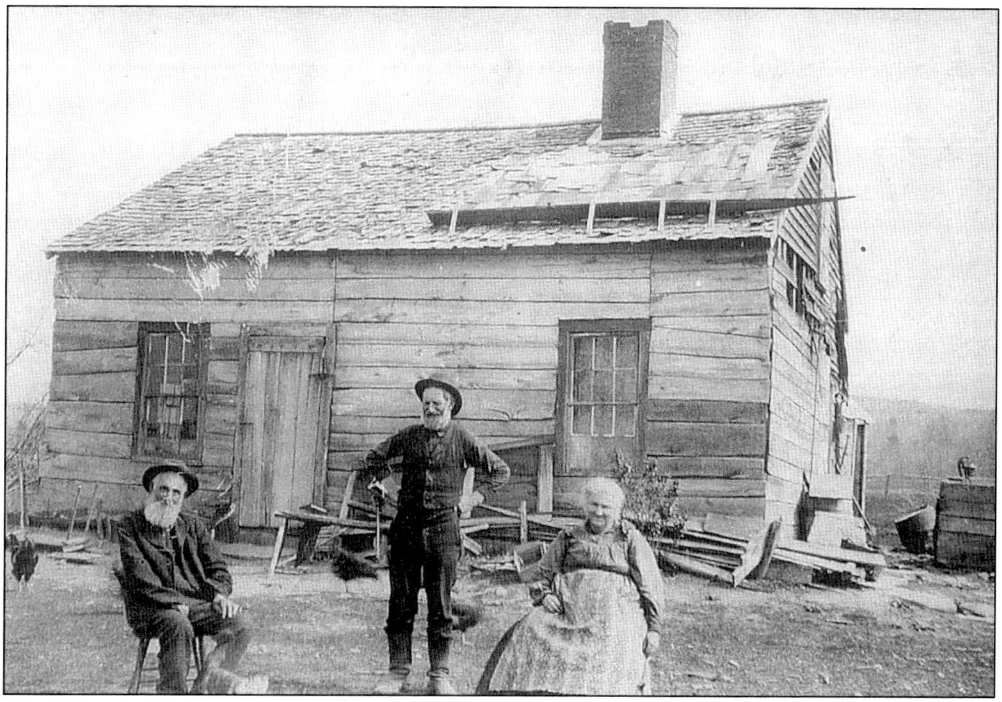

The Quartus Fisk House, Lyon Street, c. 1901. Pictured from left to right are Monroe Horr, Quartus Fisk, and Mrs. Quartus Fisk. Quartus's son Ed, who was friends with Frank Ellison, used to man the fire tower on Tower Road.

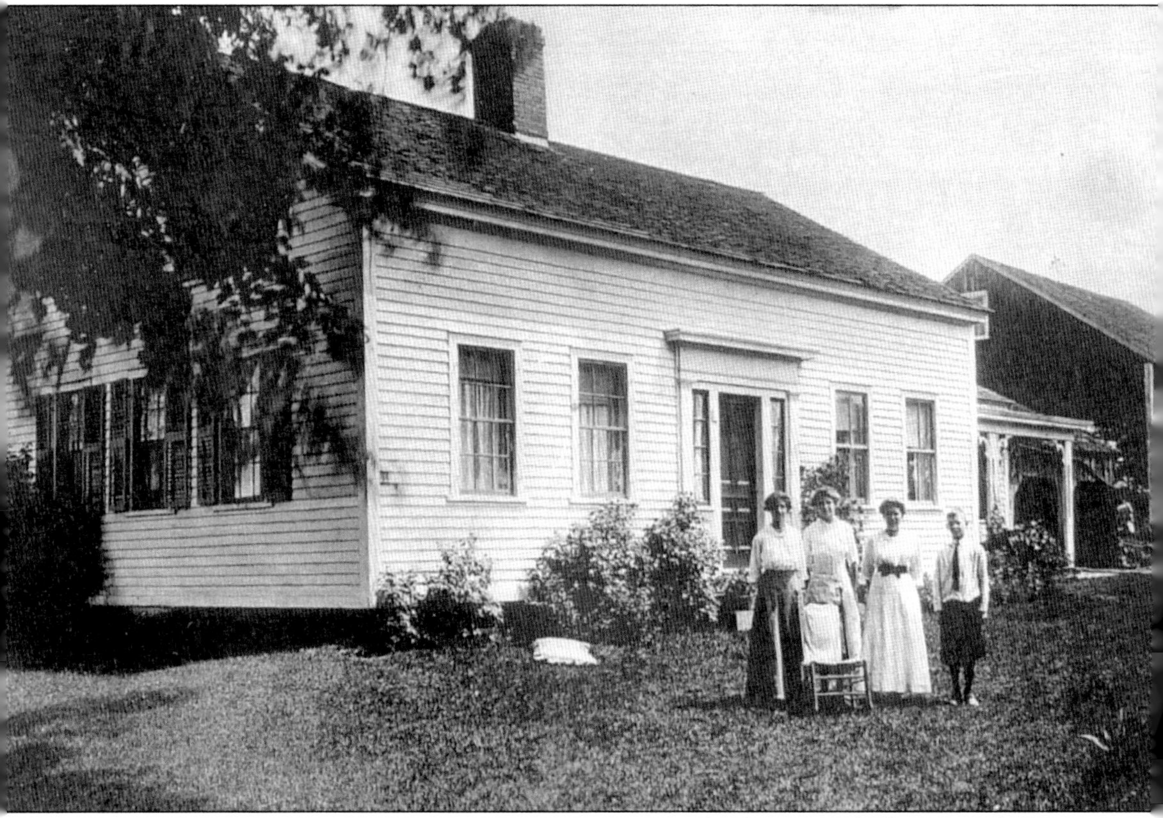

THE R. ASHWELL HOUSE, CENTER STREET, JULY 1915. This house was built in 1841 by Henry Charles. Shown here, from left to right, are Josephine A. Pease, Isabel Pease, Minnie (Mrs. William A. Ashwell), and Raymond Ashwell.

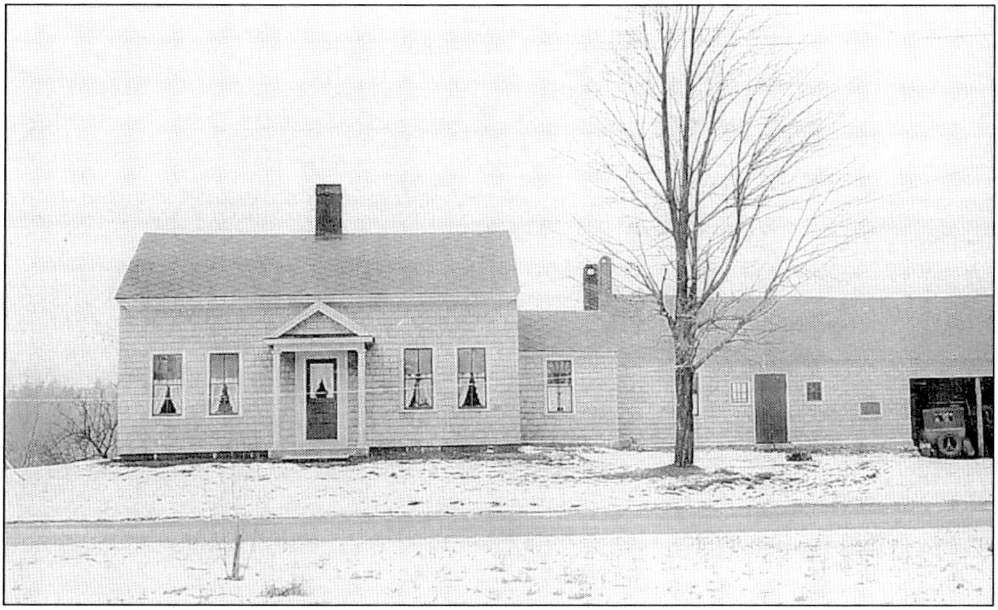

The Goden House, 1065 Center Street, c. 1930.

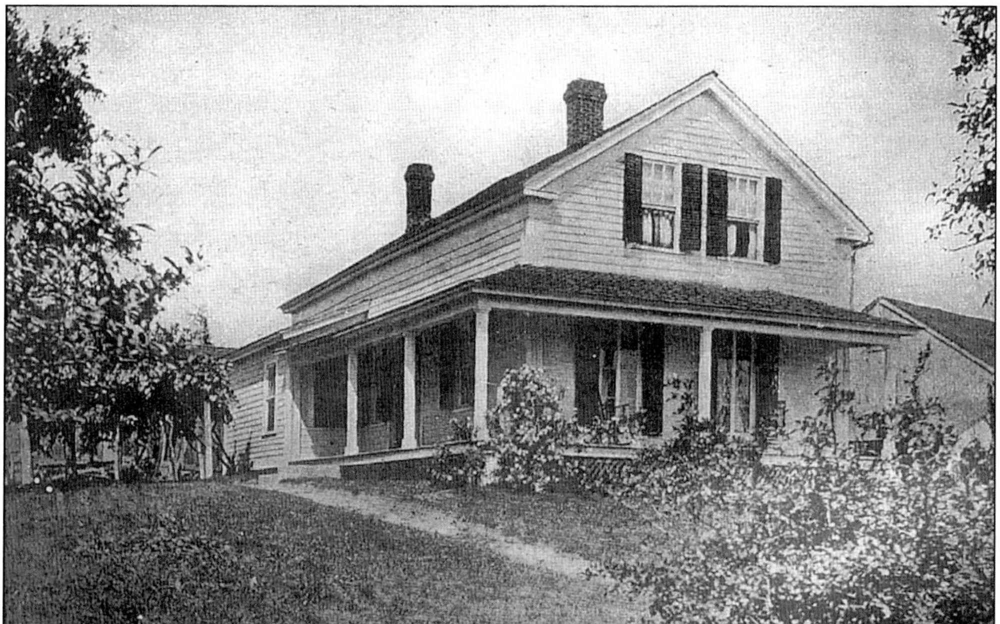

The Franklin Nash House, Fuller Street, 1900. Former owners of this house include Davenport Fuller (who enlarged and remodeled it), Warren Hubbard, Elijah Munsell, Newton Fisher, Charles Syriac, and George Streeter.

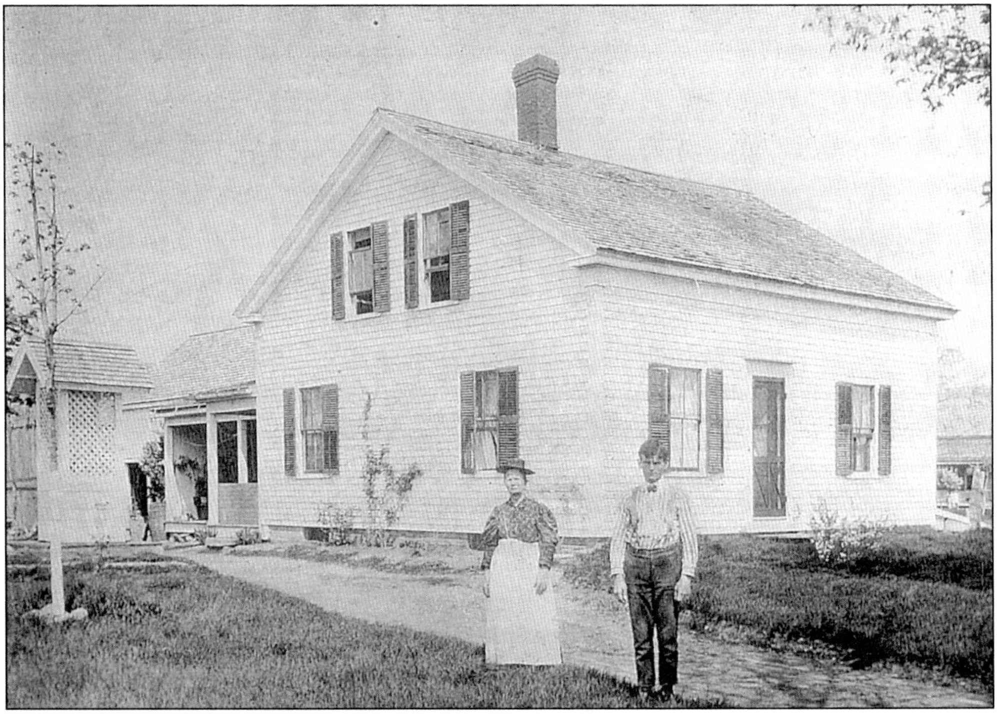

The Mike Clifford House, c. 1900.

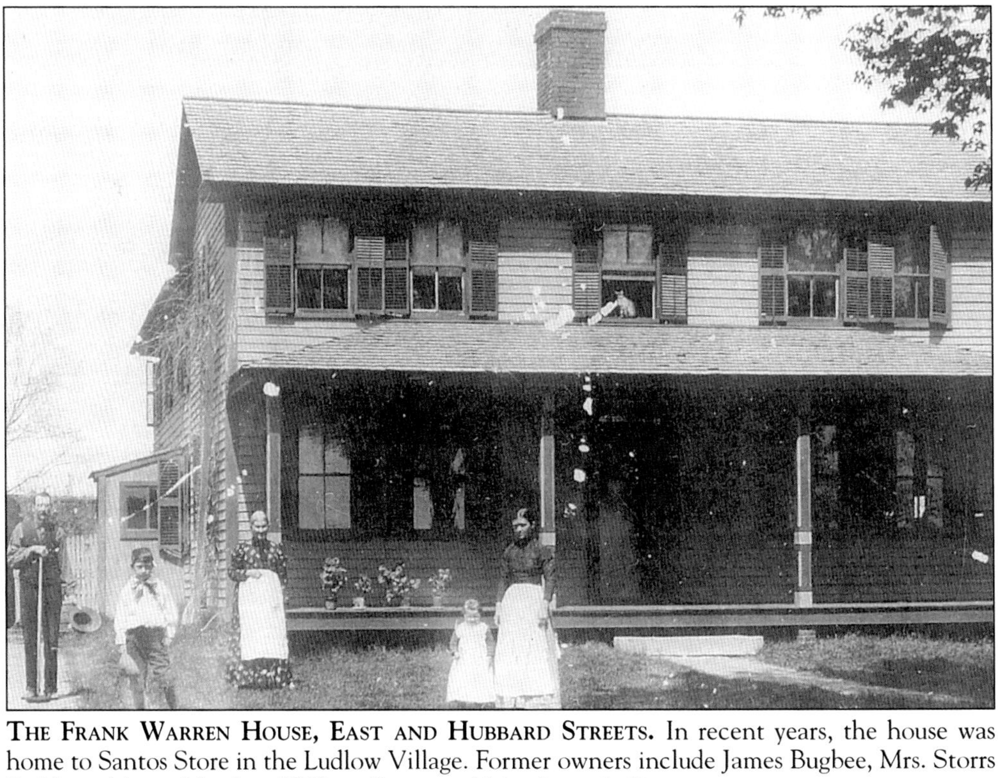

The Frank Warren House, East and Hubbard Streets. In recent years, the house was home to Santos Store in the Ludlow Village. Former owners include James Bugbee, Mrs. Storrs Stebbins, Myron Hayden, William Pease, and Mrs. Lucy A. Pease.

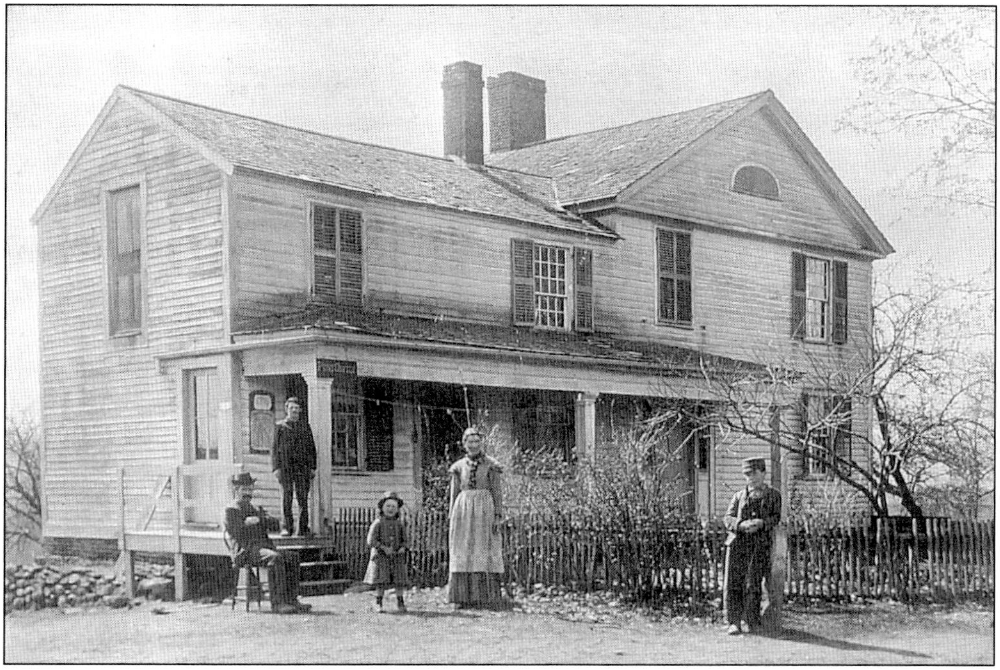

The Leavitt Perham House, 854 Center Street, Opposite First Church. The house, built by Theodore Sikes, was the sight of the Ludlow Post Office from 1892 to 1919. Former owners of the home include Dr. Washington B. Alden, Lucius Simonds, Elizur Hayes, and Gordon Pinney, who willed it to Mrs. Perham in January 1892.

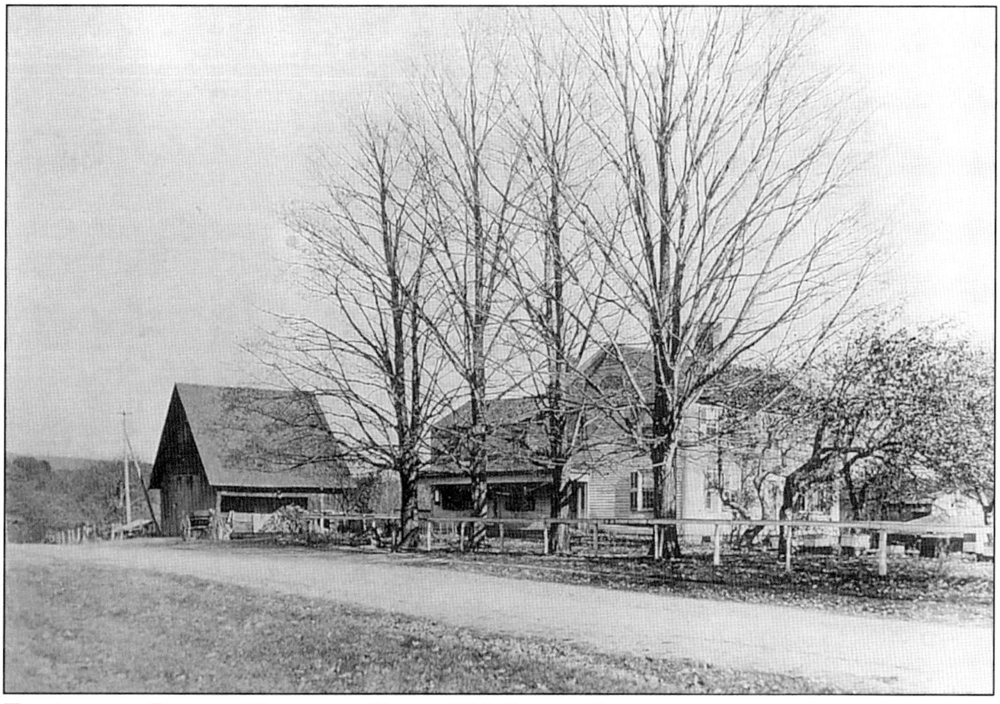

The Leavitt Perham House and Barn, 854 Center Street.

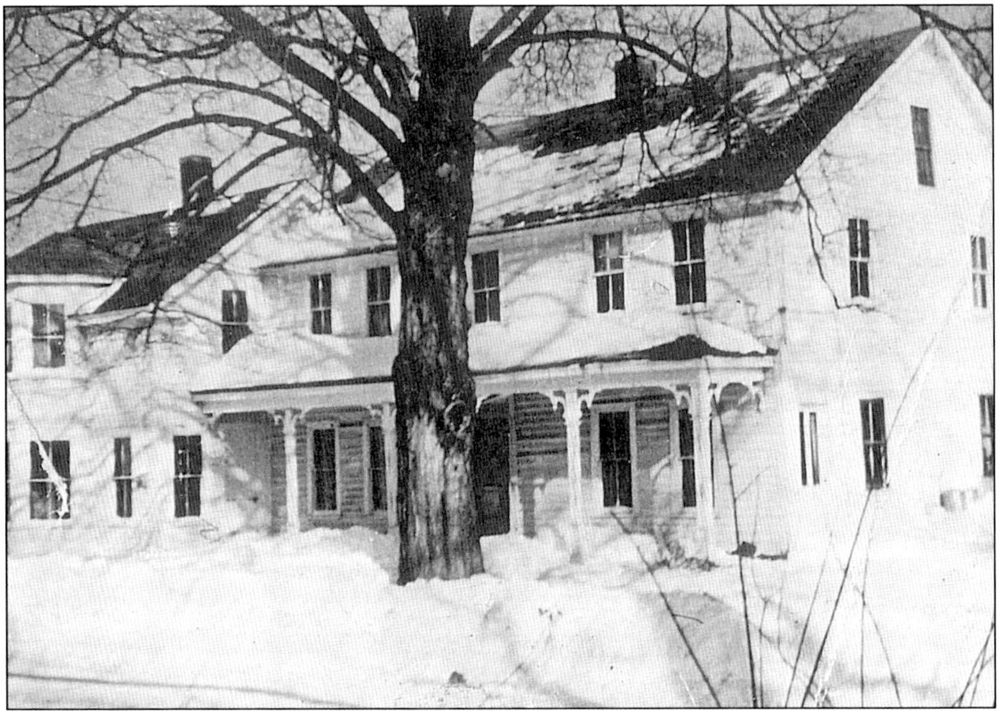

THE ELAM WRIGHT HOUSE, 476 FULLER STREET, C. 1960. Elam Wright used the house as a tavern. Former owners include George N. Hubbard, Joel Clark, Noah Clark, George Smith, Charles S. Bennett, Franklin Bennett, and Henry Granger.

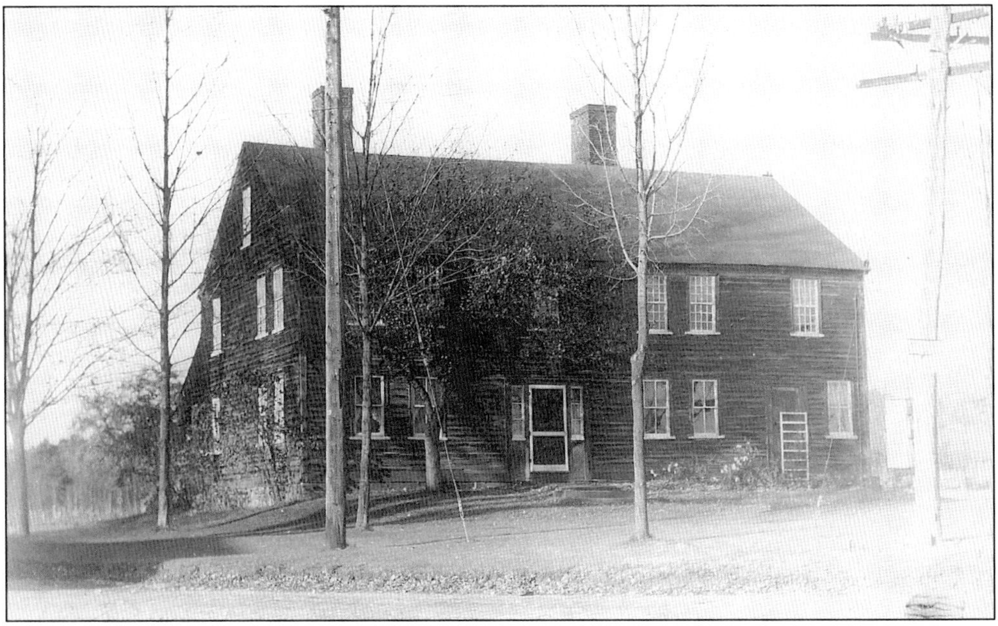

THE ELY FULLER HOUSE, 943 CENTER STREET, C. 1934. Probably built by Ely Fuller, the house was used as a hotel, tavern, and meeting place. A grand ballroom once spanned the second floor. Former owners include Mrs. Ashbel P. Chapin, Jerusha Fuller (Ely's widow), Caroline (Fuller) Warner (their daughter), Isaac Plumley, and Ashbel P. Chapin.

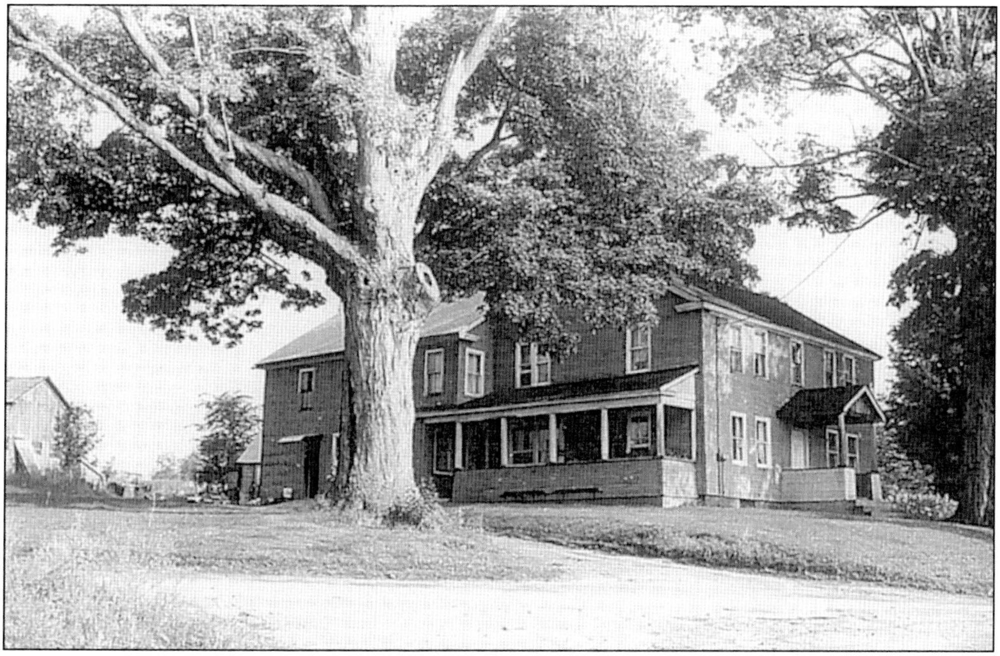

313 Fuller Street, July 1977. Located on Fuller Street, at the end of Kendall Street, this house was torn down when that end of Kendall Street was redesigned. The house was formerly owned by Szarlan.

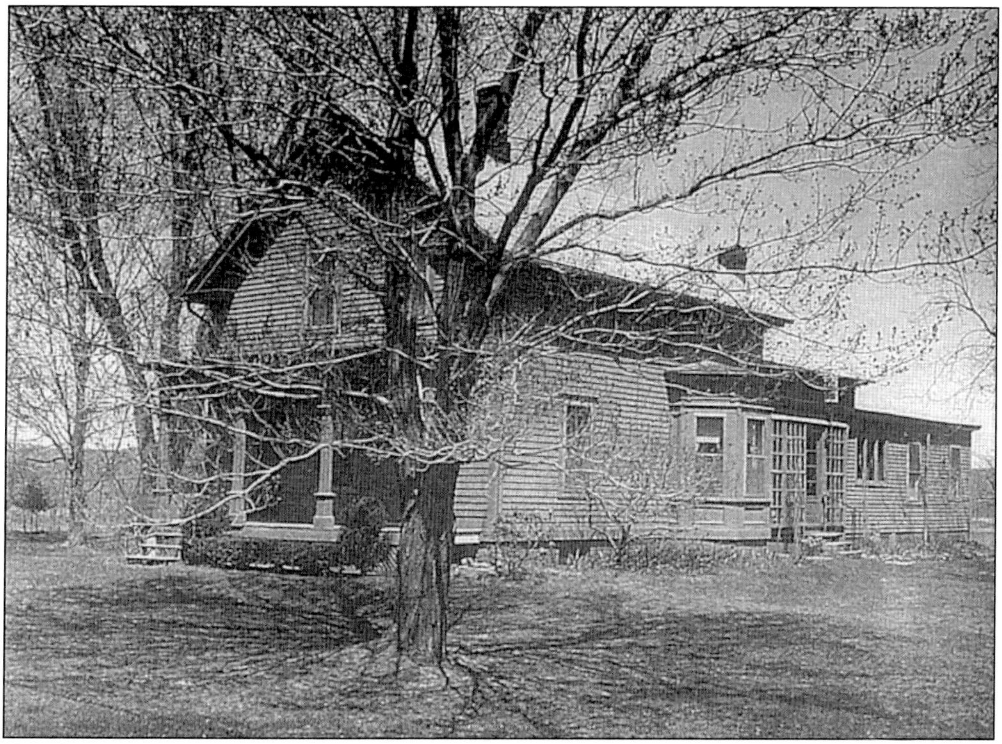

The Chauncey Buell House, 392 Fuller Street. The house and barn were built by Albert Fuller. Former owners include Albert Fuller and Mrs. Lucy A. (Fuller) Pease.

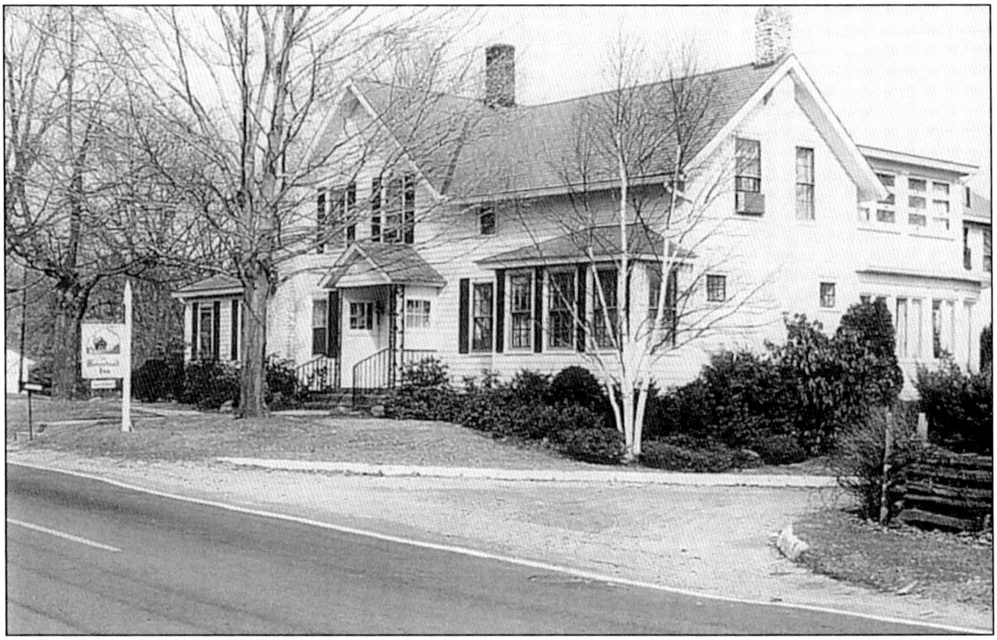

The Homestead Inn, 782 Center Street, 1976. This used to be called the Charles Jones Farm. Mr. Jones provided ice-cold milk to the marchers being transported by truck to the soldiers' monument at Ludlow Center. These units marched on Memorial Day in the downtown area, then disbursed to various cemeteries for ceremonies there.

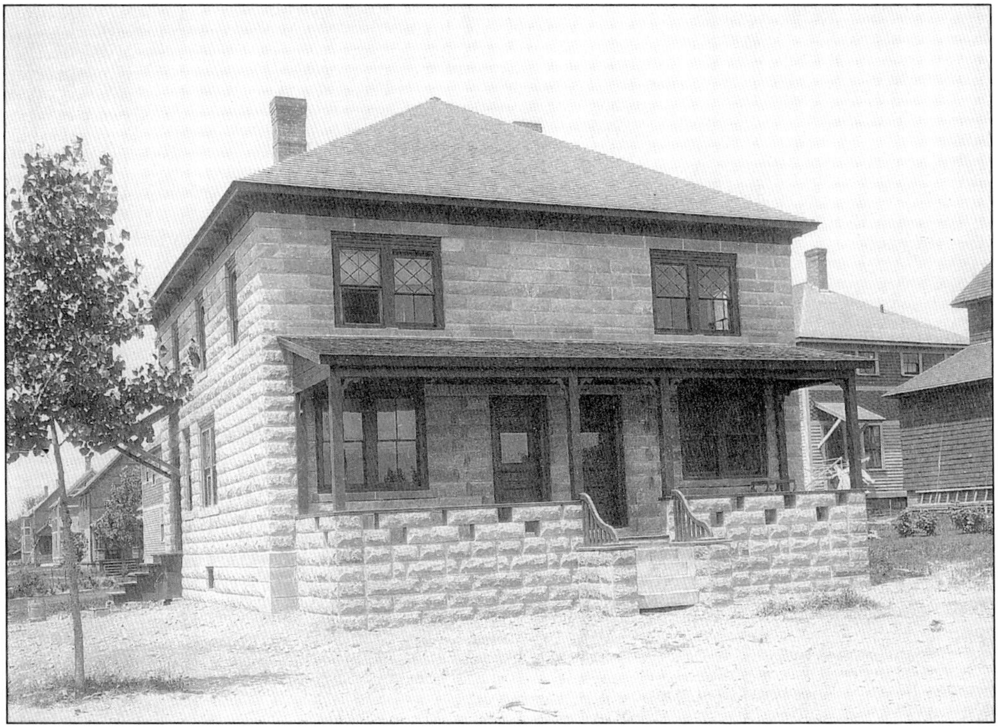

Cement Block House, c. 1901. This example of LMA-provided housing is located in the Ludlow Village area.

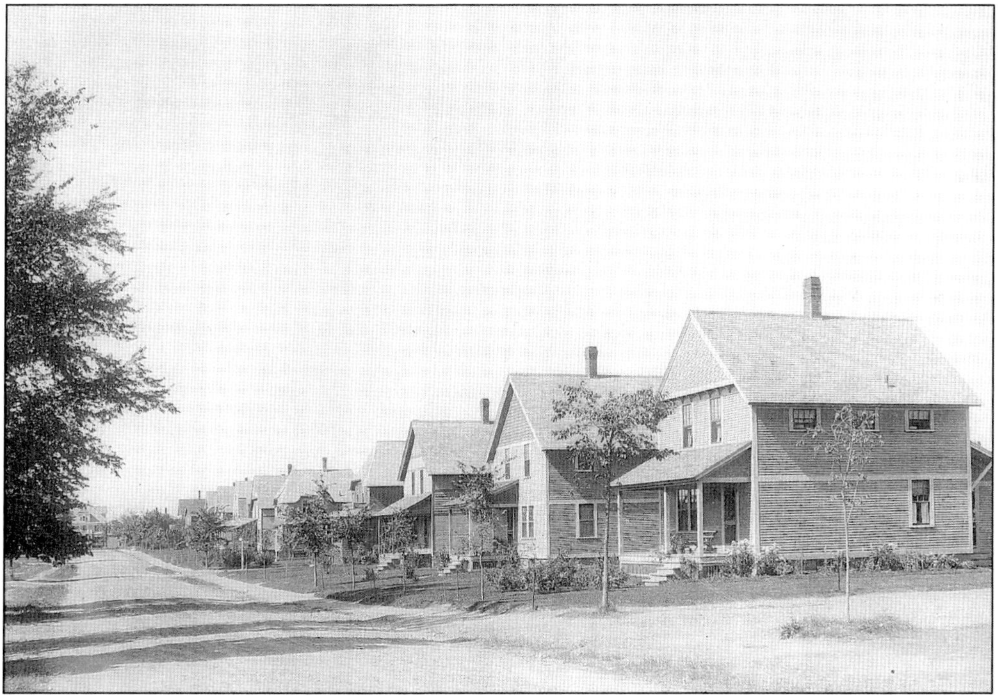

LMA Housing, October 1901. This is a view looking toward North Street (Center Street) on Hubbard Street, between Sewall and North Streets. All houses were constructed in a similar design to speed construction and keep costs low.

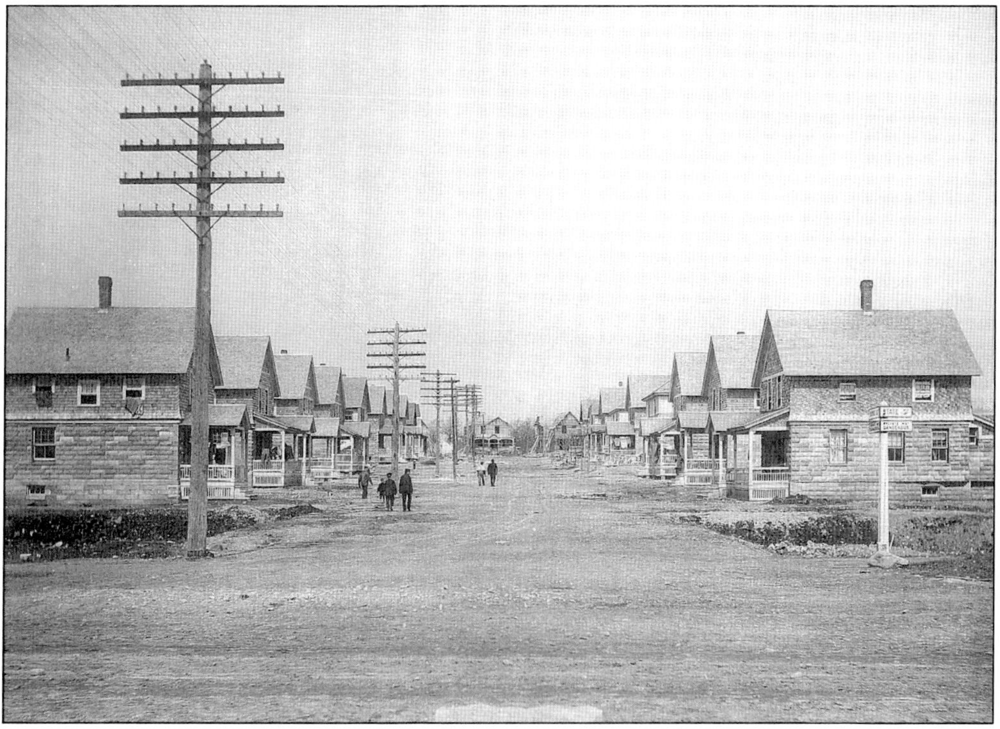

More LMA Housing. Here are Duke and State Streets, probably c. 1910.

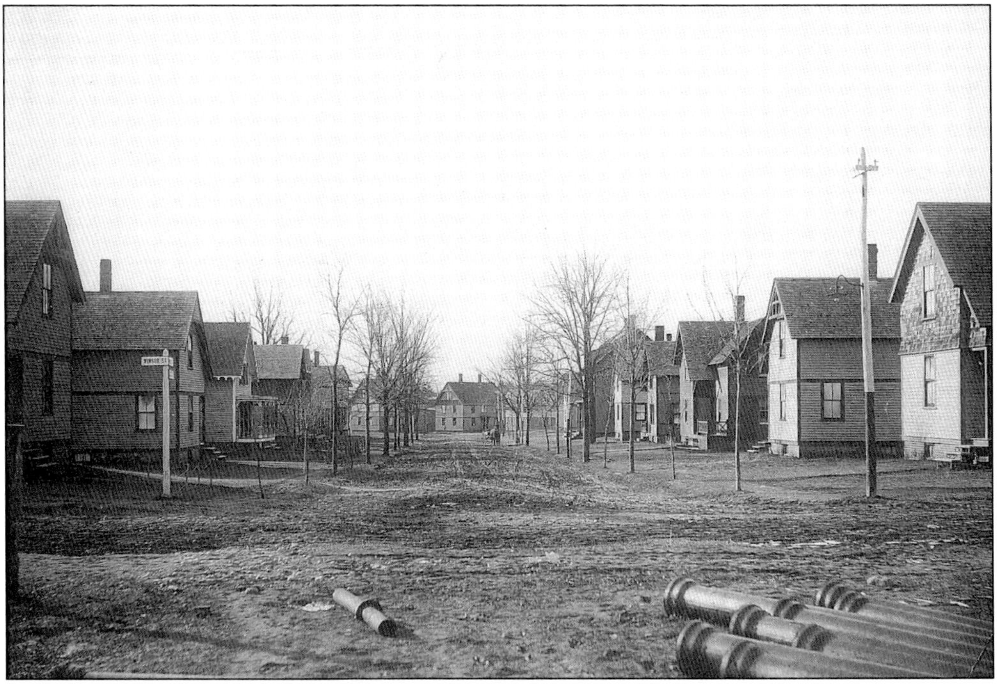

LMA HOUSING, WINSOR AND STATE STREETS, C. 1910.

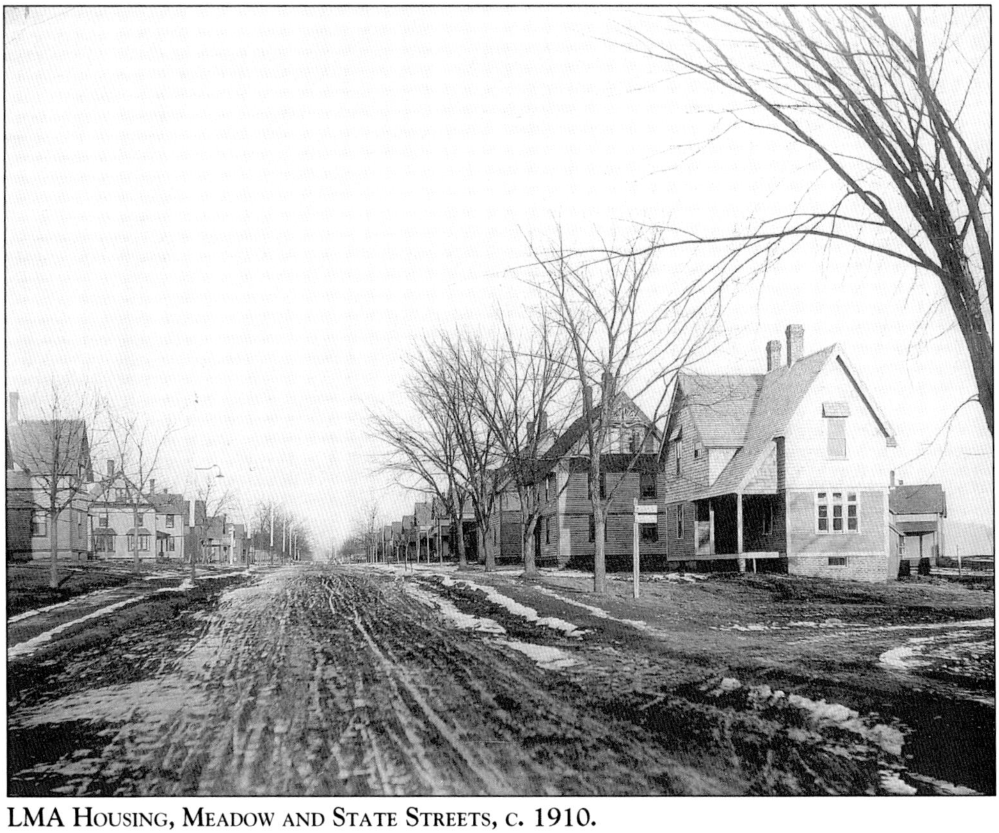

LMA HOUSING, MEADOW AND STATE STREETS, C. 1910.

Five

Recreation, Events, and Natural Disasters

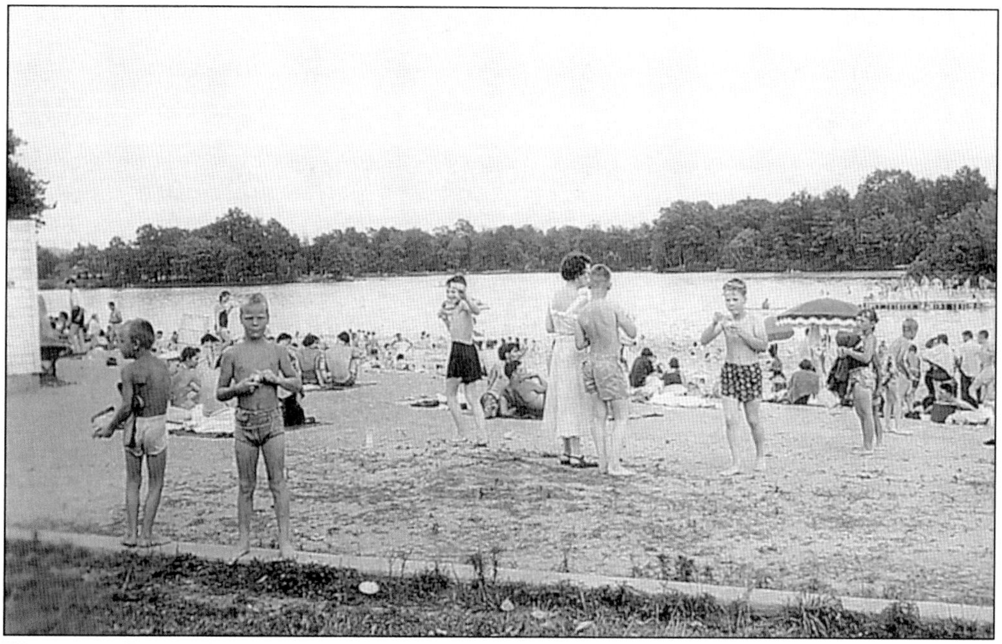

Haviland Pond, Center Street, c. 1950. Haviland Pond was a summer gathering place, with a raft for patrons to swim out to. In 1894, the town acquired water rights and allowed the use of a beach for public swimming. Use today is limited due to an influx of Canadian geese and their debris.

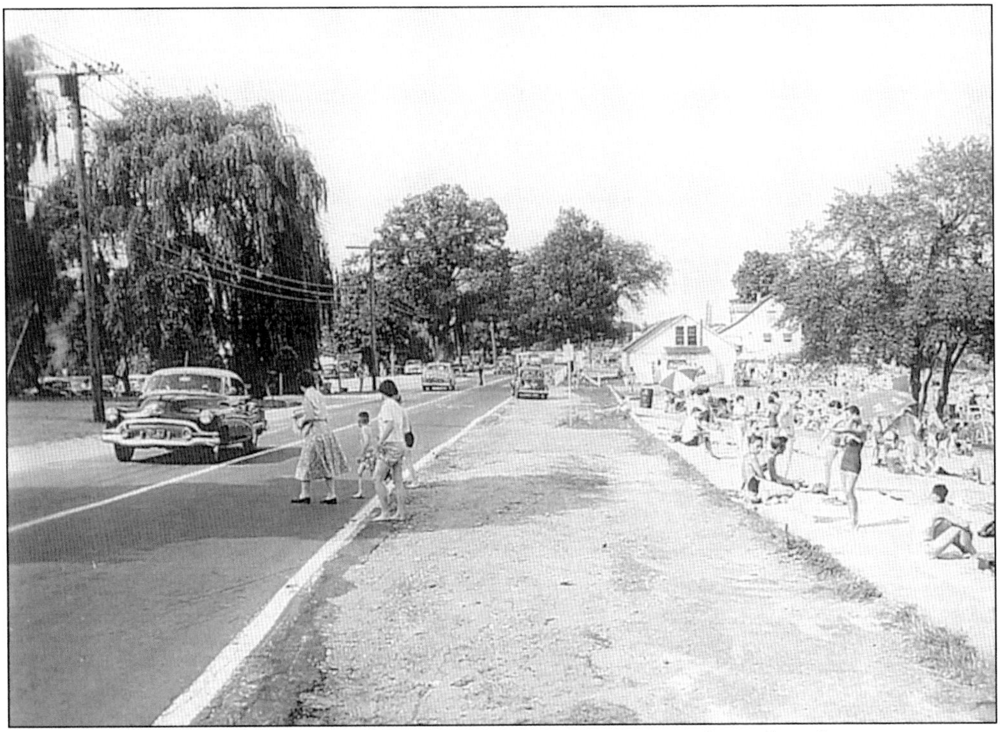

HAVILAND POND, CENTER STREET, 1950. Crossing Center Street after a day of swimming is not something easily or safely done today!

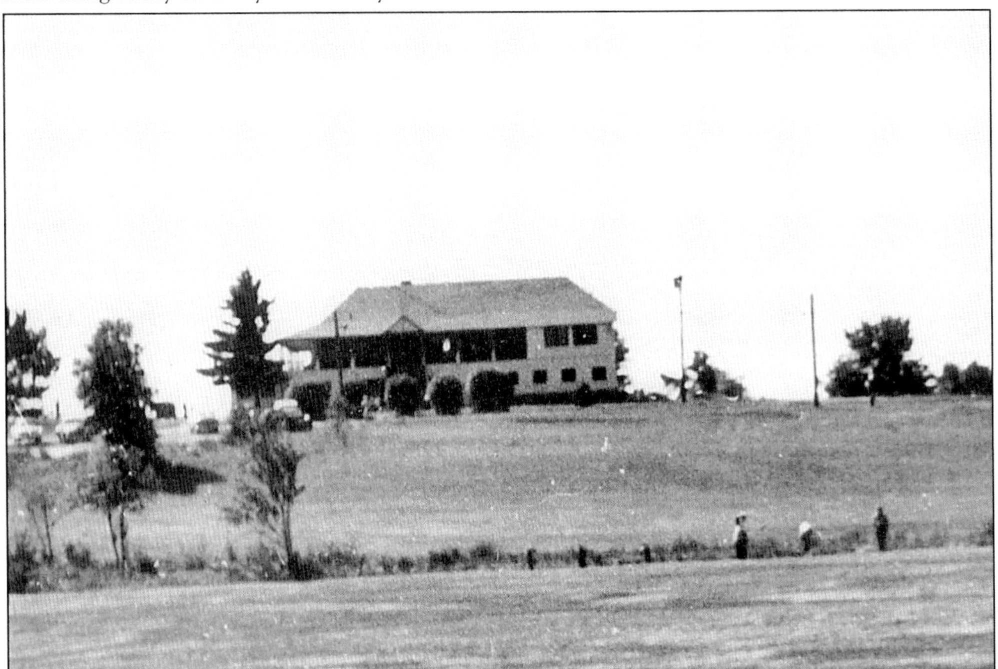

THE LUDLOW COUNTRY CLUB. Built on LMA-donated land, this area was once the "poor farm." People who could not physically or financially care for themselves stayed here.

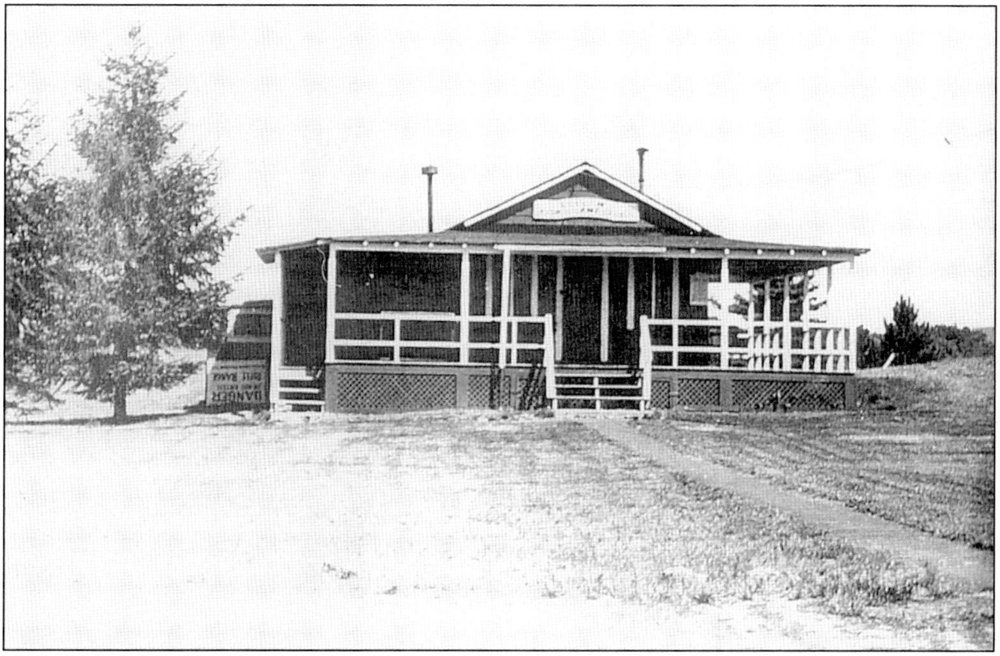

The Ludlow Fish and Game Club, Sportsman's Road. This was the first clubhouse until 1970. Members could hunt and fish pheasants, rabbits, and trout. The program was expanded after 1950 to include archery and gun handling.

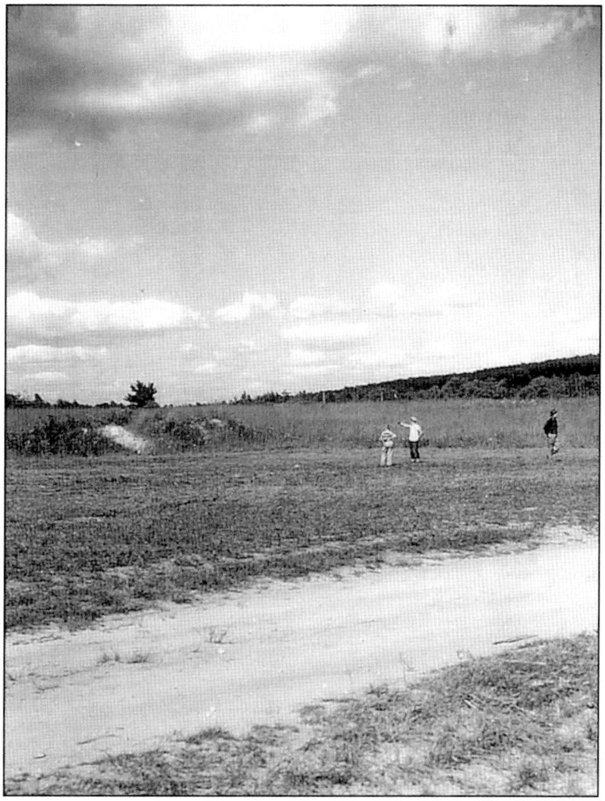

The Rifle Range at the Rod & Gun Club, Sportsman's Road. As part of the Fish and Game Club, members of the Rod & Gun Club could learn fly-tying, archery, and safe gun handling.

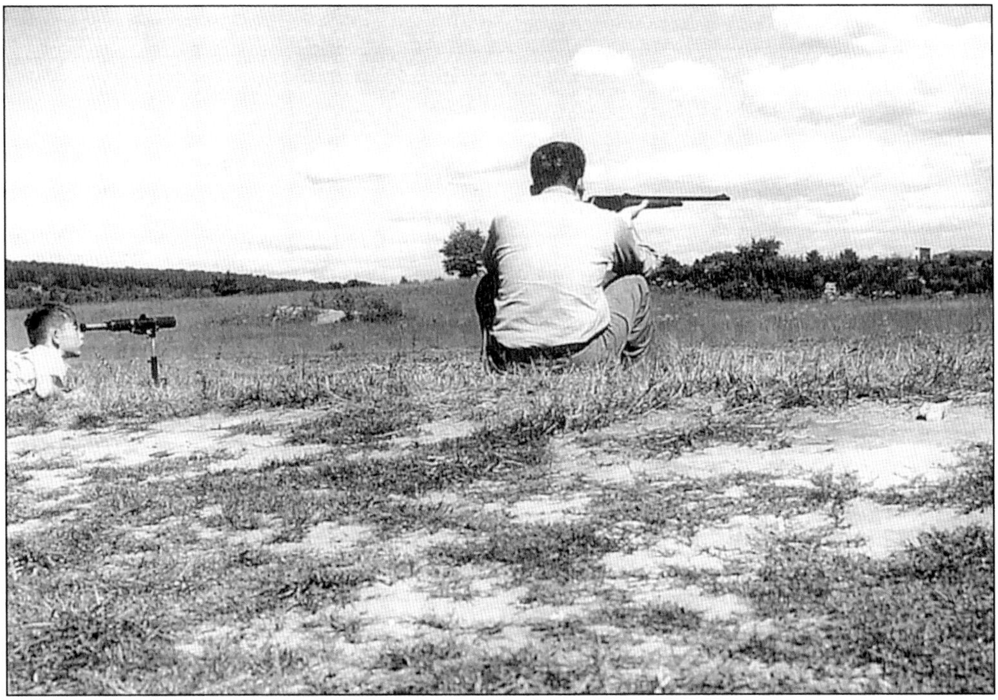

THE RIFLE RANGE, ROD & GUN CLUB, SPORTSMAN'S ROAD, C. 1950.

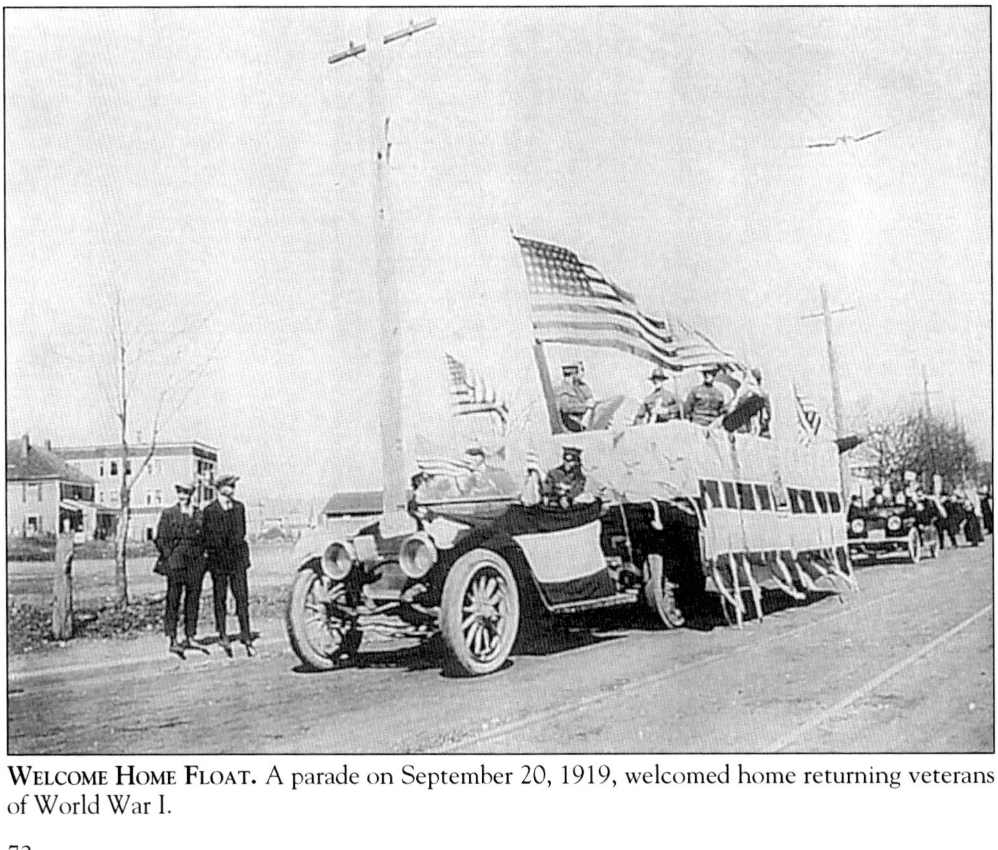

WELCOME HOME FLOAT. A parade on September 20, 1919, welcomed home returning veterans of World War I.

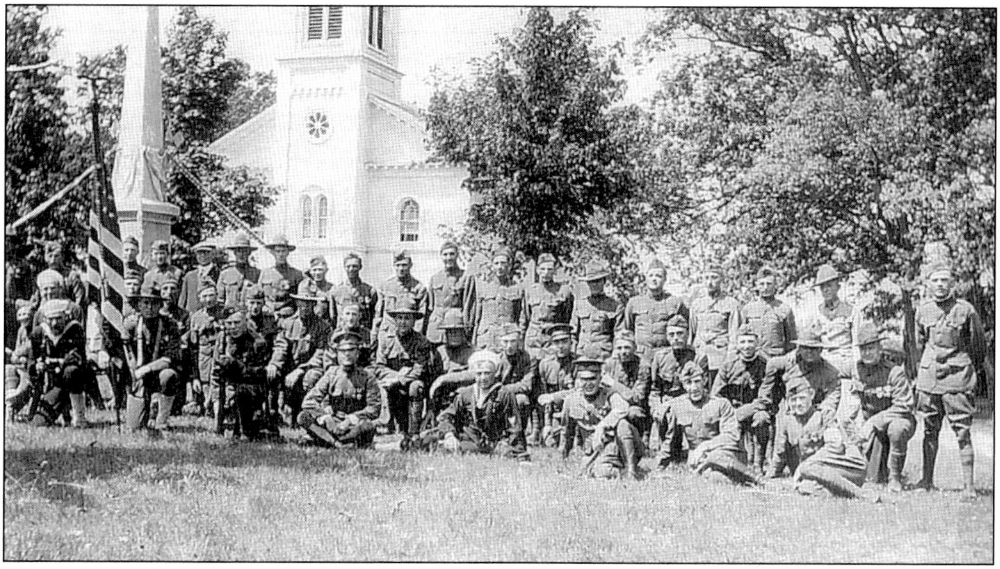

WORLD WAR I VETERANS, C. 1920. This photo, taken by Frank Ellison, shows World War I vets in front of the First Church on Center Street.

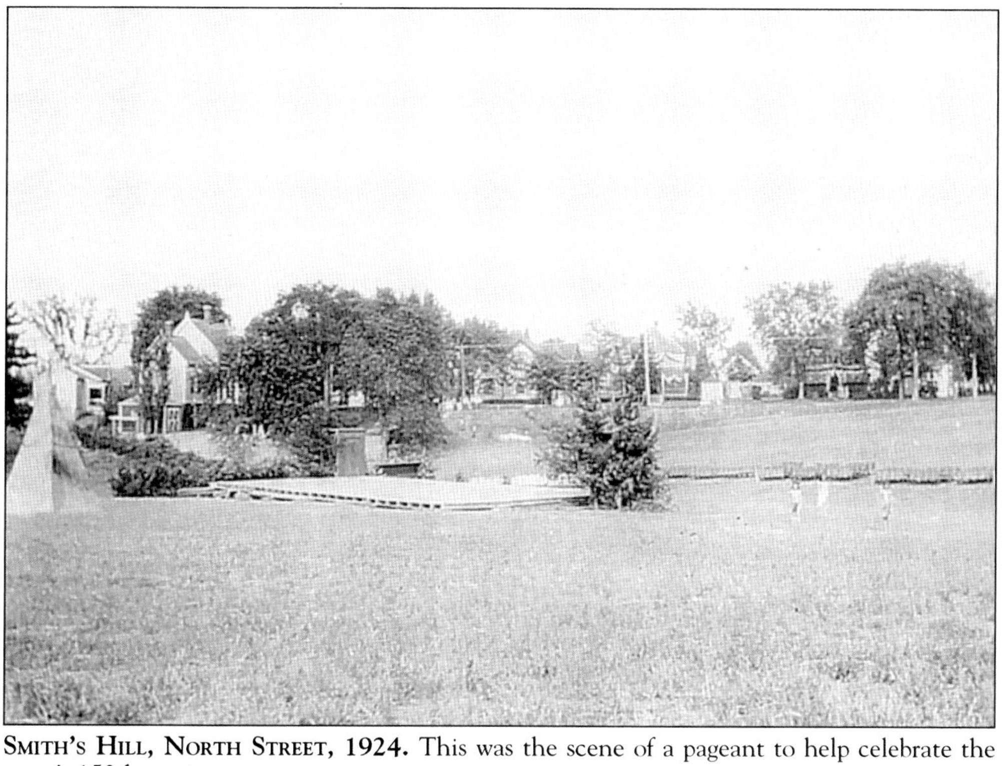

SMITH'S HILL, NORTH STREET, 1924. This was the scene of a pageant to help celebrate the town's 150th anniversary.

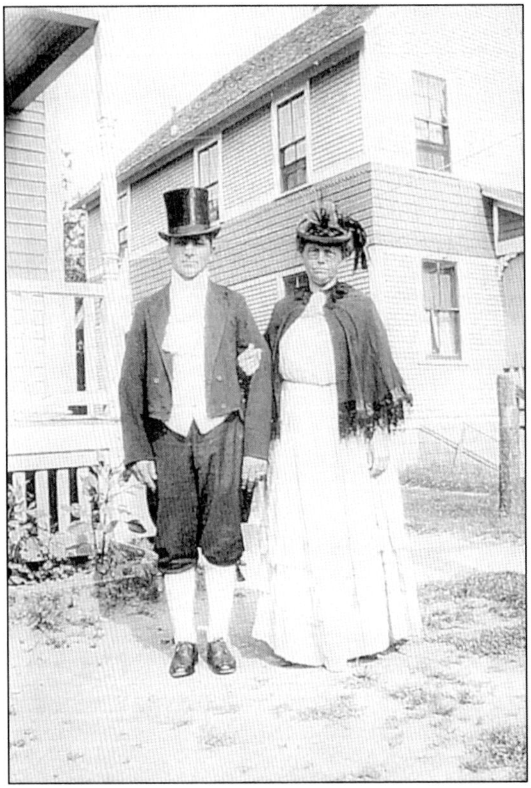

ALBERT AND ALBINA GAGNE, 1924. Dressed for the pageant of the 150th anniversary, this photo was taken in a backyard on Highland Avenue.

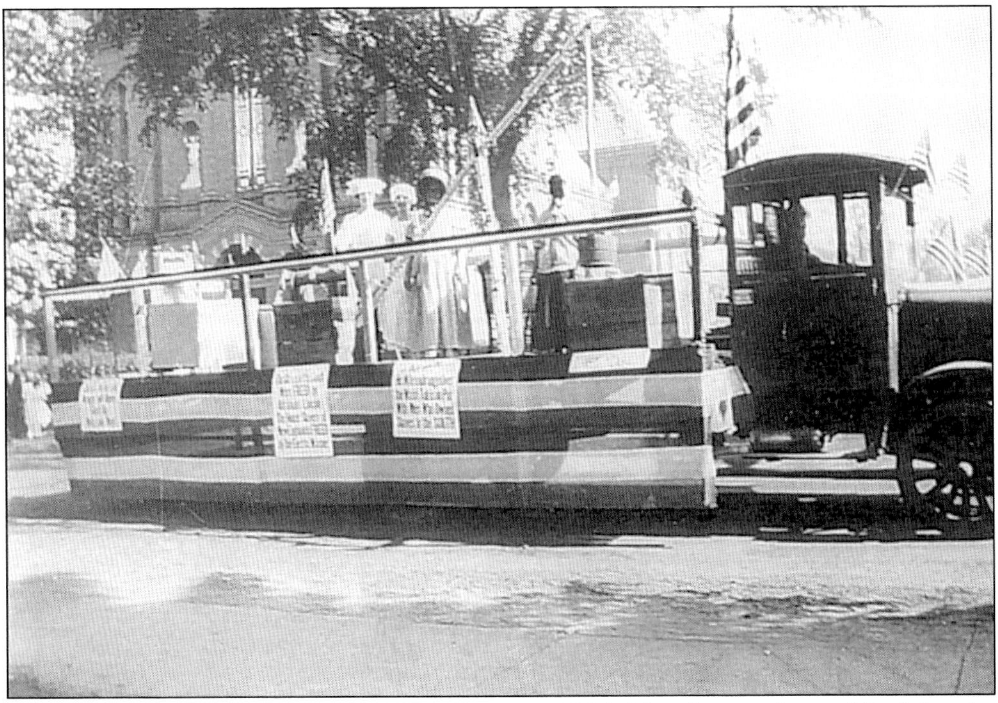

TOWN OF LUDLOW, 150TH ANNIVERSARY PARADE, 1924. This float in front of St. John the Baptist Church reflects early washing methods.

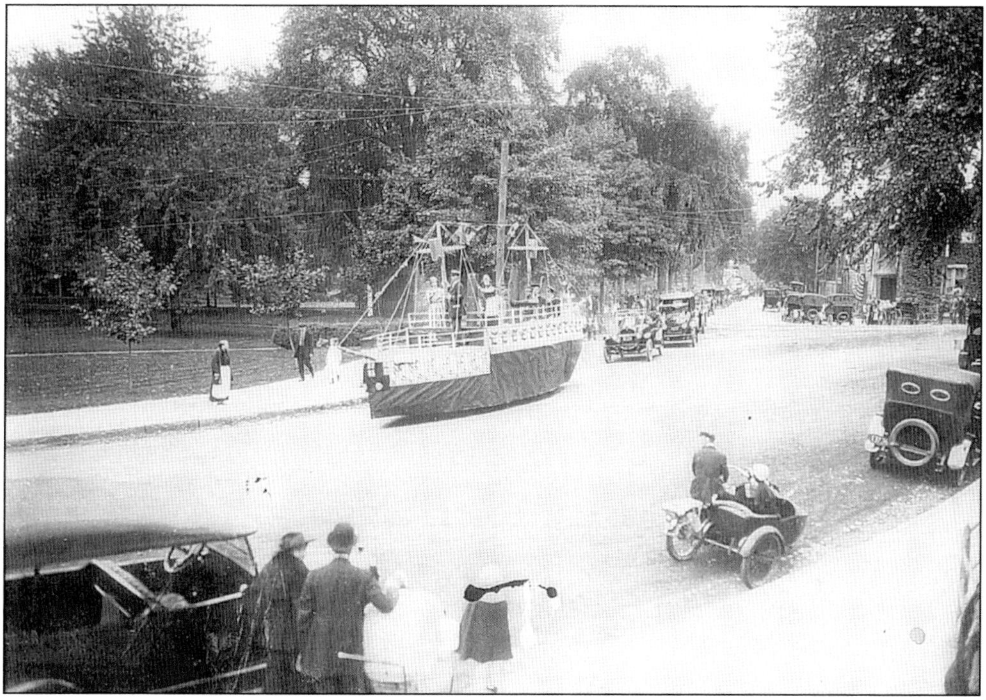

PARADE AT CENTER AND HOLYOKE STREETS. This parade is most likely the 150th anniversary celebration.

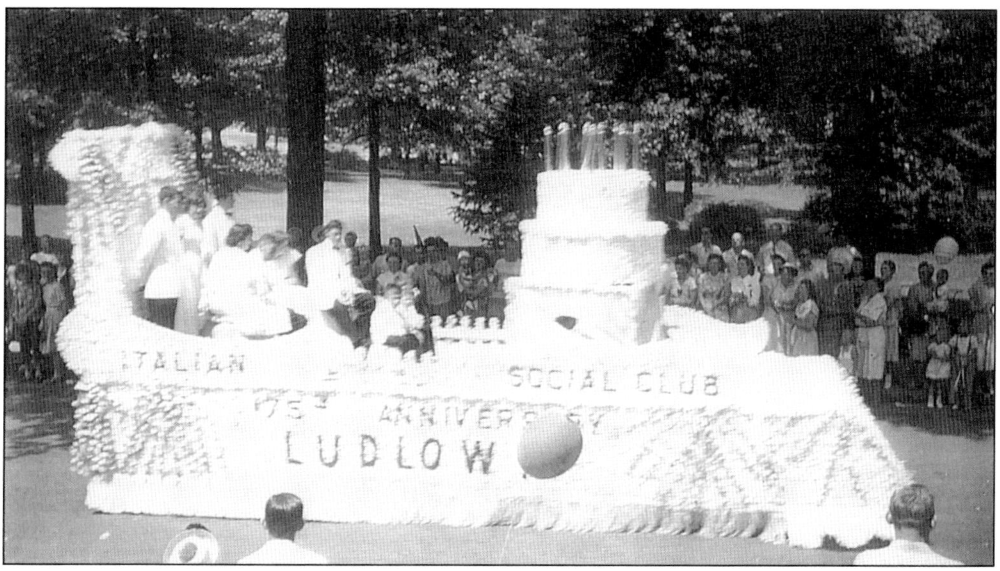

LUDLOW LOVES A PARADE. Shown here is the Italian Social Club's float in the 175th anniversary parade in 1949. (Photo courtesy Ruth Gilman.)

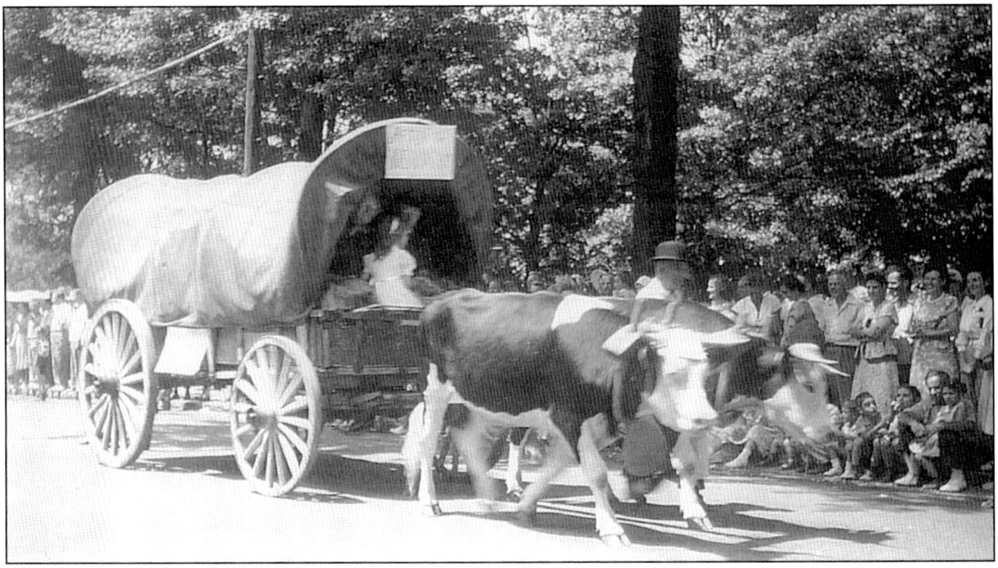

Ludlow's 175th Anniversary Parade, 1949. Oxen and wagon depict how early settlers got around. (Photo courtesy Ruth Gilman.)

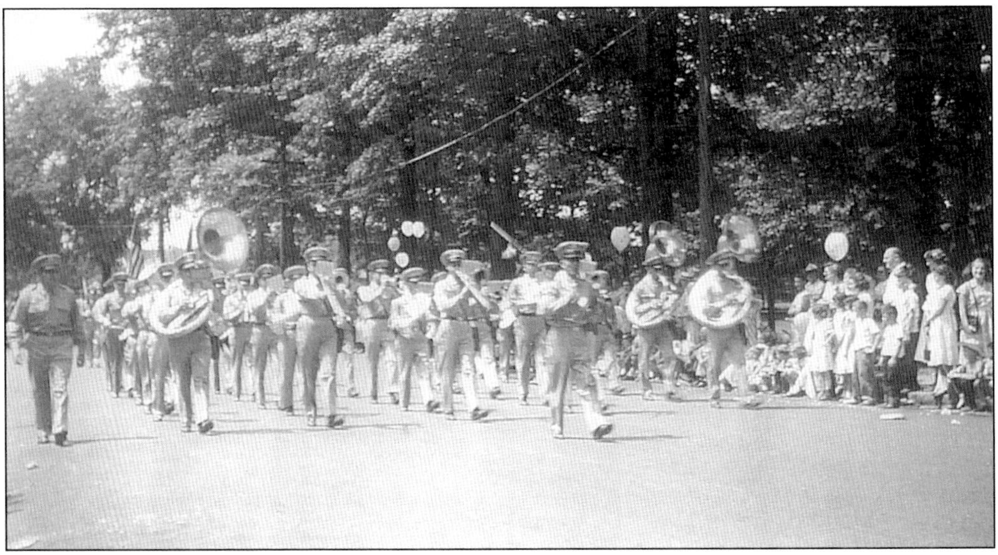

Ludlow's 175th Anniversary Parade, 1949. Pictured here is one of the many marching bands on display. (Photo courtesy Ruth Gilman.)

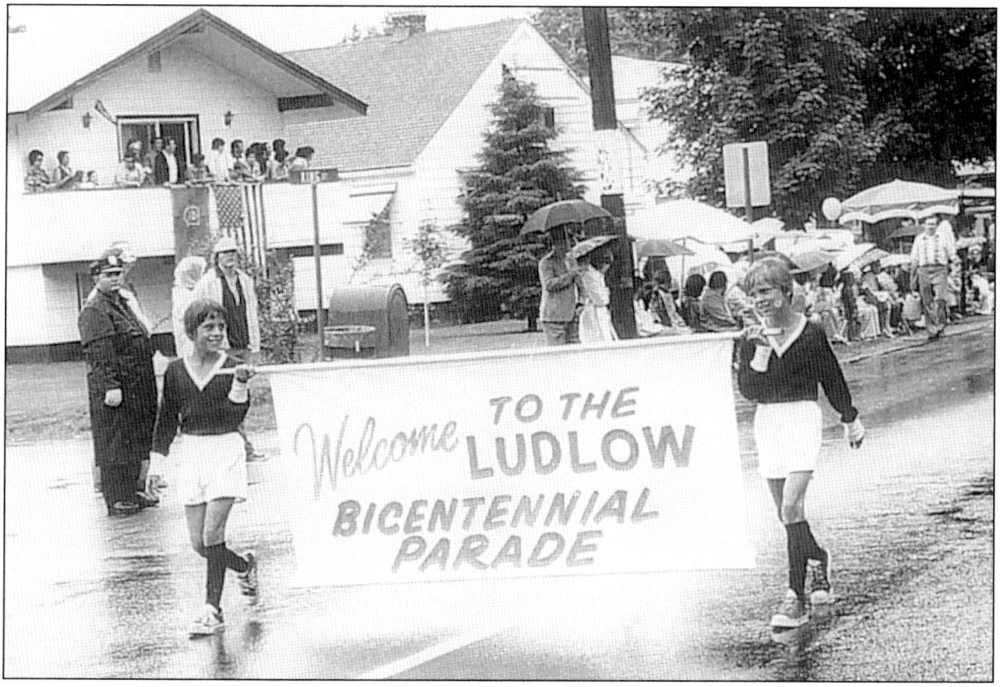

The Bicentennial Parade, June 23, 1974. The day dawned rainy and dreary for one of the biggest parades in the town's history. In spite of the bad weather, the parade went on as scheduled.

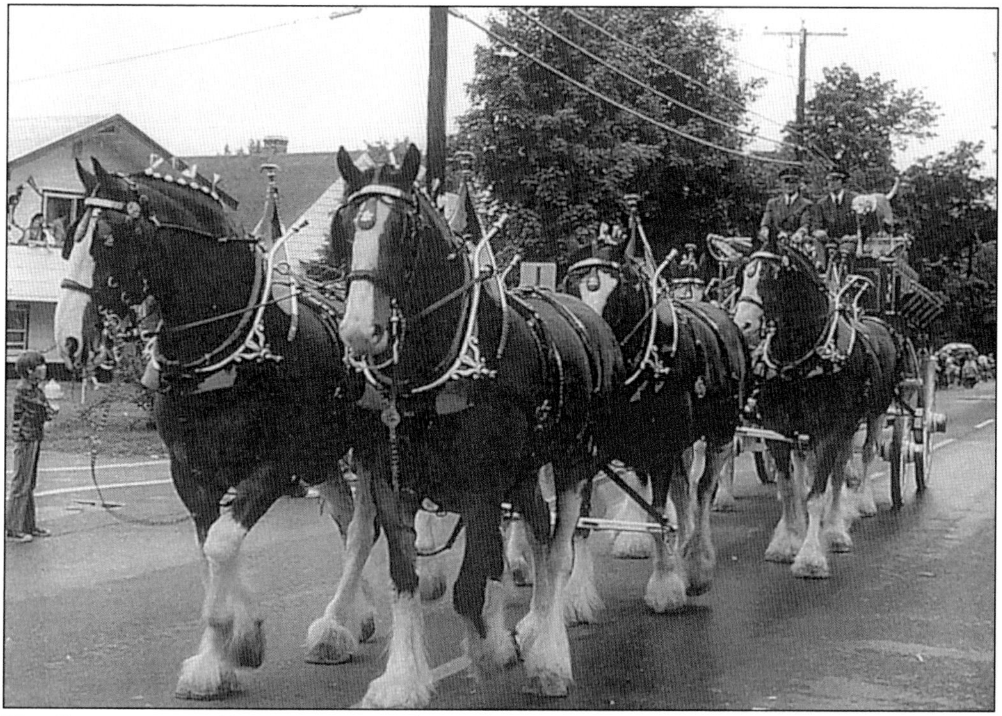

The Bicentennial Parade, 1974. The Budweiser Clydesdales helped to make a successful parade.

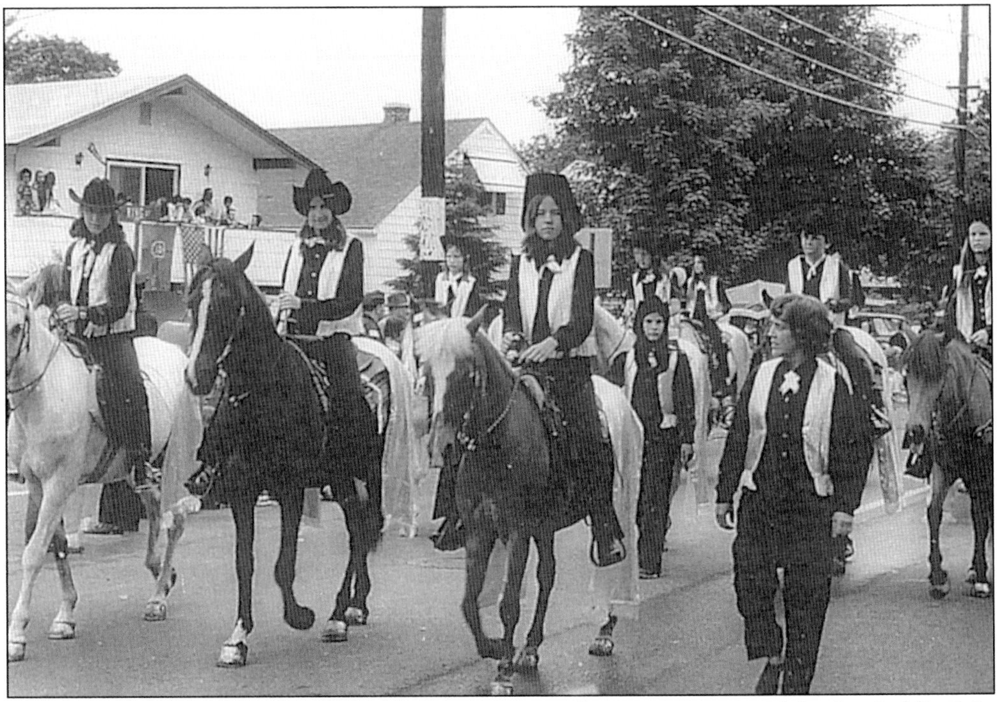

The Bicentennial Parade, 1974. Shown here is Ludlow's 4-H Horse Club, the Saddle Pals. Under the guidance of Dexter and Martha Hiersche, Ludlow's only 4-H horse club was a fixture in many town parades, including each Memorial Day Parade.

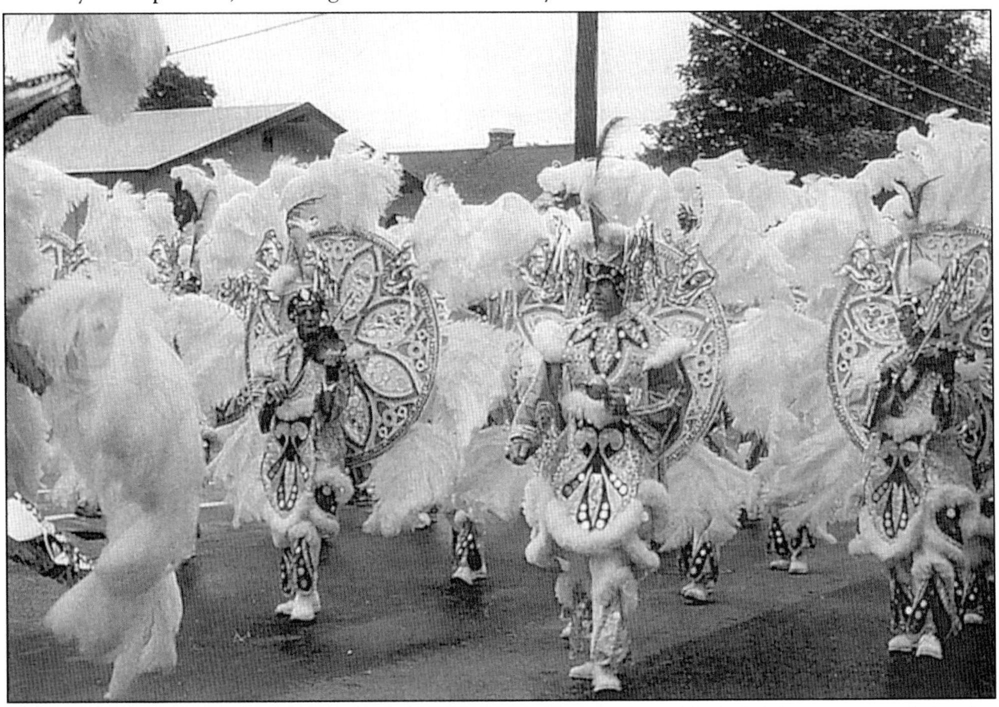

The Bicentennial Parade, 1974. The Mummers came from Philadelphia to march in the parade. Rain nearly kept them from marching.

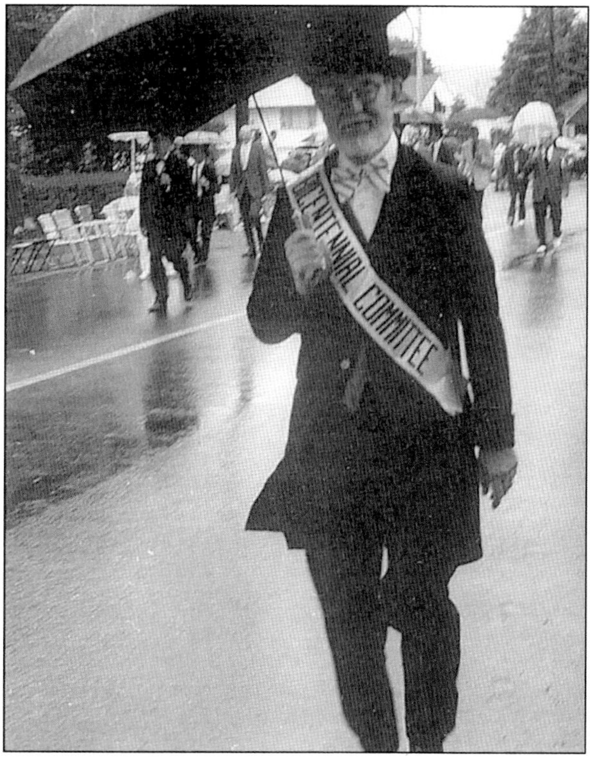

The Bicentennial Parade, 1974. Pictured in this view is the late Herbert McChesney, bicentennial committee member, town historian, and author of *A History of Ludlow, Massachusetts, 1774–1974*.

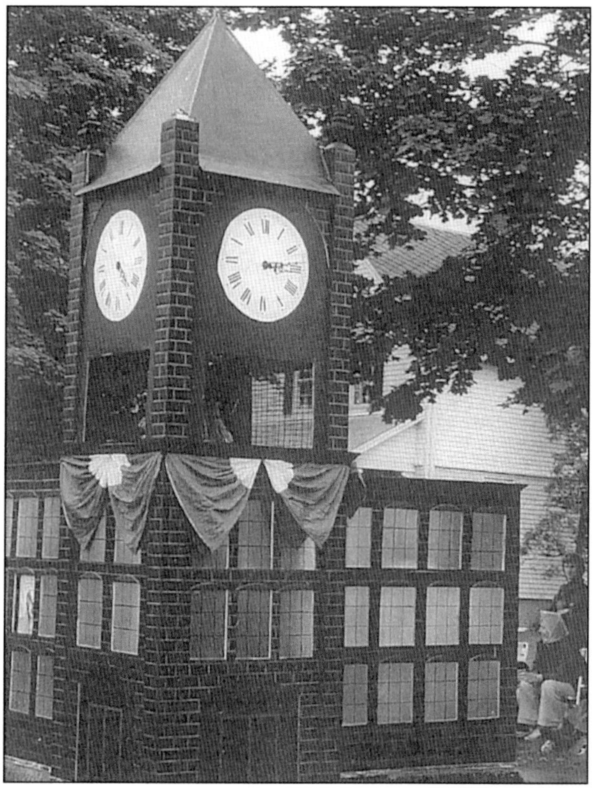

The Bicentennial Parade, 1974. Ludlow Realty's float paid tribute to mill #8 and the clock tower.

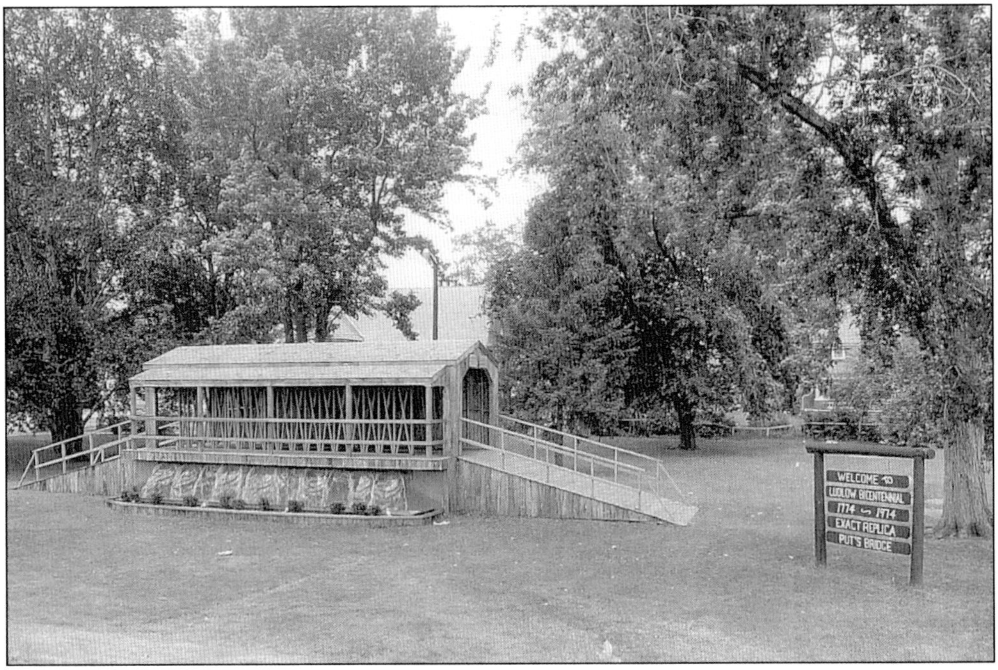

PUT'S BRIDGE REPLICA, 1974. An exact replica of Put's Bridge over the Chicopee River was constructed and set up for all to see on the grounds of the Hubbard Memorial Library.

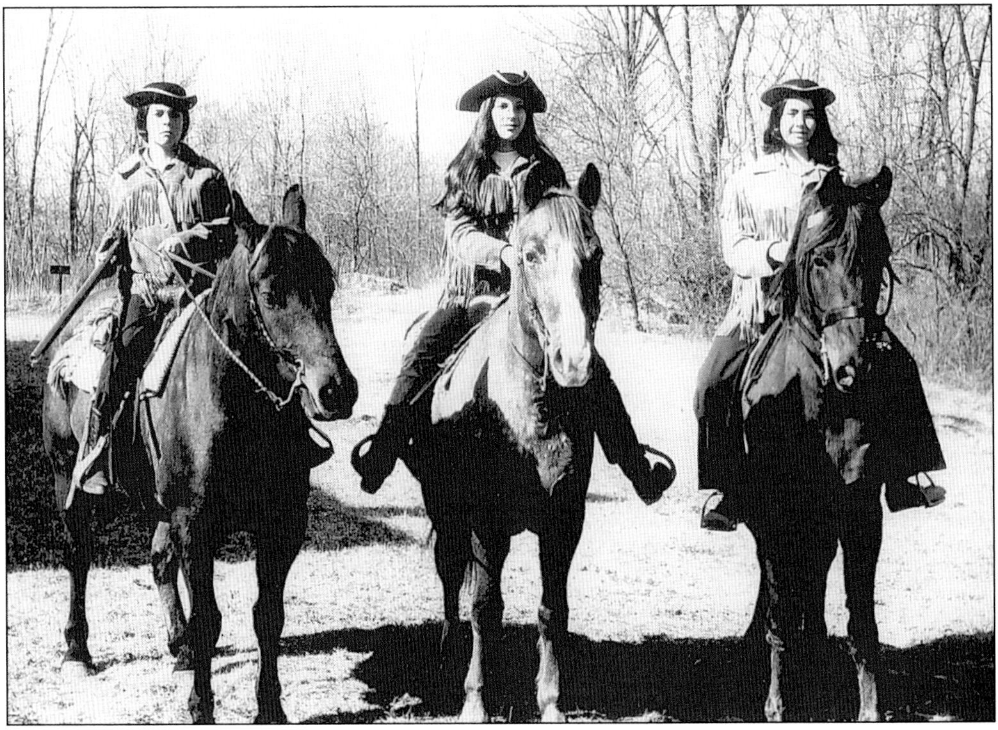

HISTORIC RIDE. During local celebrations of the national bicentennial, these riders from the Ludlow 4-H Saddle Pals re-enacted a historic ride to the town hall. From left to right are Jimmy Martins, Gail Machado, and Ann Grabowski.

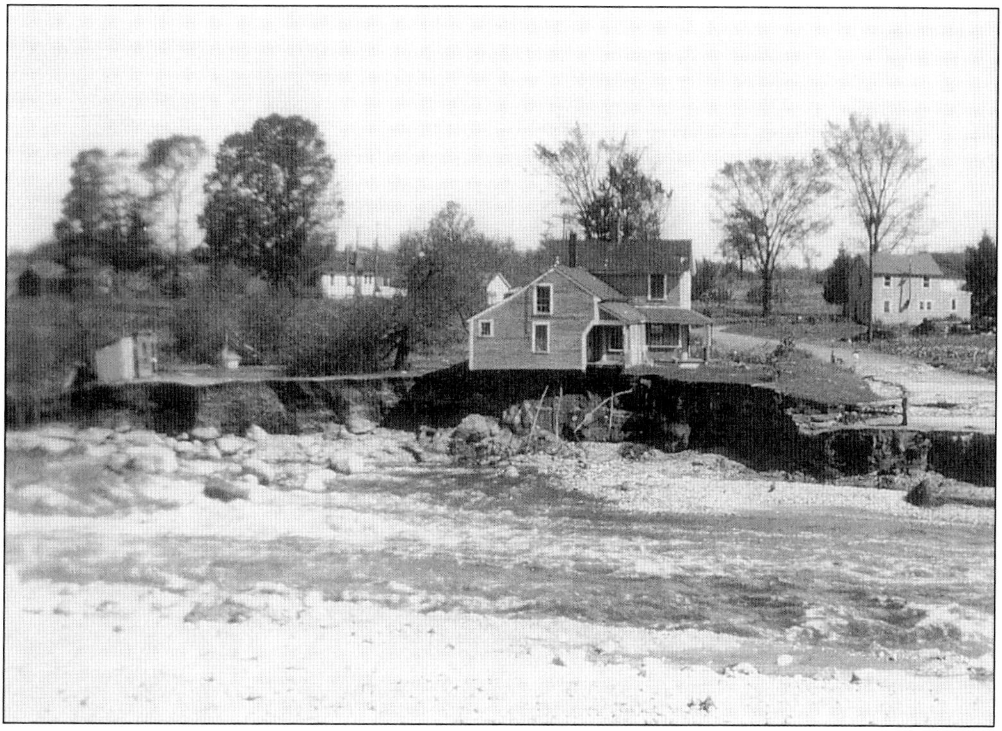

Washout on Alden Street, between Newcombs and Goldens. This washout occurred during the hurricane of 1938. This section was renamed Ventura Street when the Massachusetts Turnpike went through in the 1950s. (Photo courtesy Ruth Gilman.)

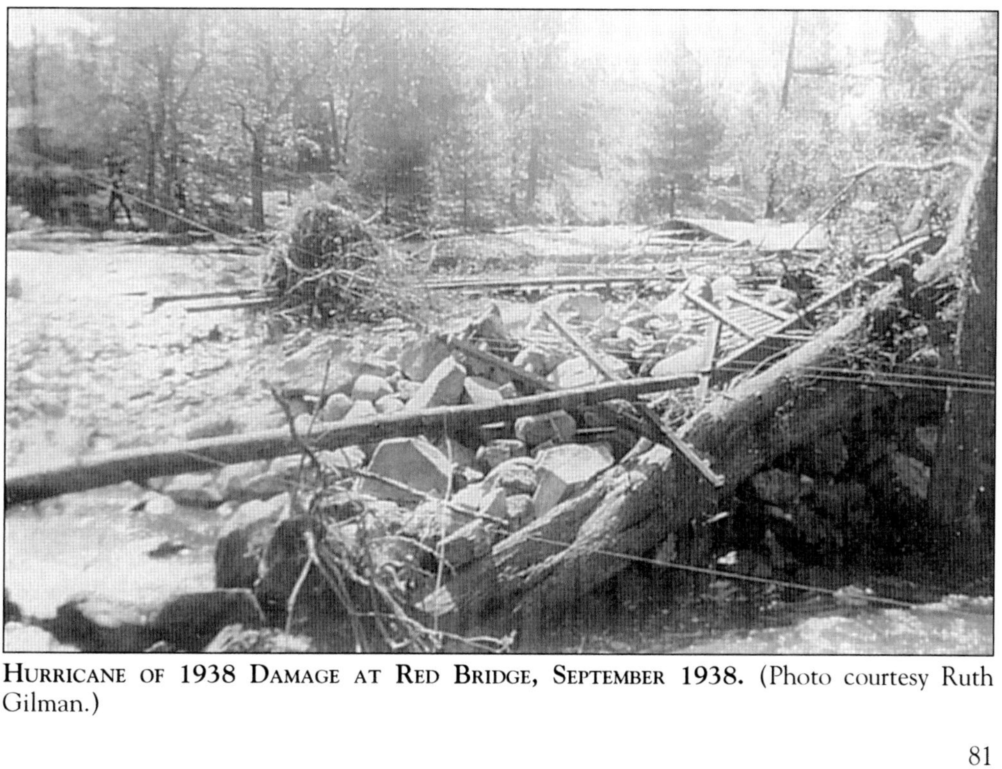

Hurricane of 1938 Damage at Red Bridge, September 1938. (Photo courtesy Ruth Gilman.)

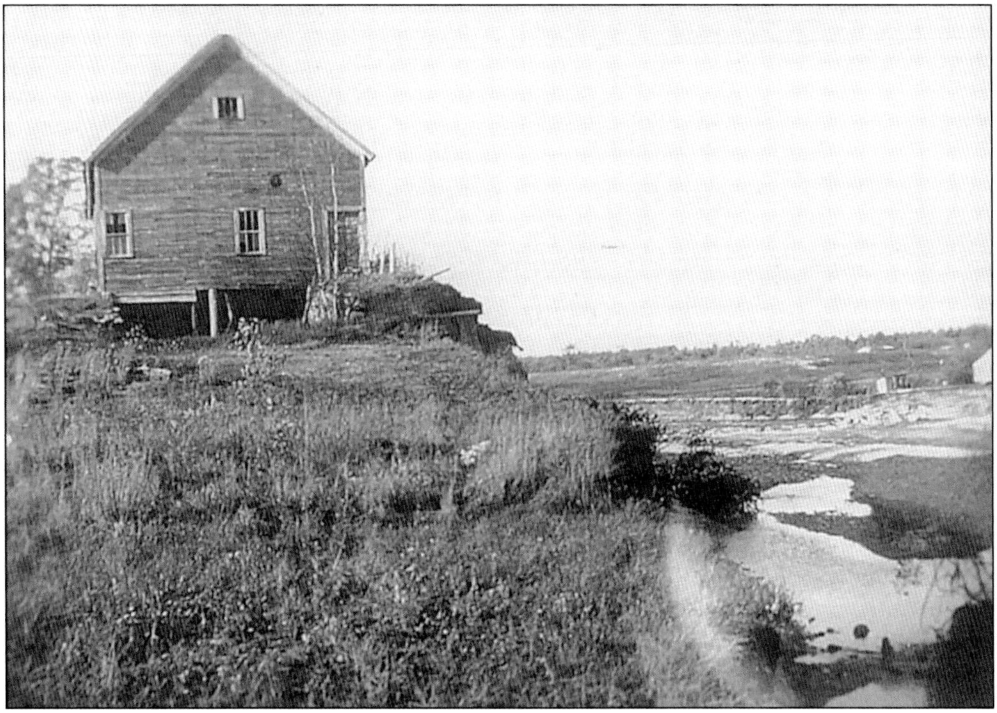

MRS. NEWCOMBS BARN, ALDEN STREET. The hurricane of 1938 left virtually no one untouched. (Photo courtesy Ruth Gilman.)

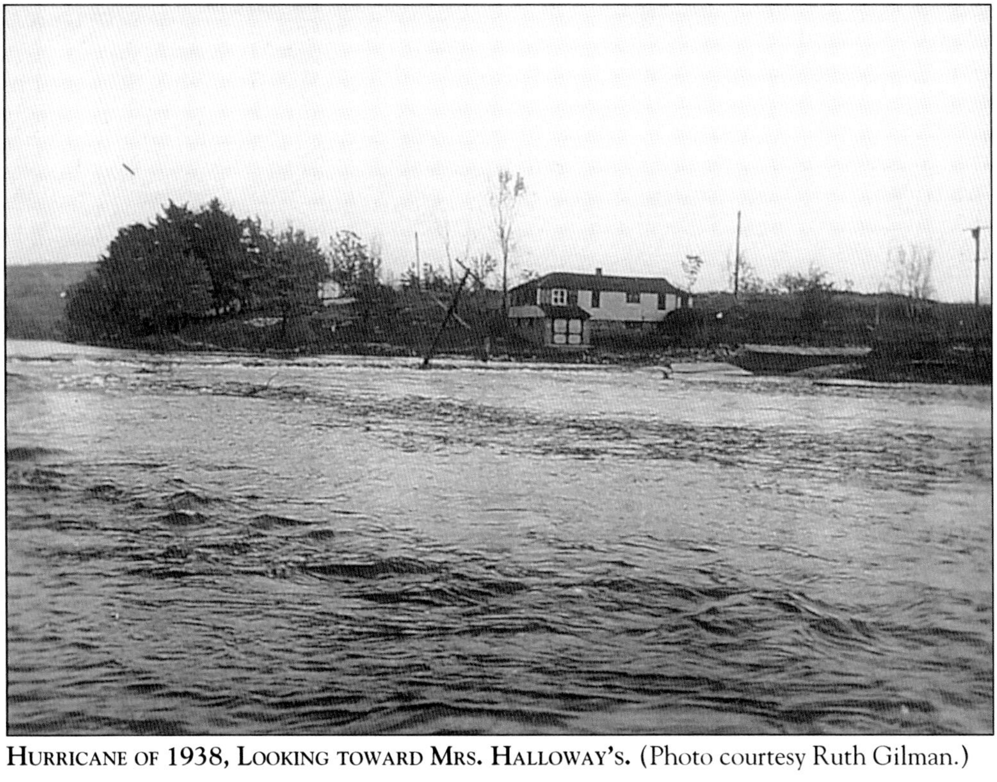

HURRICANE OF 1938, LOOKING TOWARD MRS. HALLOWAY'S. (Photo courtesy Ruth Gilman.)

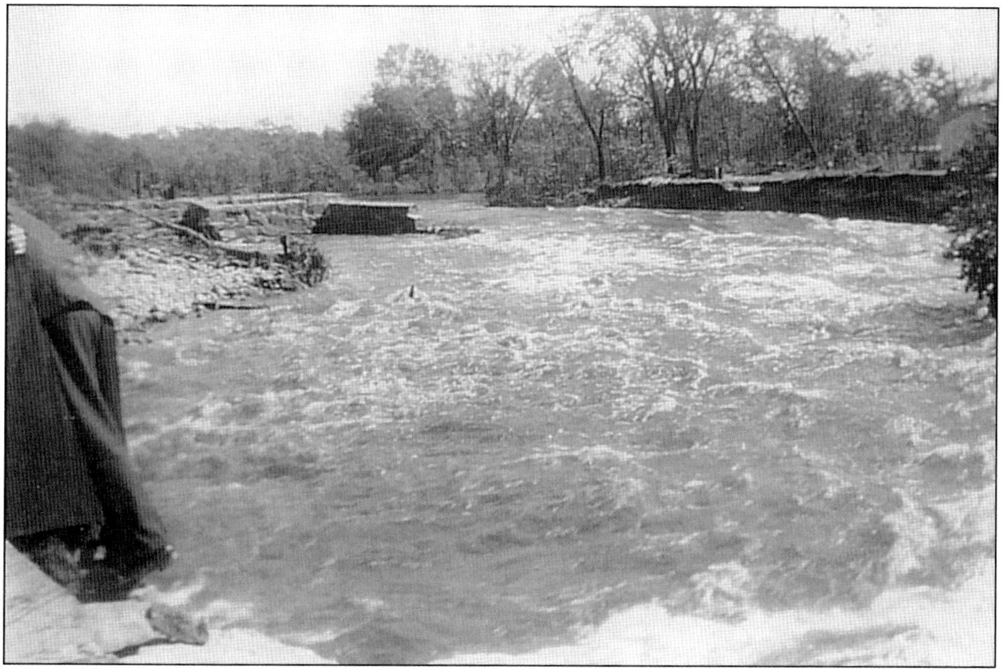

Hurricane of 1938. Flood waters in the Chicopee Rivers caused a break through the canal walls near Collins Bridge. (Photo courtesy Ruth Gilman.)

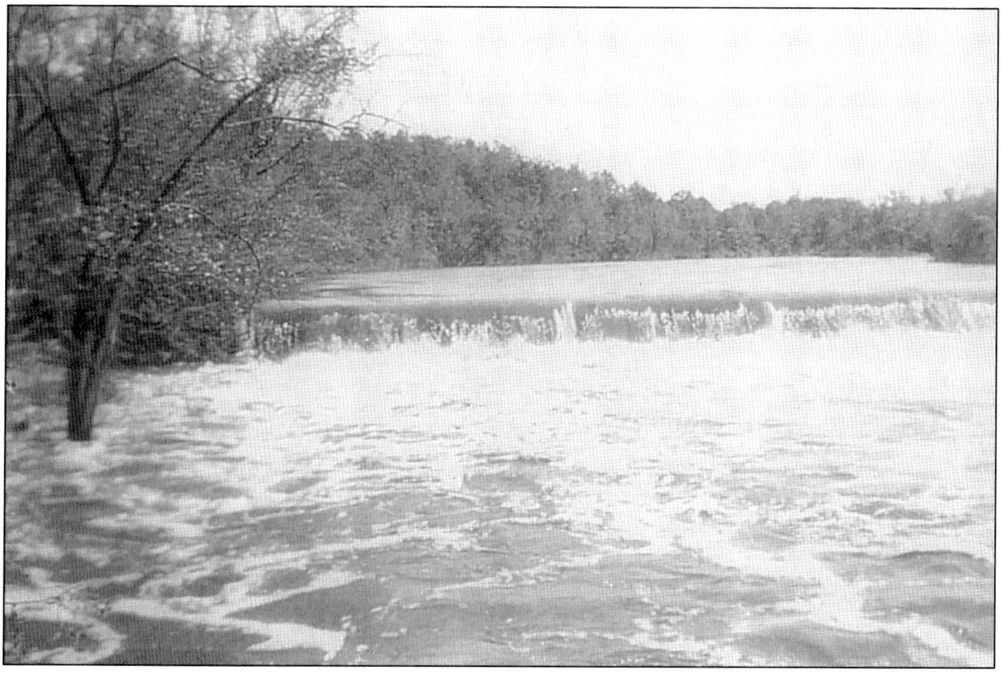

Hurricane of 1938. Shown here are rushing waters at the Ludlow end of the Collins Bridge Dam. (Photo courtesy Ruth Gilman.)

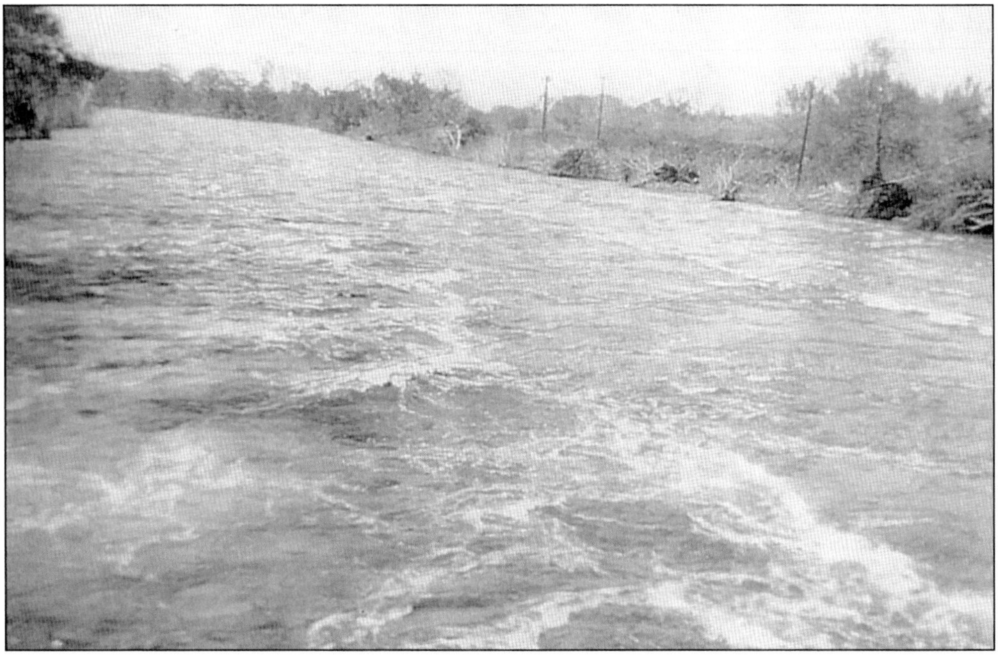

Hurricane of 1938. Pictured is the Chicopee River, down river below the Collins Bridge, on September 25, 1938. (Photo courtesy Ruth Gilman.)

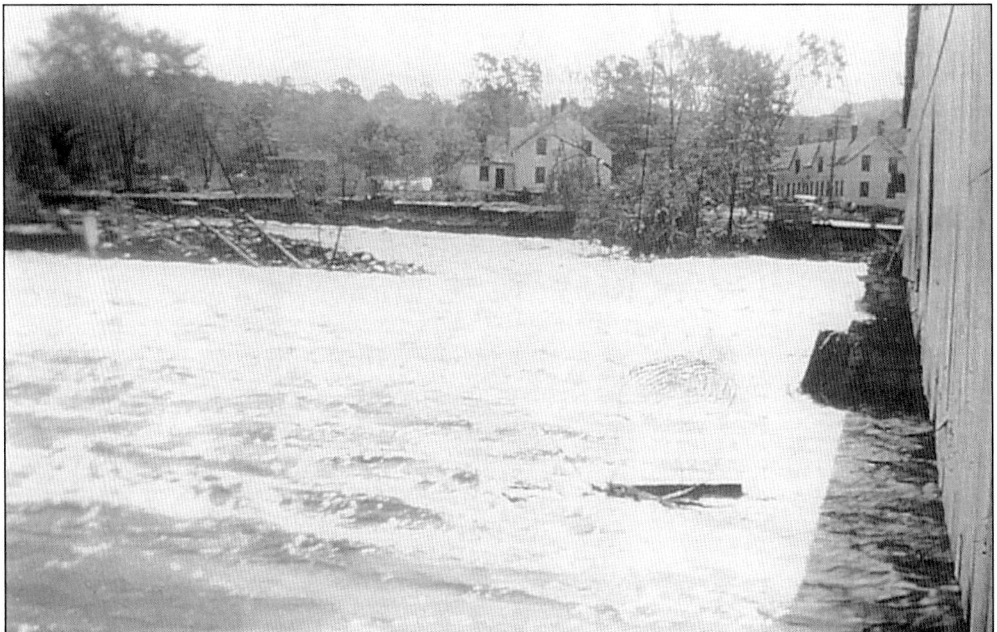

Hurricane of 1938. This is the upper side of Collins Bridge from the Ludlow side, looking towards Wilbraham. (Photo courtesy Ruth Gilman.)

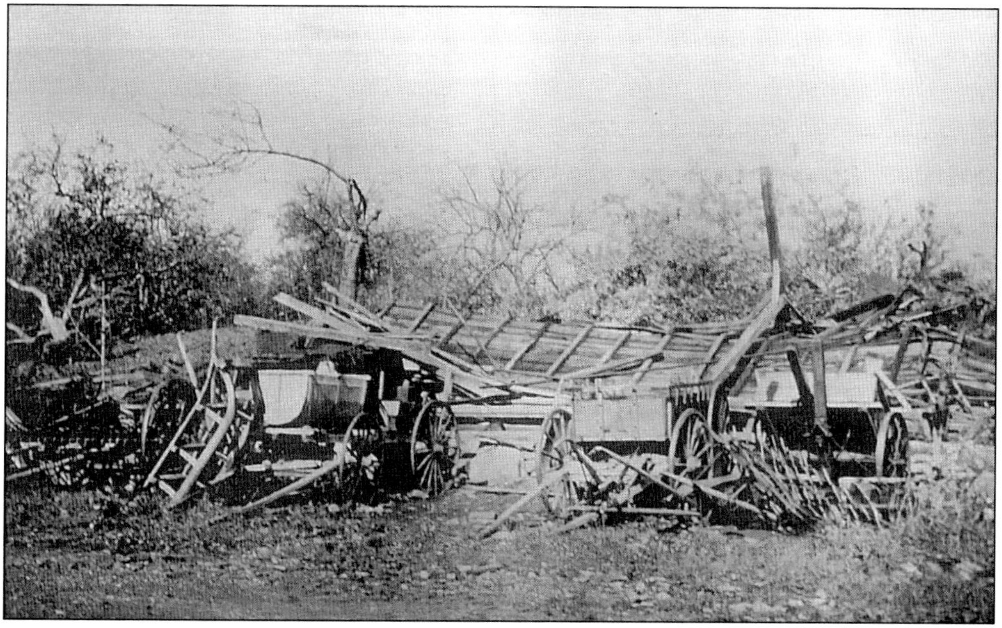

HURRICANE OF 1938. Winds completely demolished this wagon shed on Nash Farm, which was located on Fuller Street. (Photo courtesy Ruth Gilman.)

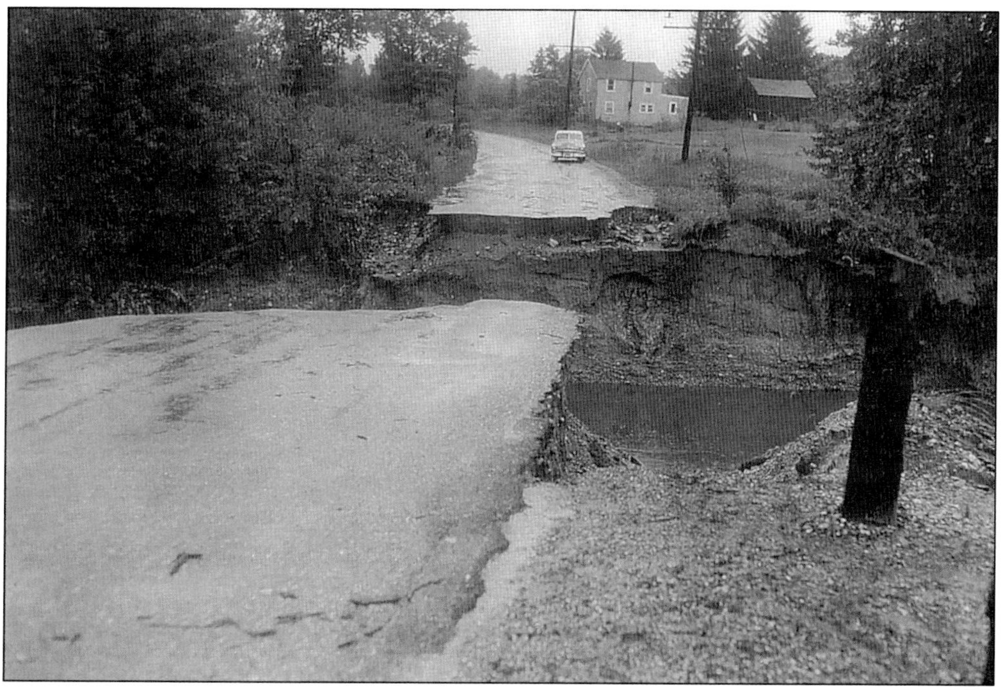

HURRICANE DIANE, AUGUST 1955. This washout on Alden Street was created by Hurricane Diane on August 19, 1955. On August 20, 1955, this author's aunt, Dorothy Pieczarka, was married to Aldo Lombardi. Her father, Michael Pieczarka, drove to the Ludlow Bridge (which was closed to automobile traffic) to pick up wedding guests. They parked their cars in Indian Orchard and walked across the bridge to be chauffeured to the reception.

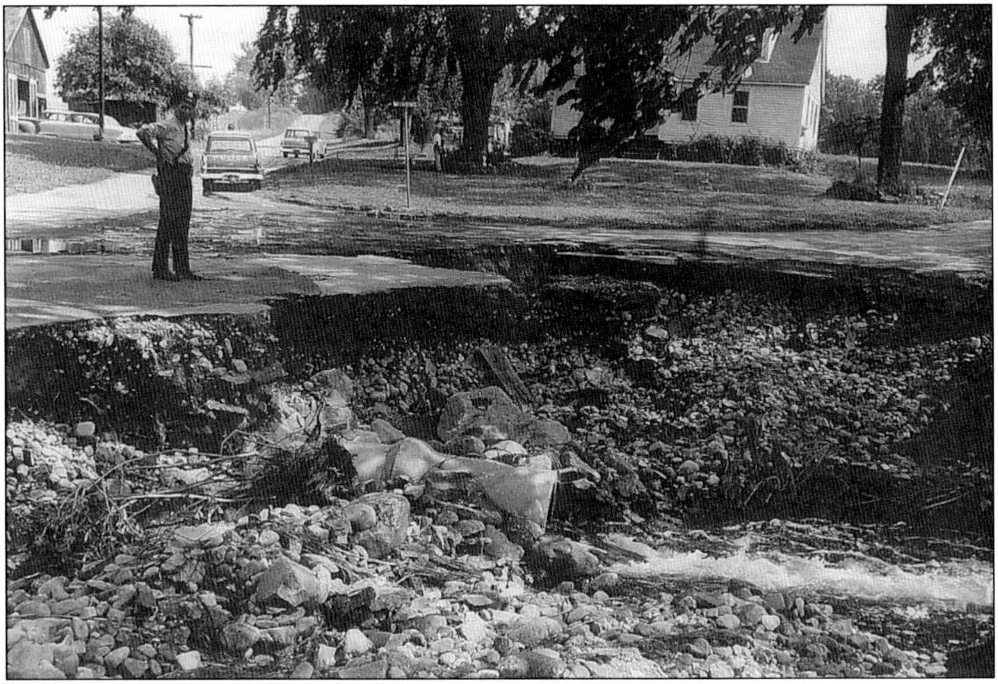

FLOOD OF 1955. The fork of Lyon and Munsing Streets was carried away by the waters of Harris Brook.

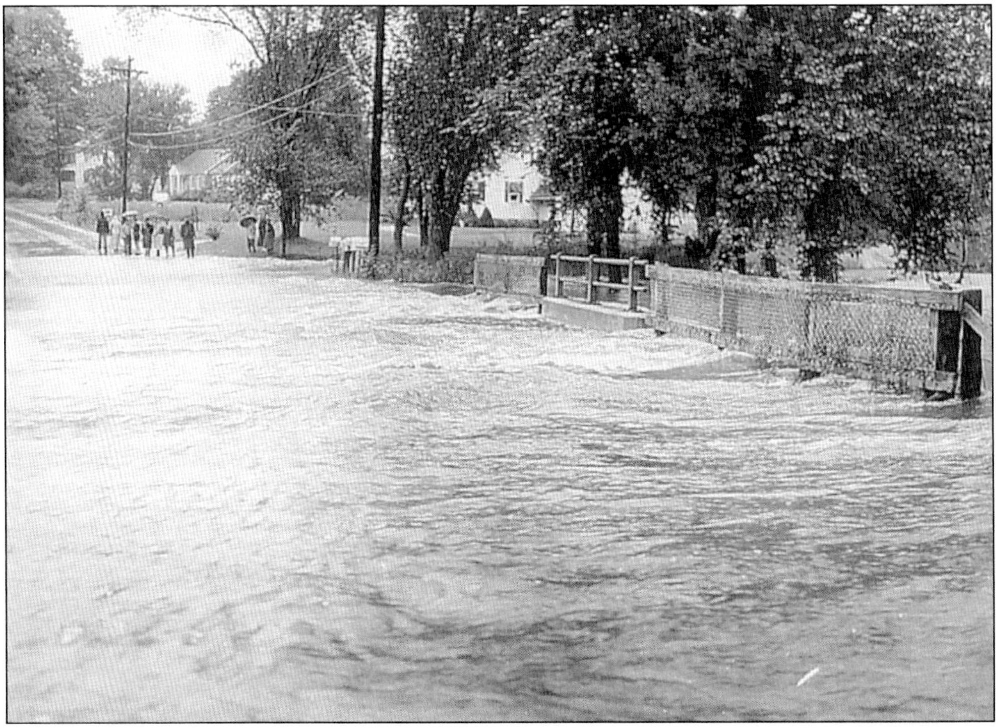

FLOOD OF 1955. Flood waters of Higher Brook are shown passing over Center Street.

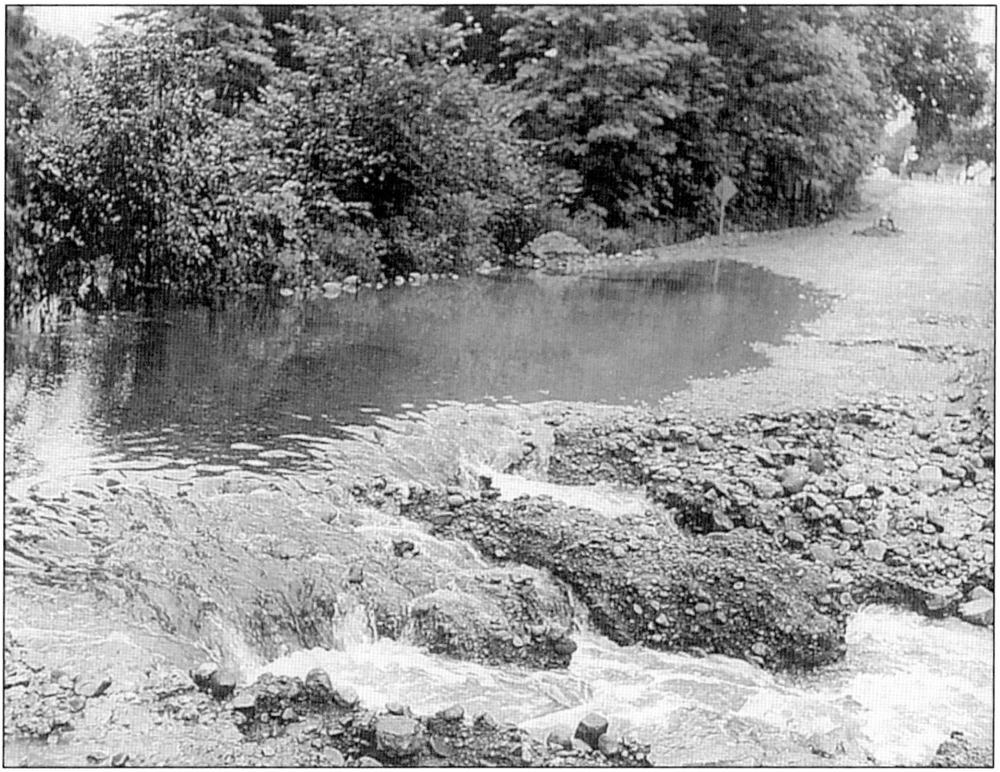

FLOOD OF 1955. This is Center Street on August 18, 1955, one day before Hurricane Diane hit.

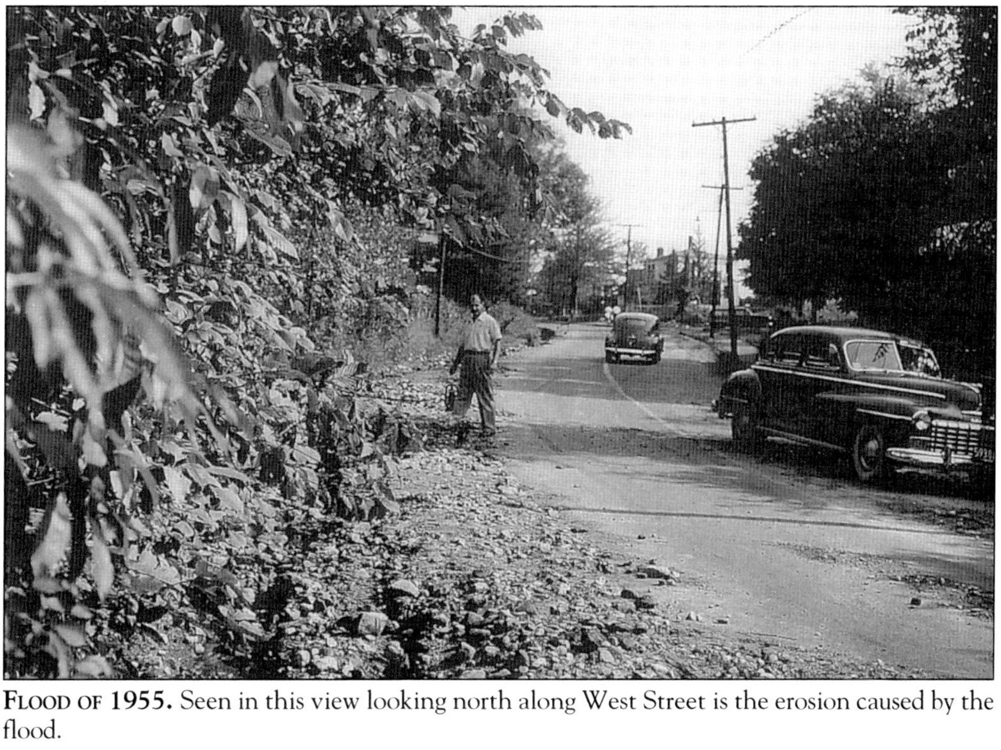

FLOOD OF 1955. Seen in this view looking north along West Street is the erosion caused by the flood.

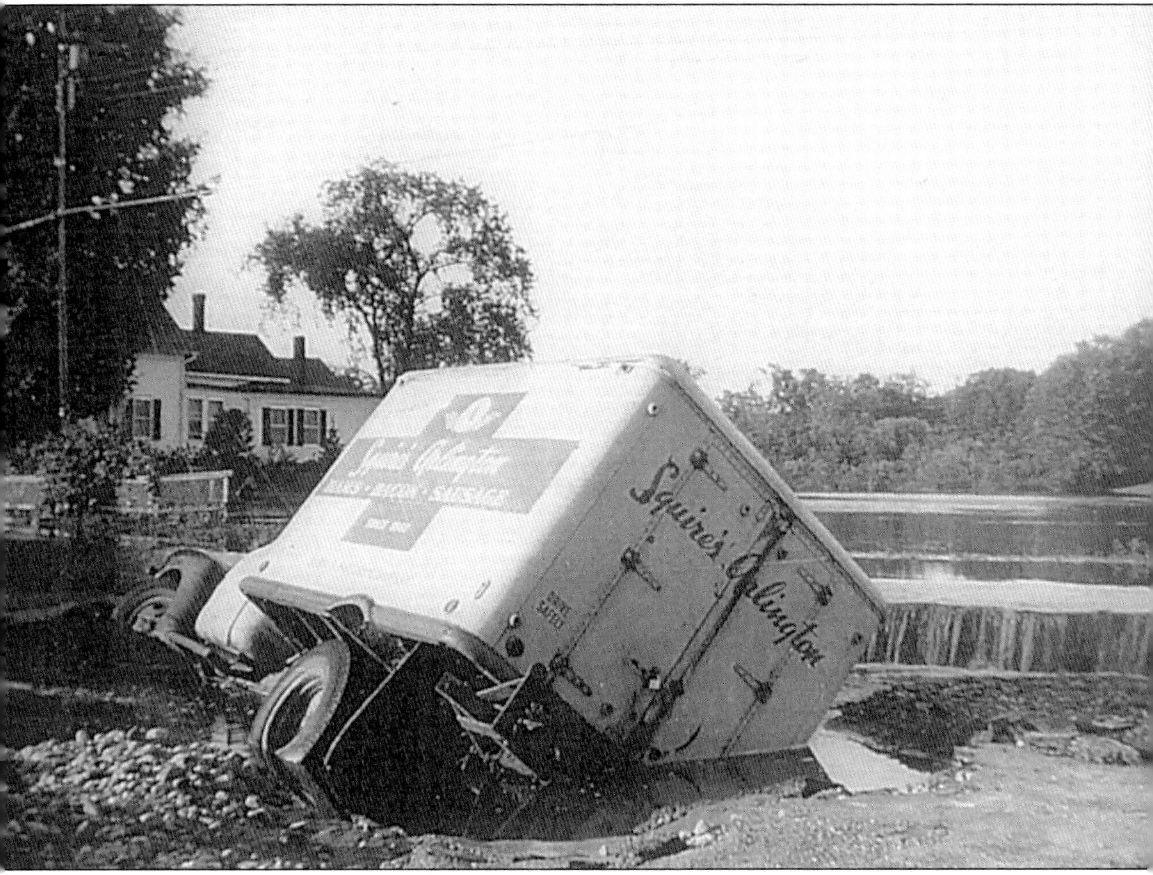

FLOOD OF 1955. Apparently, someone used poor judgement at the washout at Church and Rood Streets (Harris Brook crossing).

Six

PEOPLE

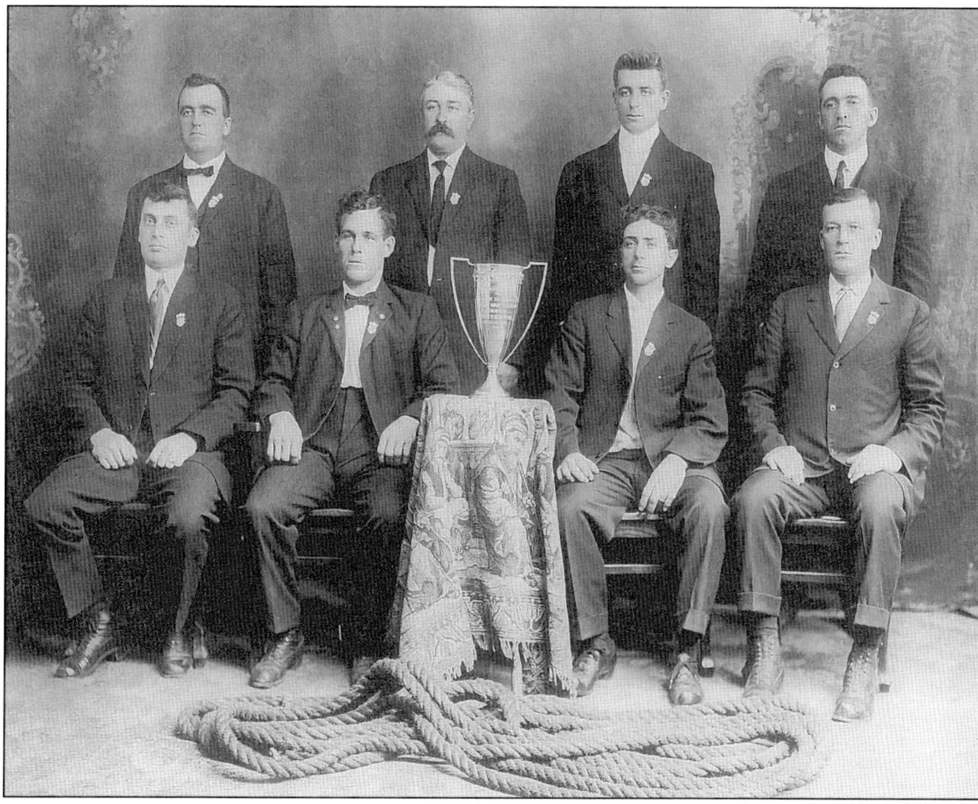

LUDLOW TUG-OF-WAR TEAM, C. 1904. The Ludlow Manufacturing Associates supported and encouraged sports teams and recreational activities. Employees benefited from this, as it gave them an outlet of tension from long days spent in the mills. Shown here is the tug-of-war team with a trophy and the jute rope they won it with.

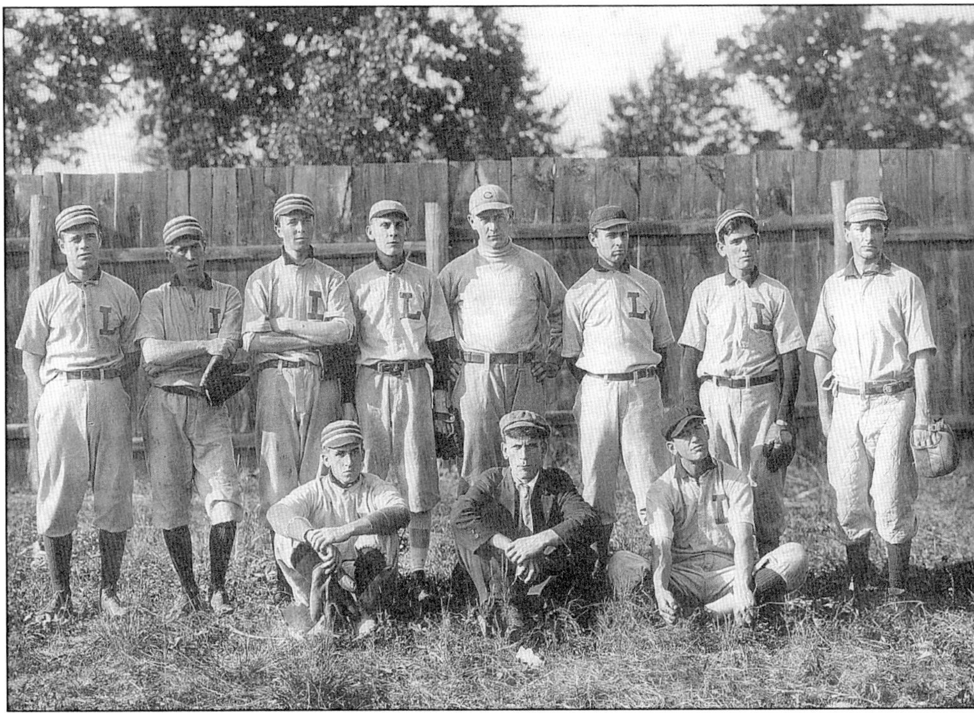

LMA Baseball Team, c. 1905. Everyone had teams back then. There were factory teams and church leagues, and different nationalities had their own teams as well. All townspeople played on, cheered for, or supported the teams in some way.

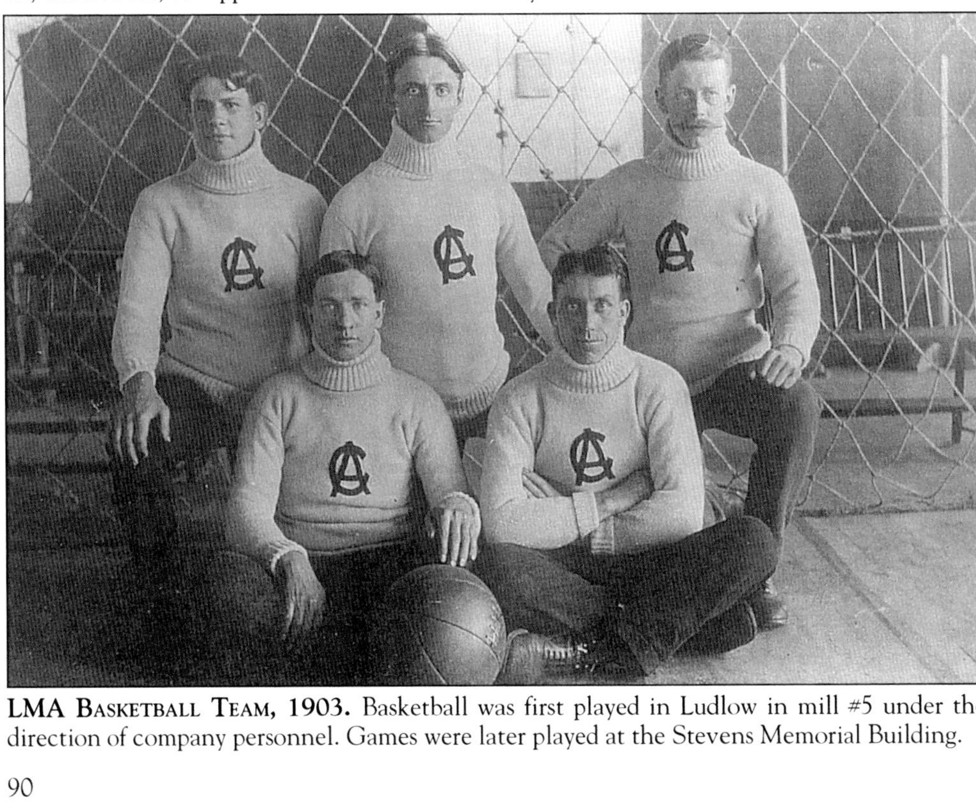

LMA Basketball Team, 1903. Basketball was first played in Ludlow in mill #5 under the direction of company personnel. Games were later played at the Stevens Memorial Building.

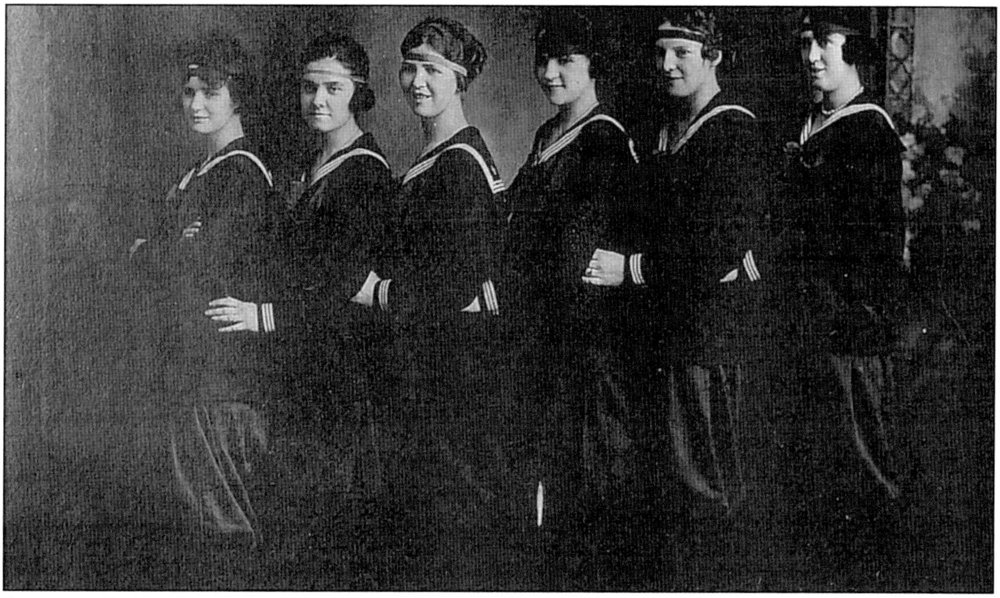

LUDLOW RECREATION ASSOCIATION, WOMEN'S BASKETBALL TEAM, 1920. Women were not allowed to participate in sports other than basketball. Pictured from left to right are Mary Beatson, Geraldine Rooney, Joan Gordon, Mabel Hoarle, Bella Wilkie (team captain), and Margaret Dougherty.

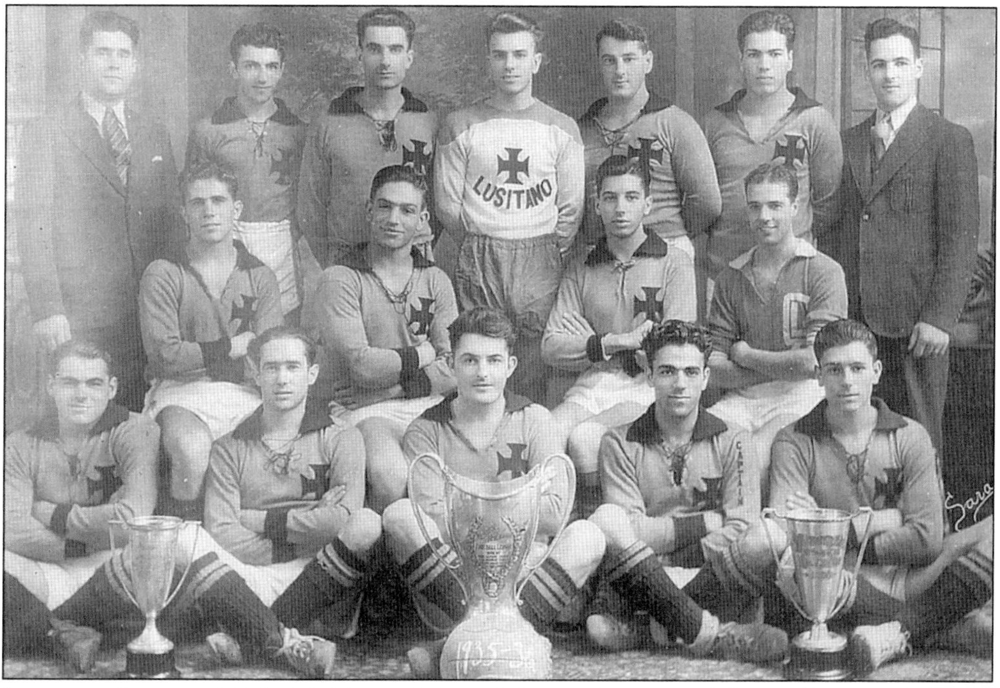

LUSITANO SOCCER, 1935–36. Pictured, from left to right, are as follows: (front row) Joseph Silva, Vitorino Silva, Joseph Cargill, Antonio Esteves, and Antonio Montaro; (middle row) Victor Costa, Domingues Francisco, Antonio Fidalgo, and Olimpio Fidalgo; (back row) Luiz Olivera, Fermino Esteves, Joseph Ricardi, Edwardo Lopes, ? Arsenio, ? Goncalves, and Simon Santos.

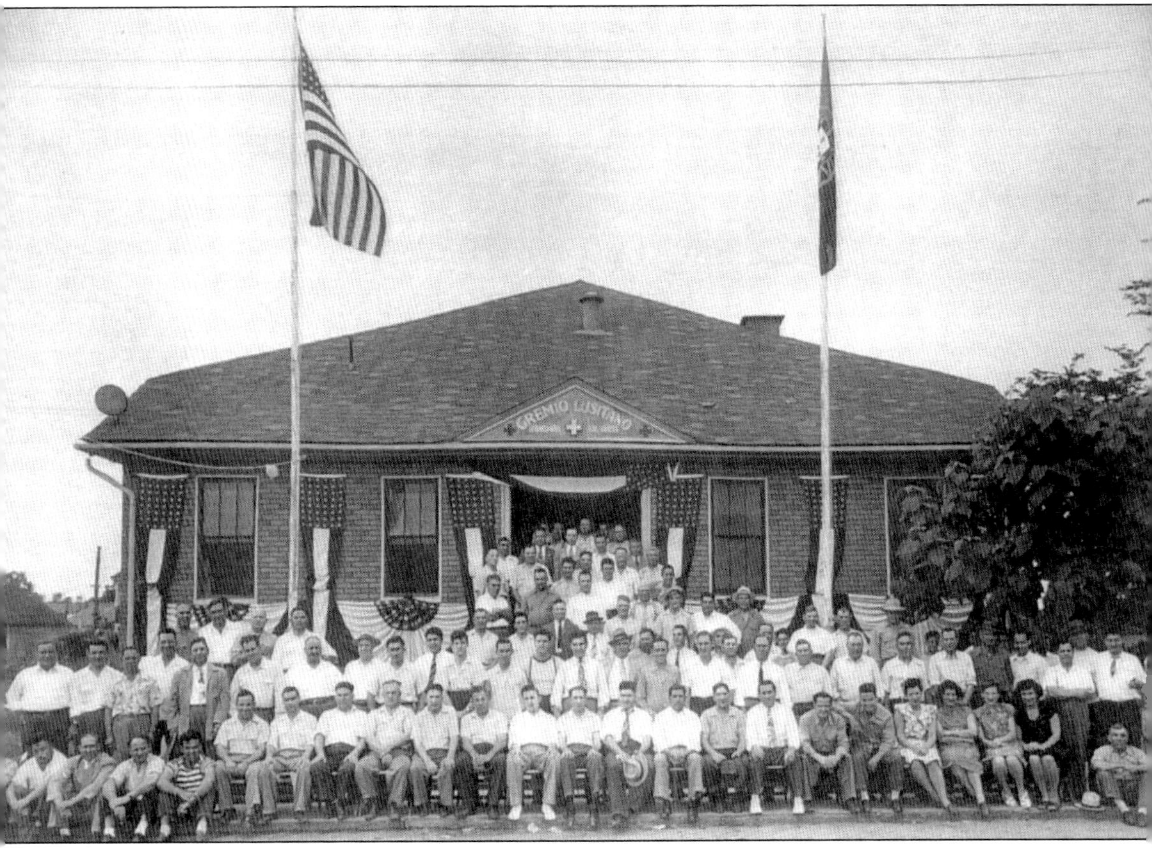

GREMIO LUSITANO CLUB, C. 1950S. This Portuguese club was founded in 1922, and the building shown here served as their clubhouse until a fire in 1951 severely damaged it. It was renovated and used until 1971, when the present and larger clubhouse was built.

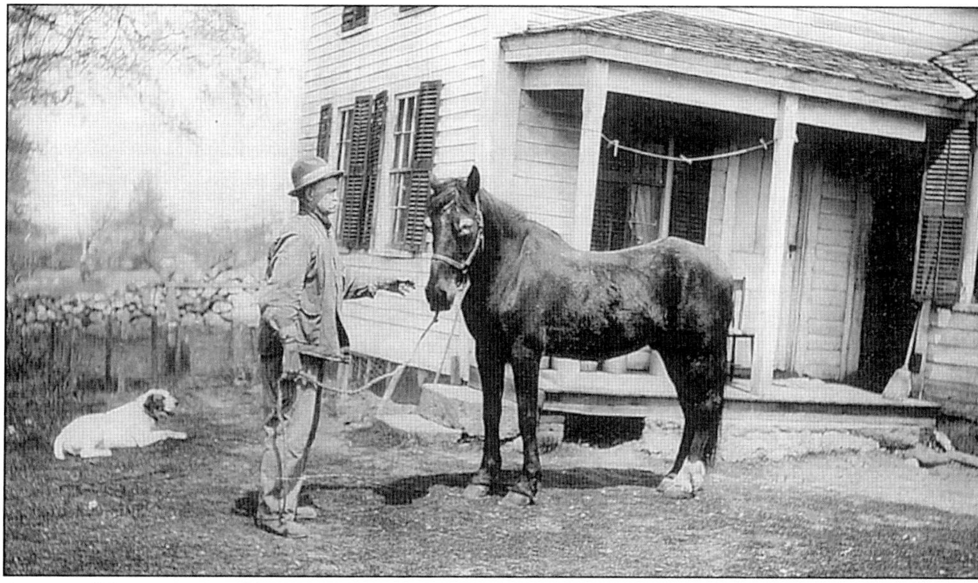

Albert Wilson and Horse outside Funeral Door, Miller Street. Families often had a funeral door in their houses; it was used as a passage for caskets being brought into or taken out of the home.

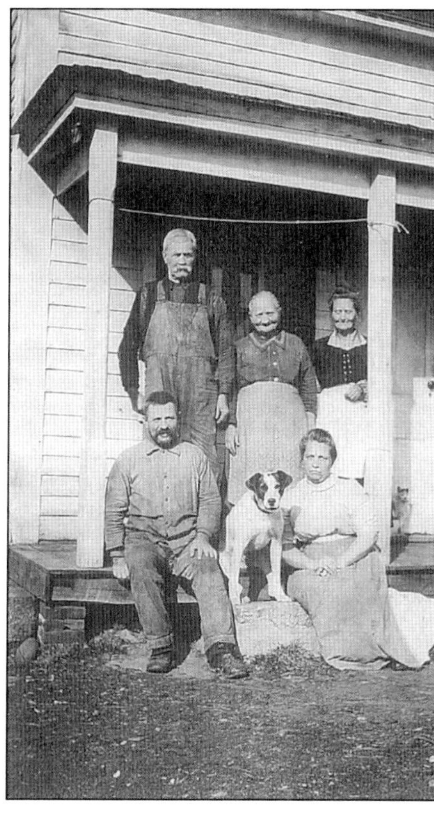

The Wilson Family. Pictured from left to right are as follows: (front row) Austin Wilson, family dog, and sister Clara Wilson; (back row) father Albert Wilson, Mrs. Albert Wilson, and Mrs. Wilson's sister.

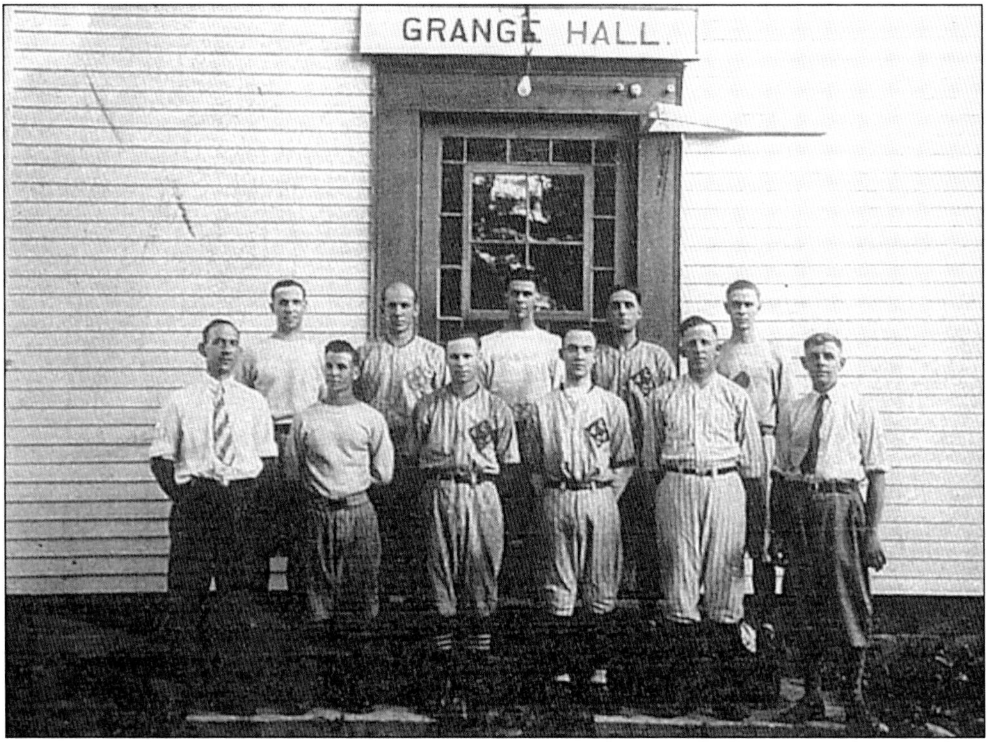

THE GRANGE BASEBALL TEAM, c. 1927. Pictured from left to right are as follows: (front row) Walter Pease Sr., Jim White, Millard White, Raymond Cottini, Warren Fuller, and Raymond Harris; (back row) Rutherford White, William Walker, Leon Harris, Ken Taylor, and Leslie Harris.

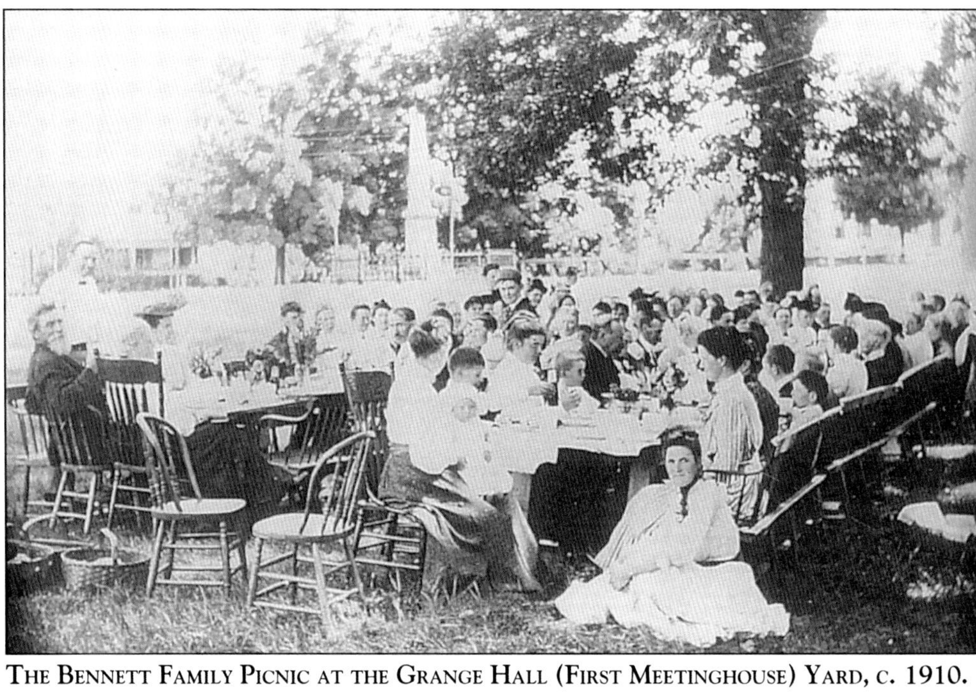

THE BENNETT FAMILY PICNIC AT THE GRANGE HALL (FIRST MEETINGHOUSE) YARD, c. 1910.

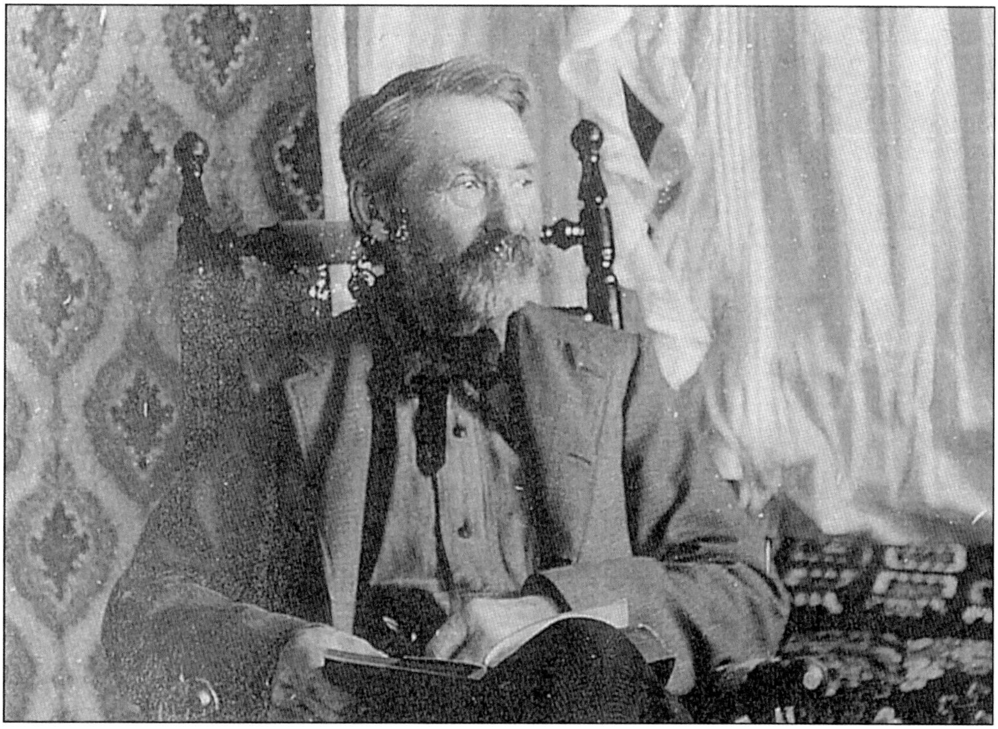

CHARLES FAIRBANKS, C. 1910. (Photo courtesy Don and Betty Kibbe.)

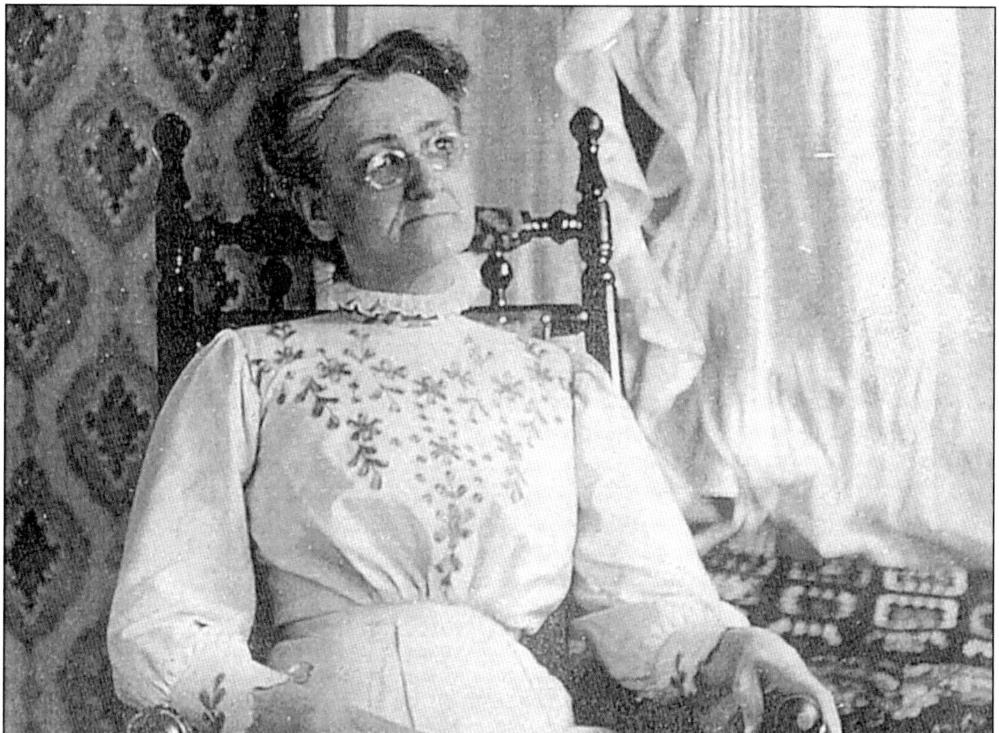

MRS. CHARLES FAIRBANKS, C. 1910. (Photo courtesy Don and Betty Kibbe.)

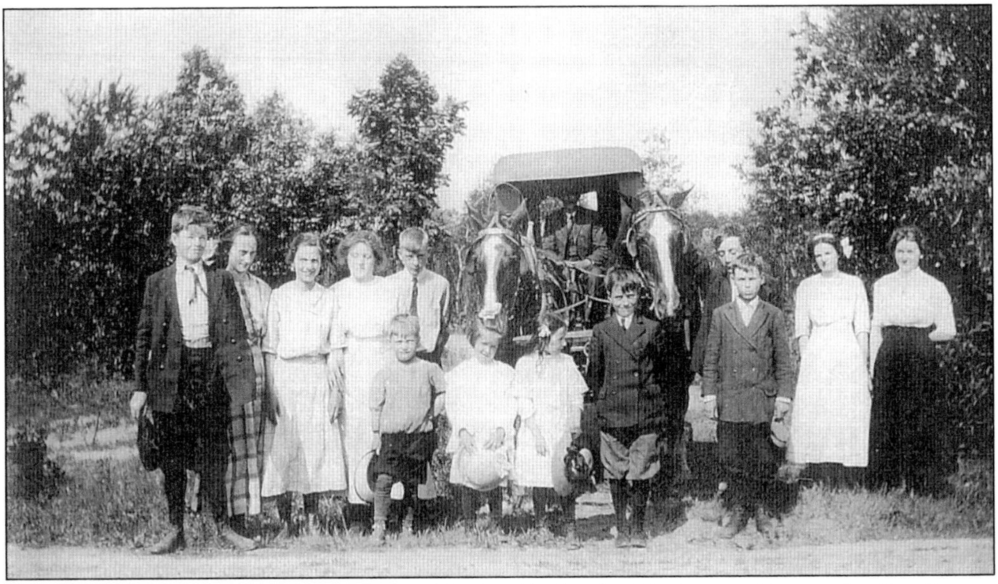

Family Picture, c. 1910. This is possibly the Fairbanks, Taylor, or George family. (Photo courtesy Don and Betty Kibbe.)

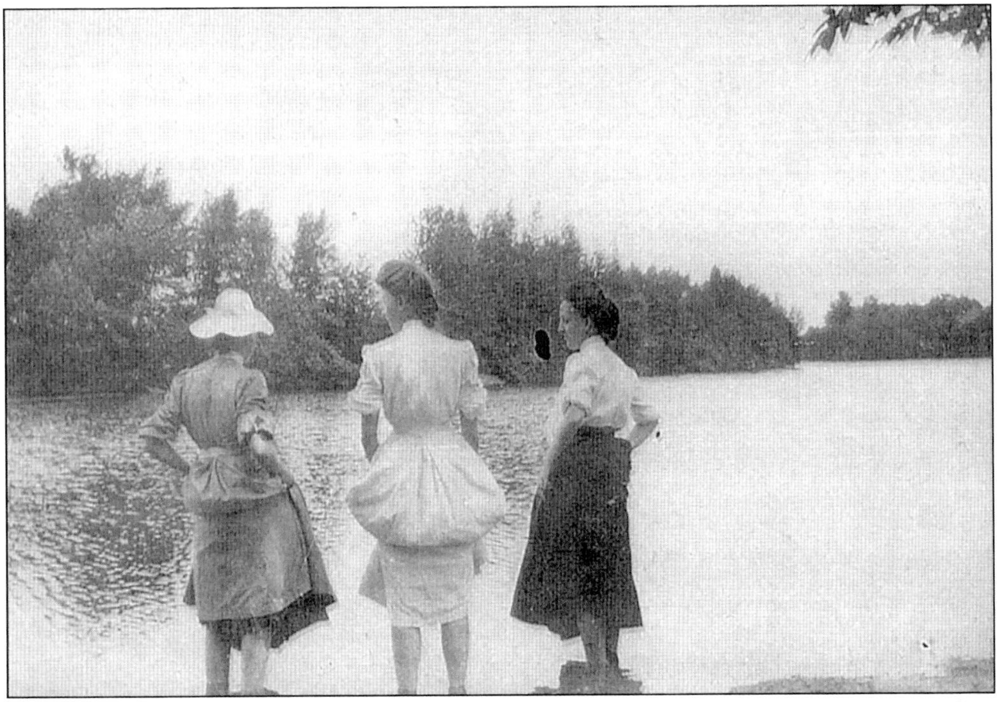

Summertime Beach Fun. This photo was taken either in Haviland Pond or Harris Pond, c. 1910. (Photo courtesy Don and Betty Kibbe.)

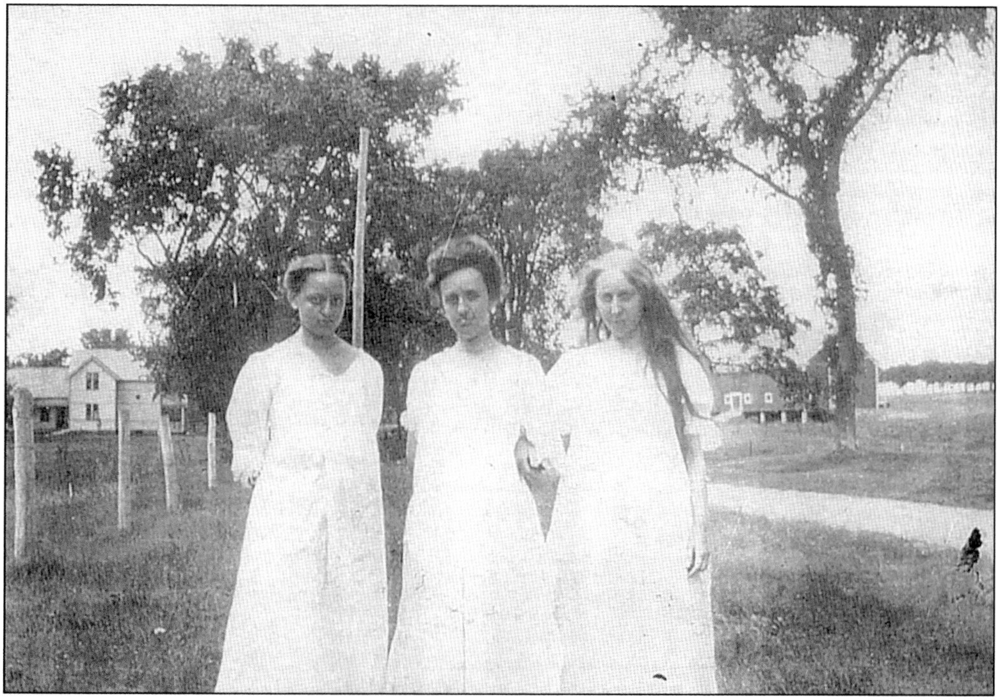

Holyoke Street, Looking toward West Street, c. 1910. The Keefe brothers' barn on the right is now gone, but the house on the left is still there. Formerly owned by the Kochanek's, the house now is part of a speed shop. (Photo courtesy Don and Betty Kibbe.)

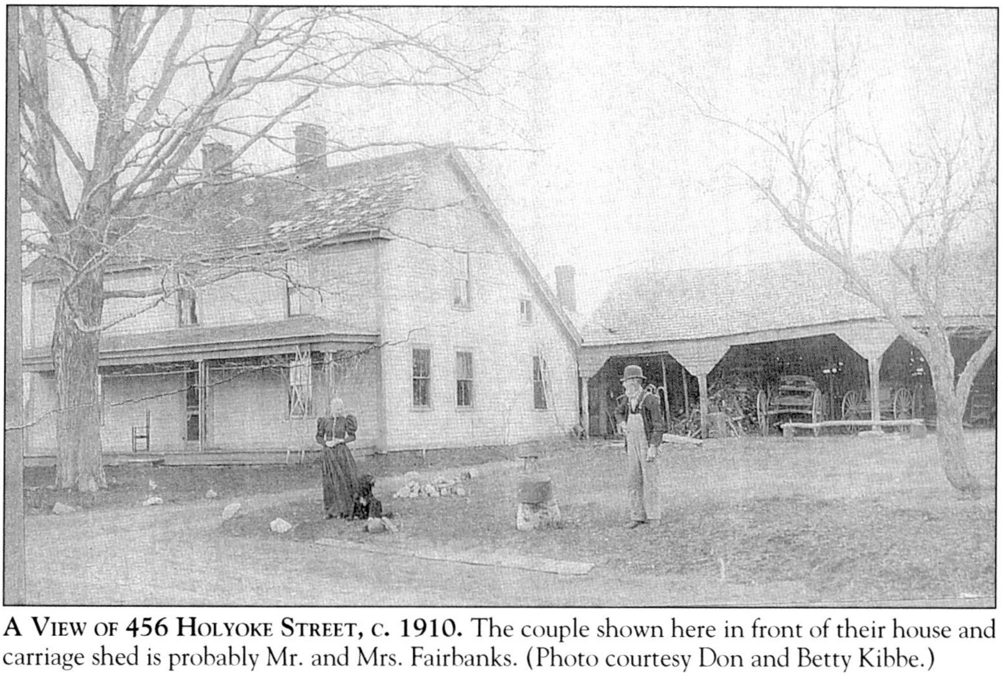

A View of 456 Holyoke Street, c. 1910. The couple shown here in front of their house and carriage shed is probably Mr. and Mrs. Fairbanks. (Photo courtesy Don and Betty Kibbe.)

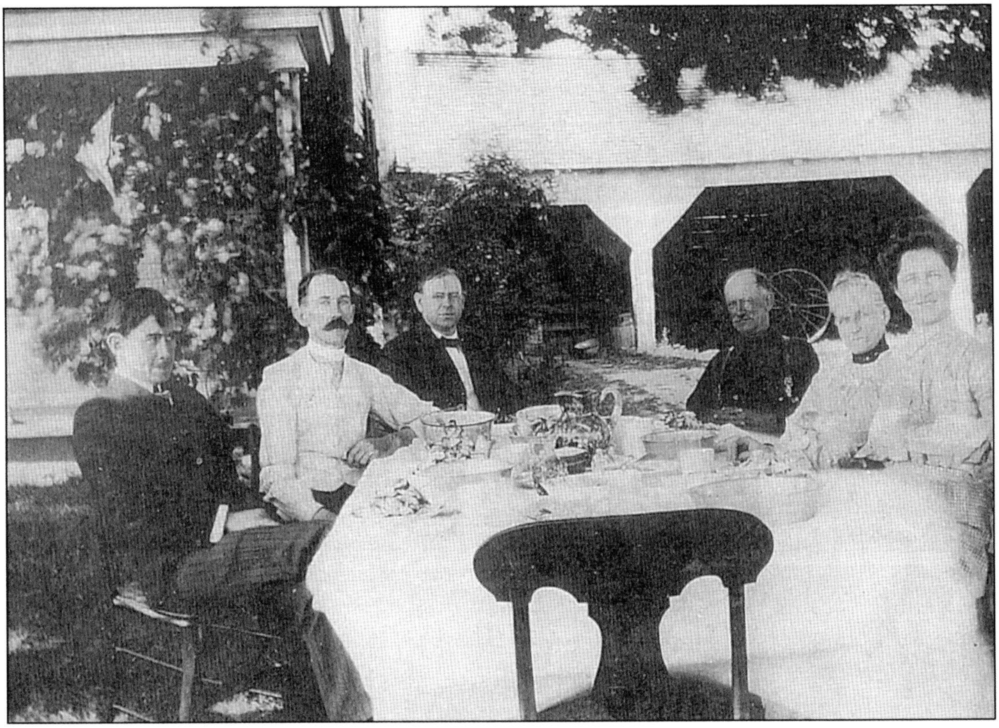

FAMILY PICNIC, 456 HOLYOKE STREET, C. 1910. The entire dining set was moved out to the front lawn in this view. (Photo courtesy Don and Betty Kibbe.)

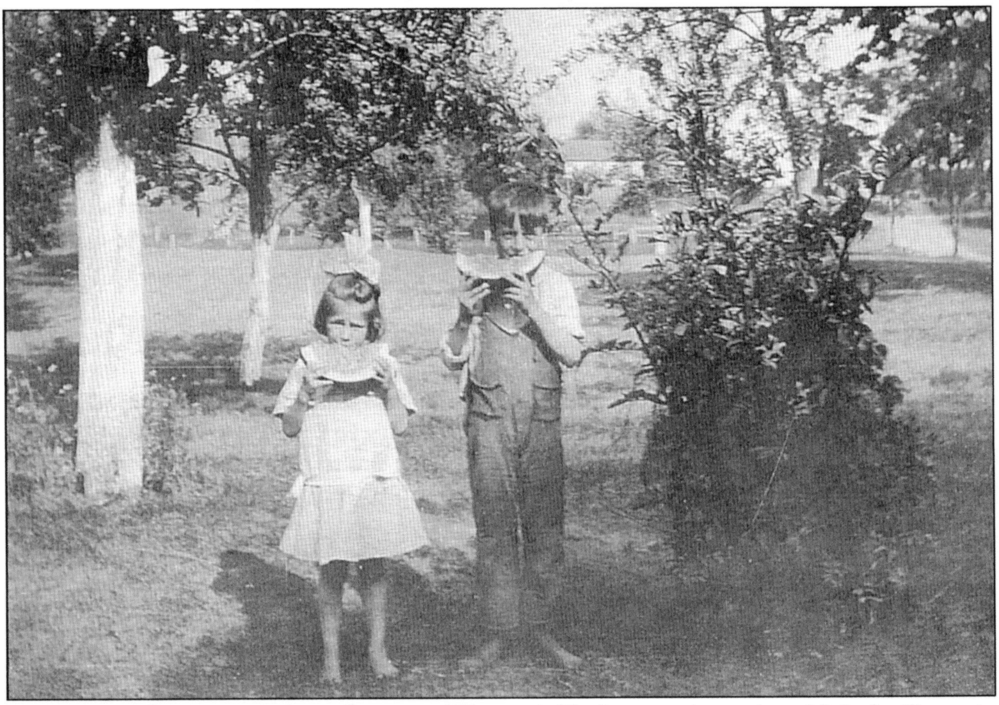

SUMMERTIME SWEETS, C. 1910. Grace and Kenneth Taylor are pictured on Holyoke Street in this view looking uphill (east) toward Kendall Street. (Photo courtesy Don and Betty Kibbe.)

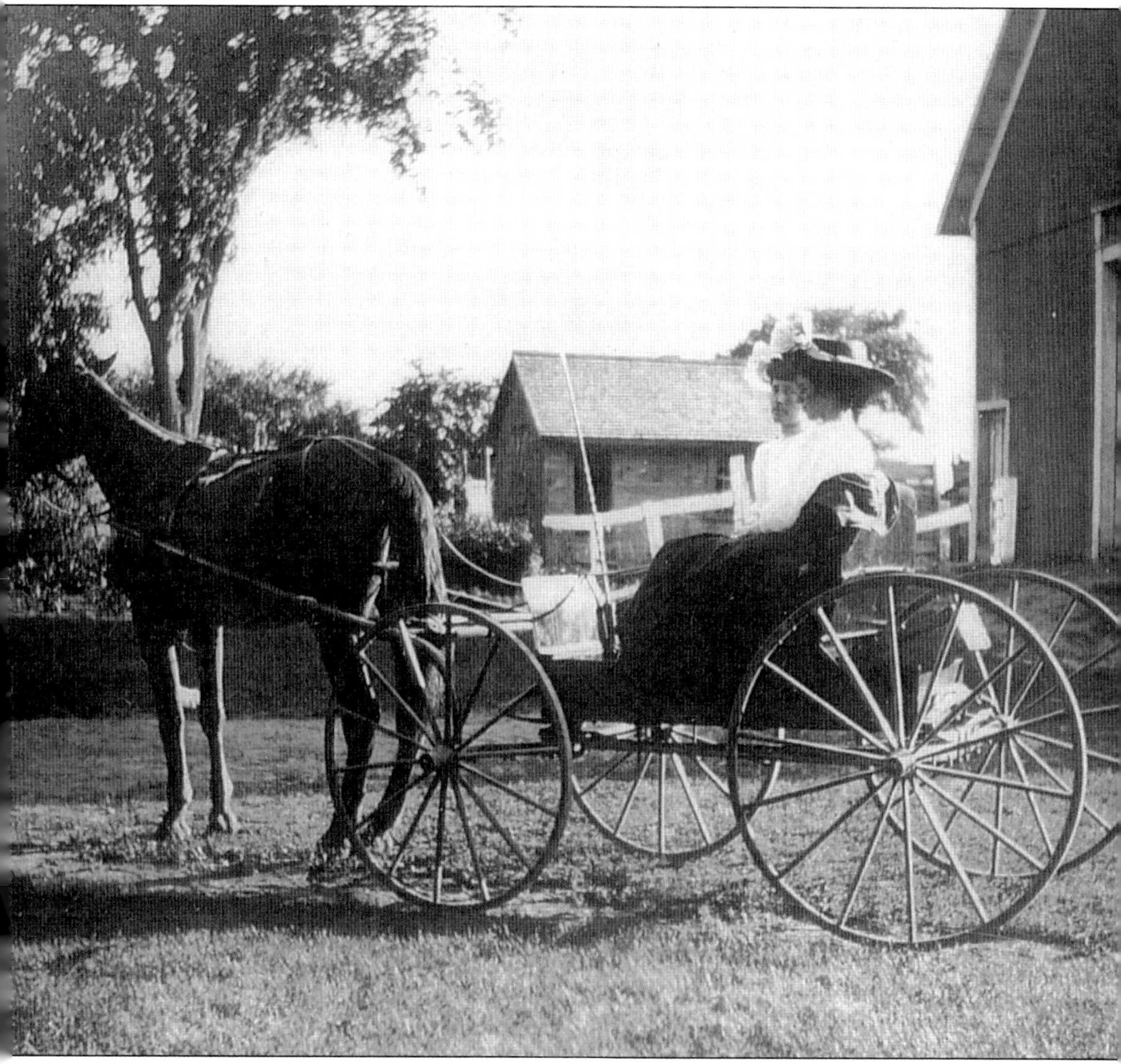

GOING OUT FOR A DRIVE, C. 1910. This barn was once located at 456 Holyoke Street, across the road. A private residence is now there. (Photo courtesy Don and Betty Kibbe.)

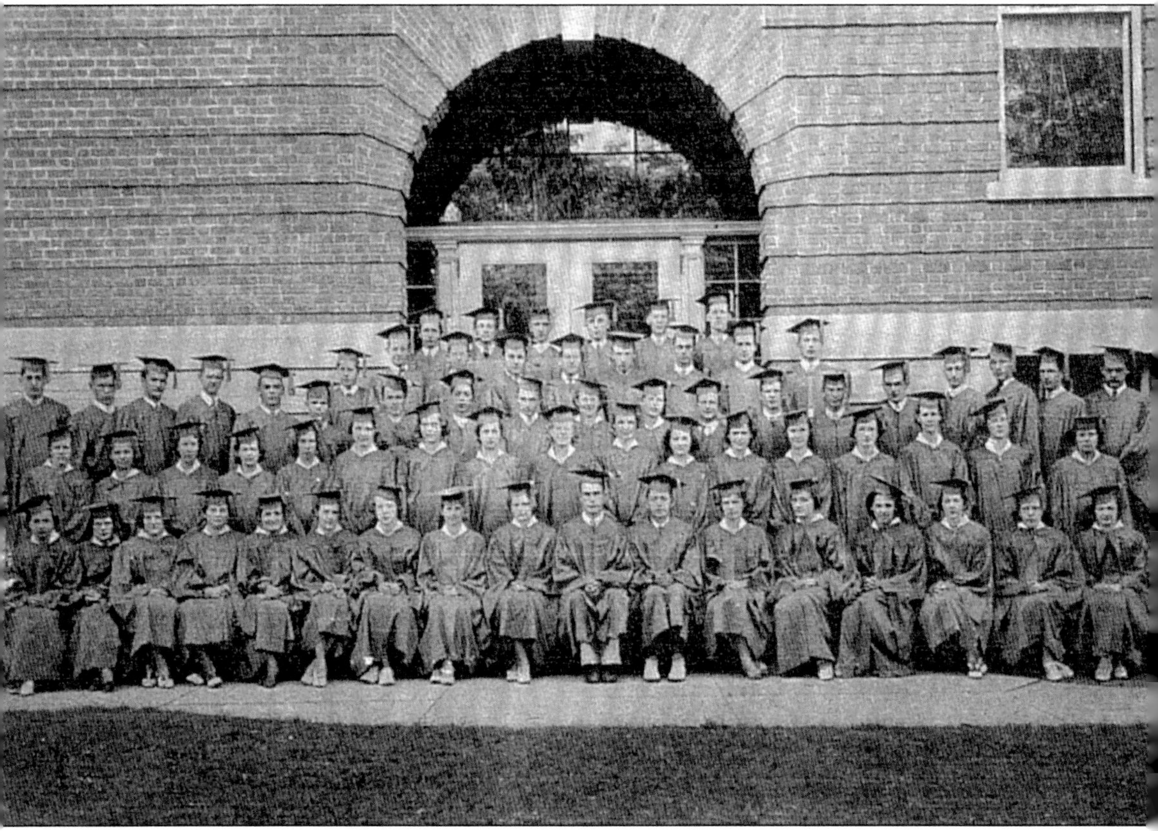

LUDLOW HIGH SCHOOL, CLASS OF 1934.

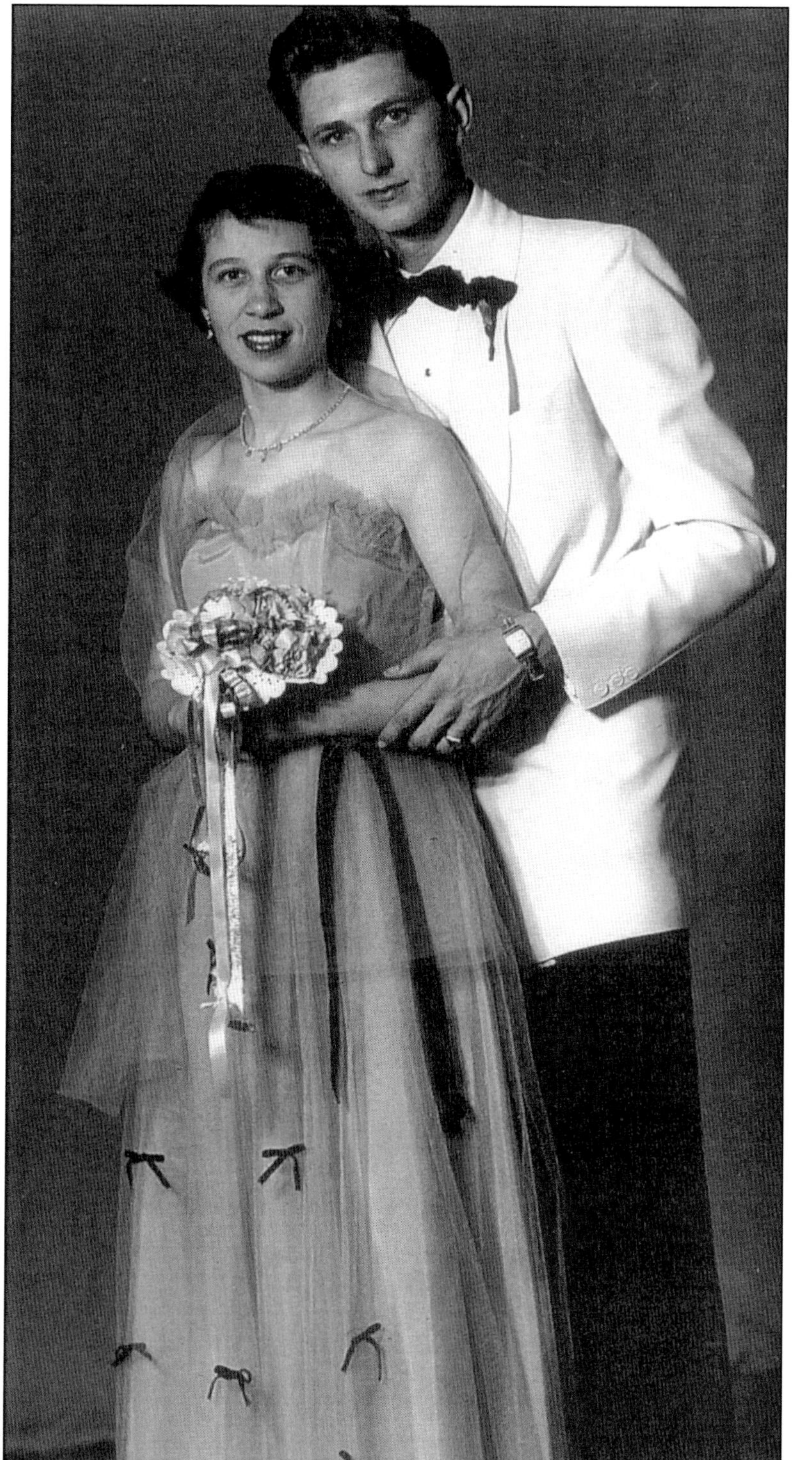

Ludlow High School Prom Night, 1951. Shown here are Dorothy Pieczarka and Bill Nichols.

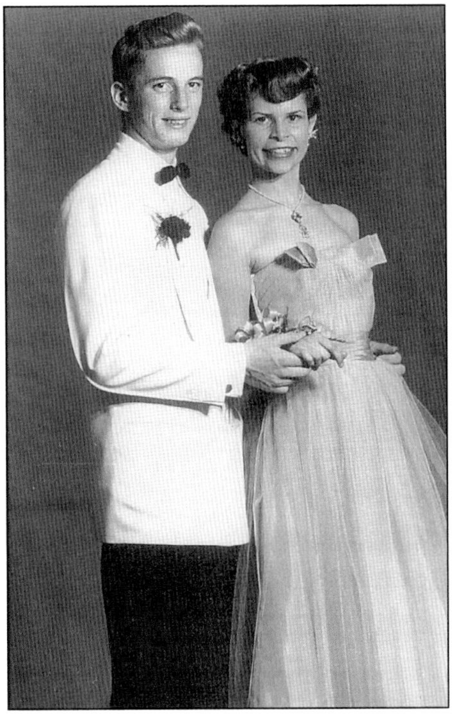

Ludlow High School Prom Night, 1951. David Bennett and Elizabeth Trombley are pictured in this prom night scene.

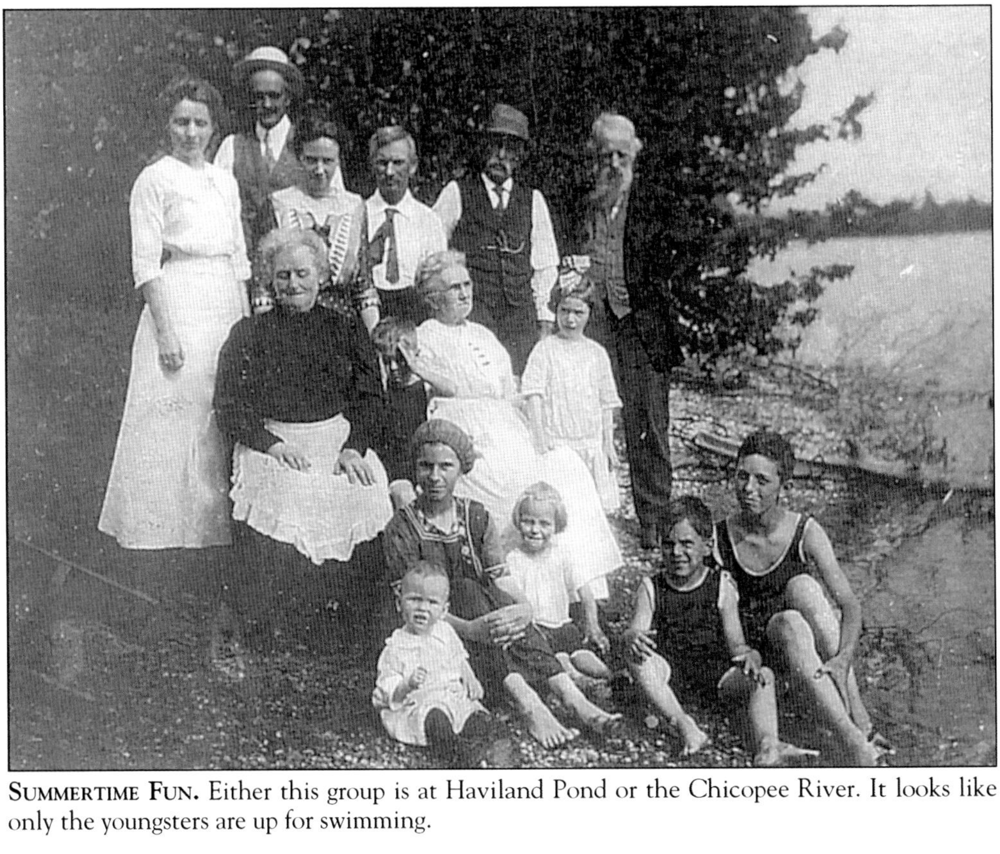

Summertime Fun. Either this group is at Haviland Pond or the Chicopee River. It looks like only the youngsters are up for swimming.

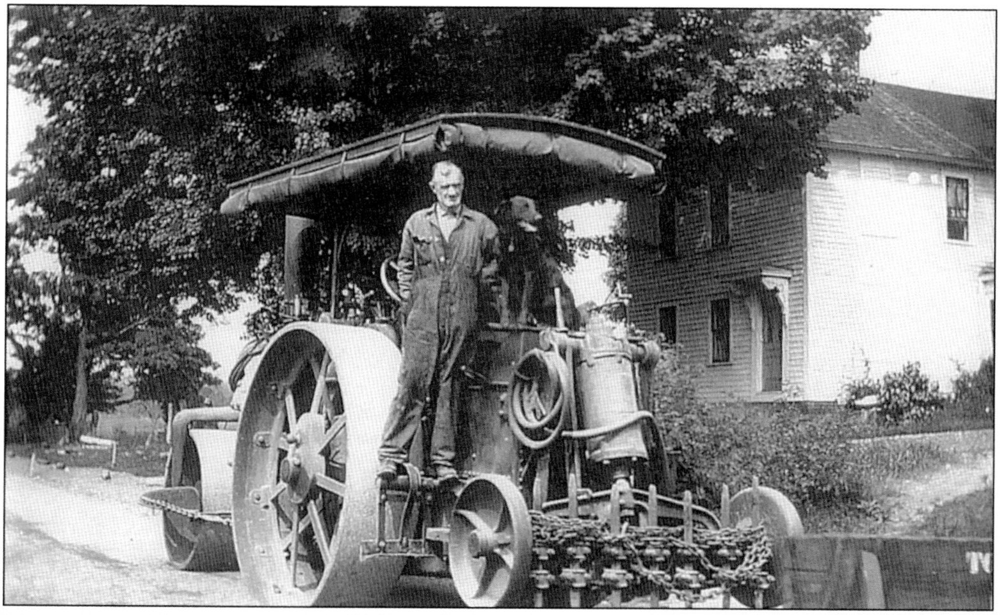

Town Steam Roller, c. 1920. William Golden Sr. is shown here with a companion.

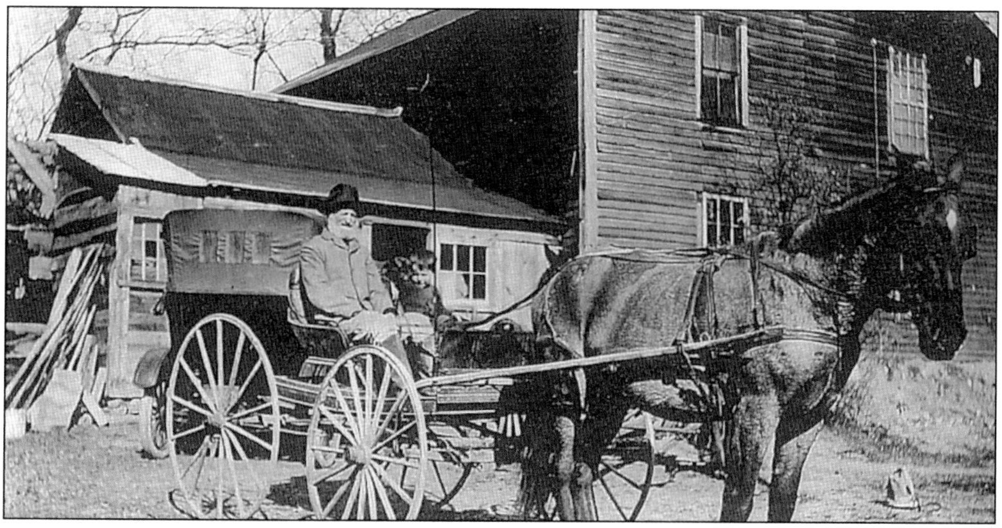

Quartus Fisk and Friend, c. 1900. This photo may have been taken at the Ely Fuller Tavern.

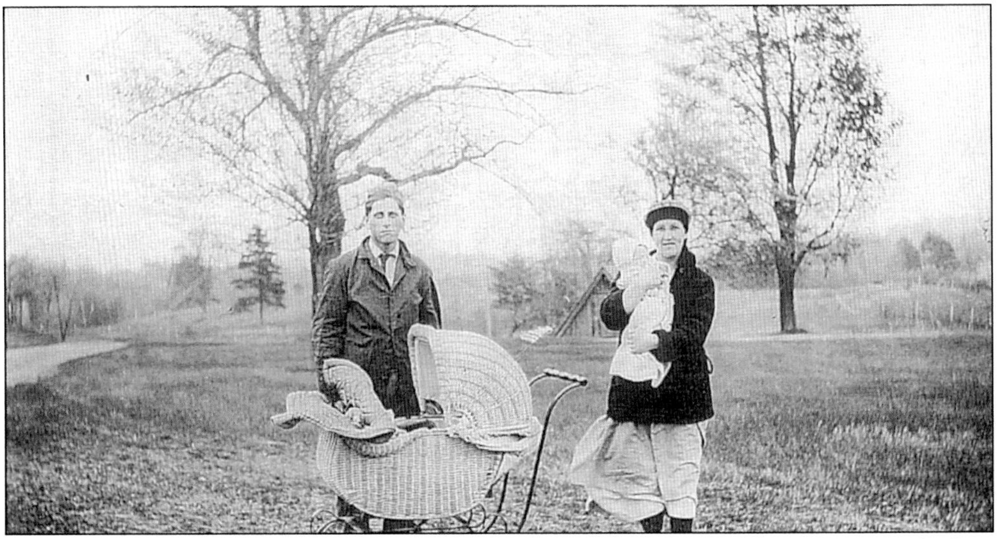

MILLER STREET, RFD #1, 1918. Mr. and Mrs. Frank H. Ellison are shown here with their baby.

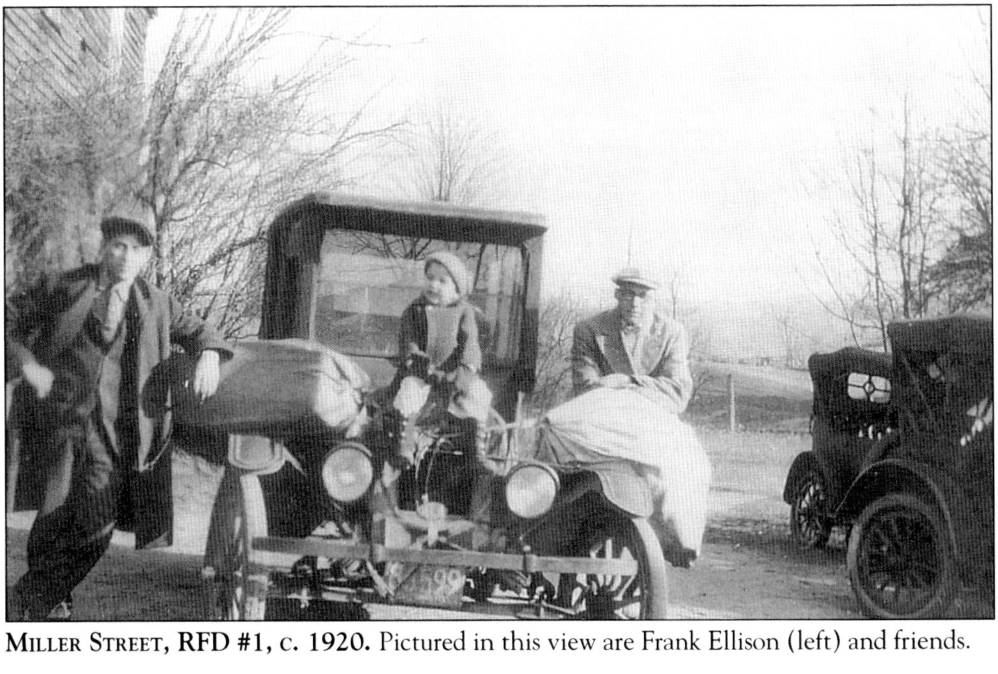

MILLER STREET, RFD #1, c. 1920. Pictured in this view are Frank Ellison (left) and friends.

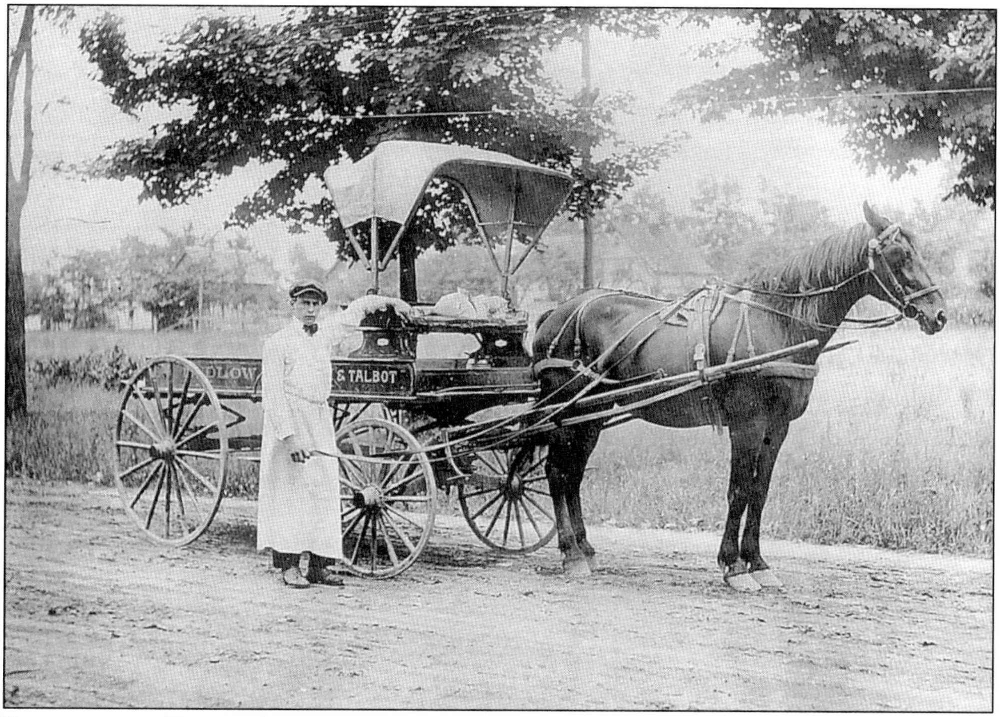

BRUNELLE AND TALBOT GROCERY WAGON, 1913. This store was located at 281/283 East Street. The driver is this photograph is Arthur Fontaine.

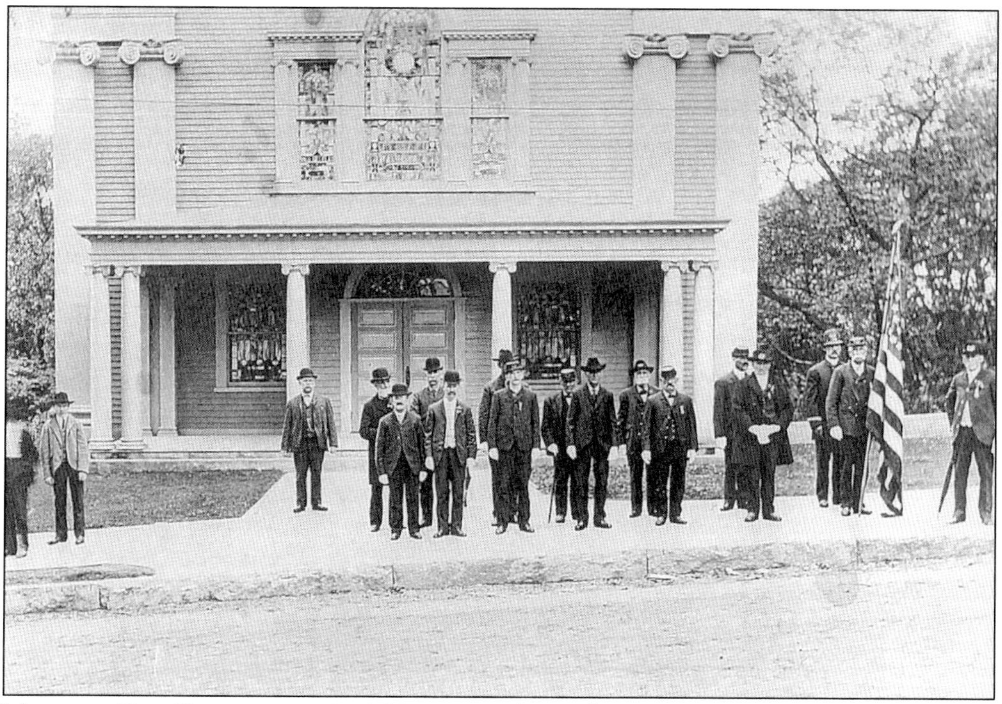

MEMORIAL DAY CEREMONIES, 1905. Veterans gather in front of the Union Church of Christ on Center Street.

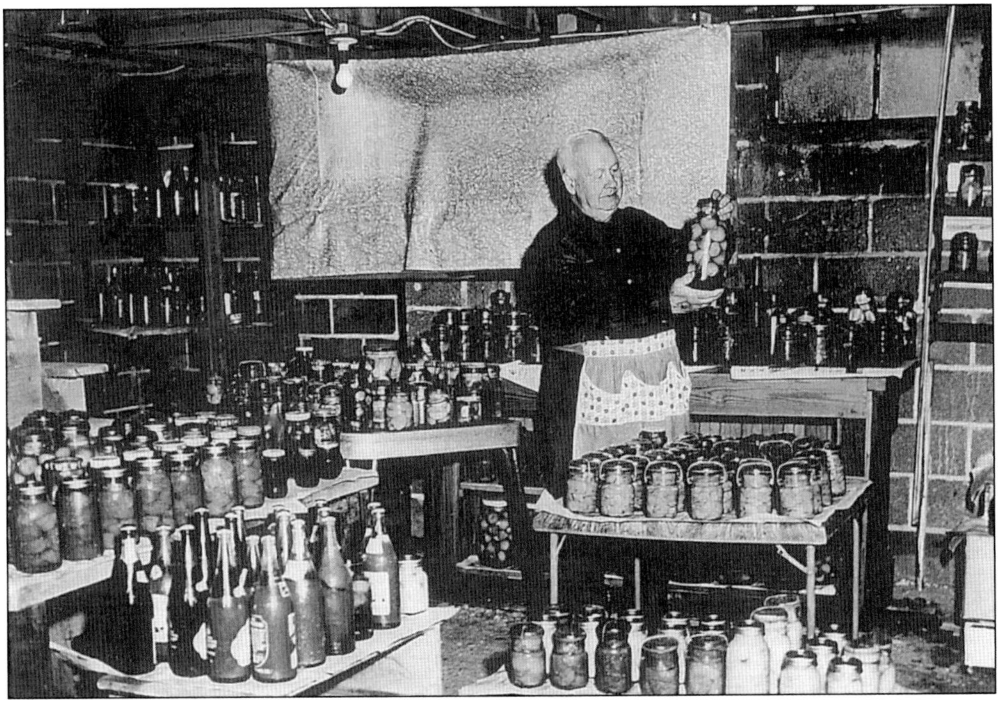

MR. STONE, HOME CANNING ON BELCHERTOWN ROAD, C. 1940.

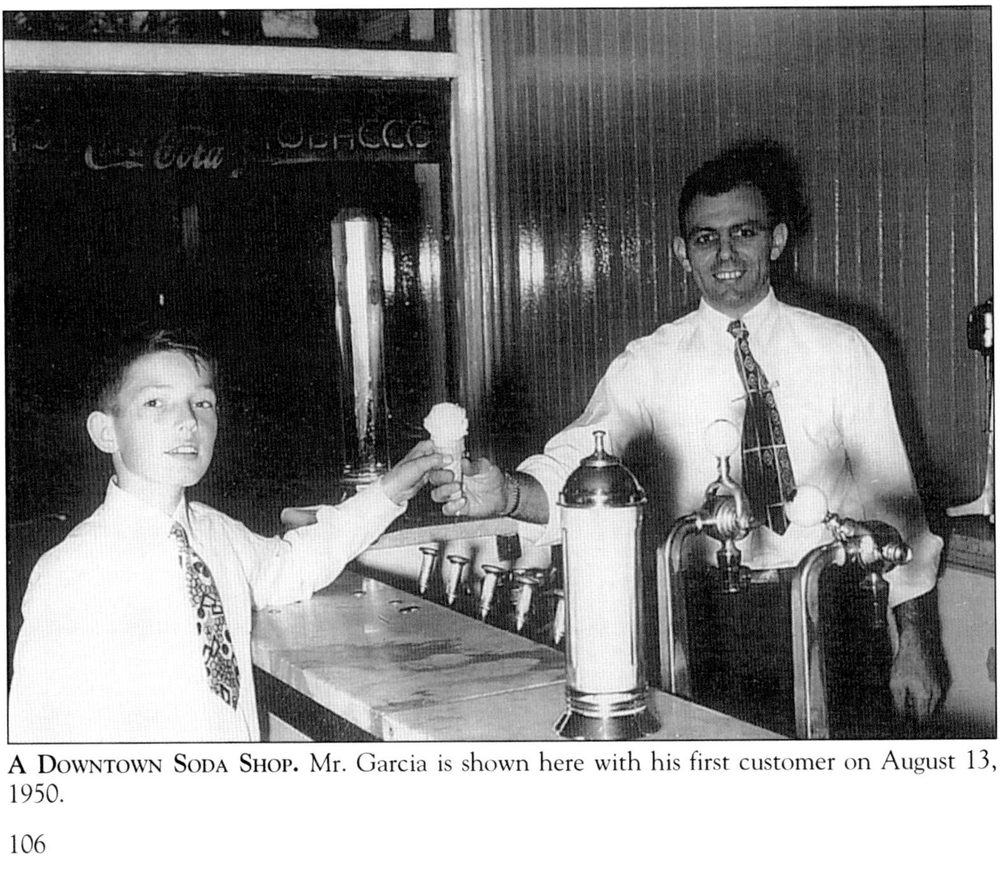

A DOWNTOWN SODA SHOP. Mr. Garcia is shown here with his first customer on August 13, 1950.

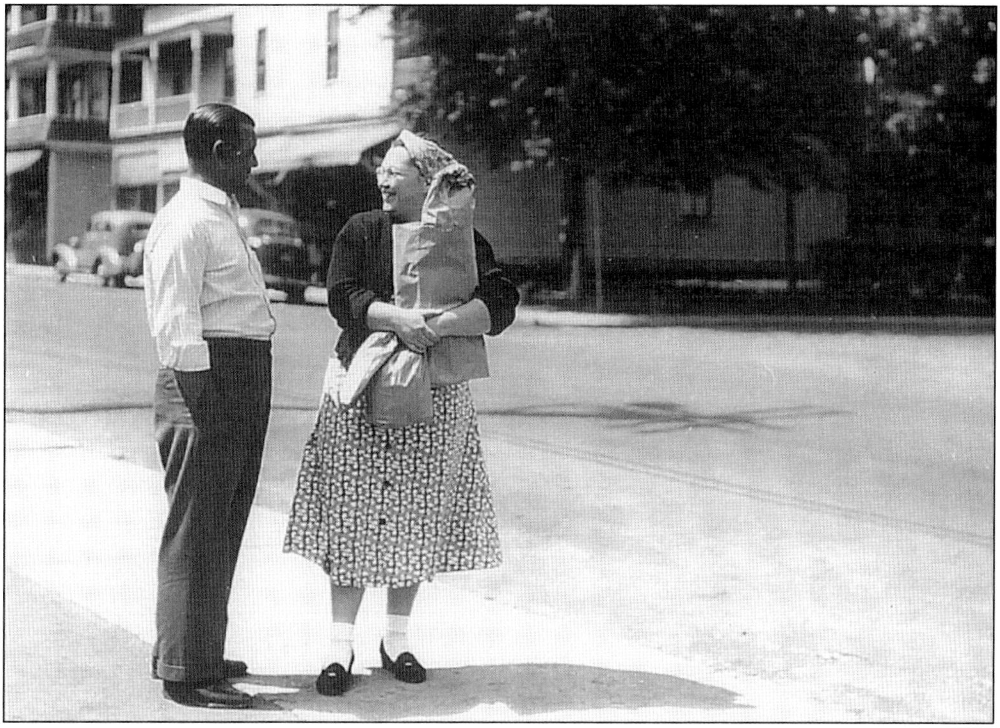

CHATTING ON EAST STREET, C. 1950.

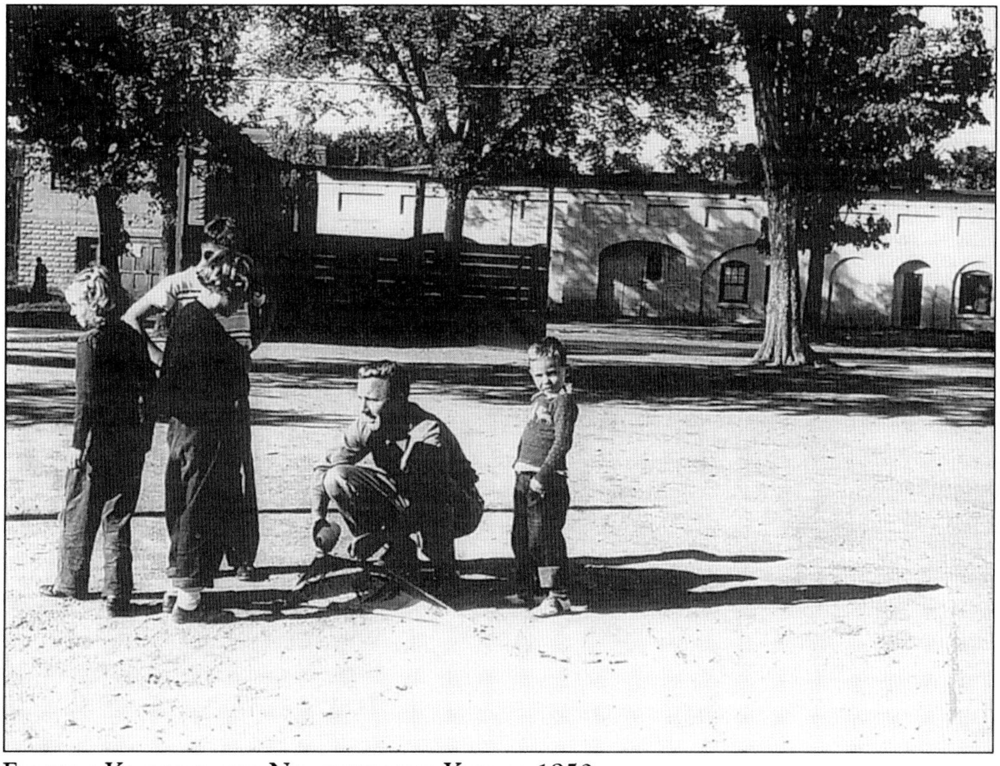

FLYING A KITE WITH THE NEIGHBORHOOD KIDS, C. 1950.

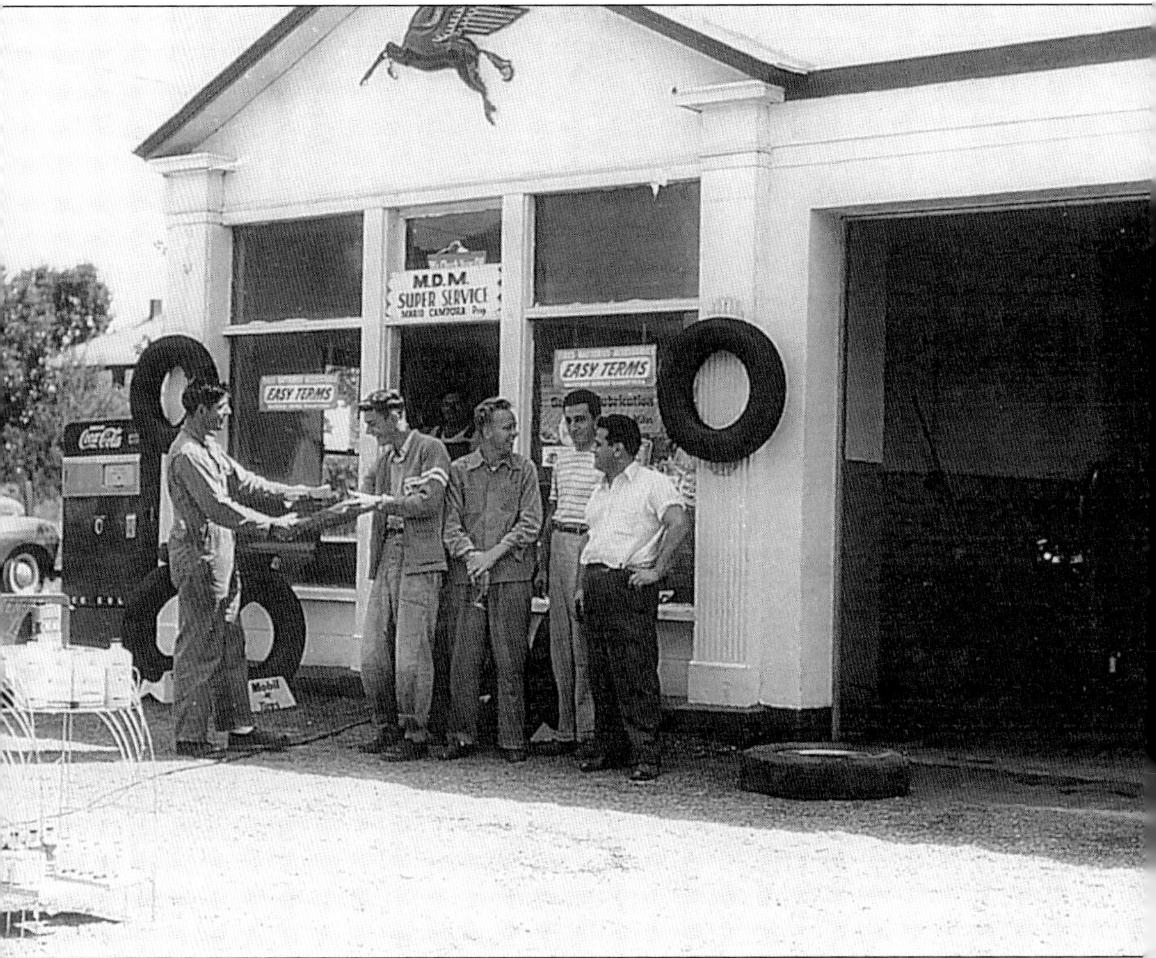

Mobile Station, East Street, c. 1950. Mario Campora was the proprietor of this business.

Seven

Ludlow, Not So Long Ago

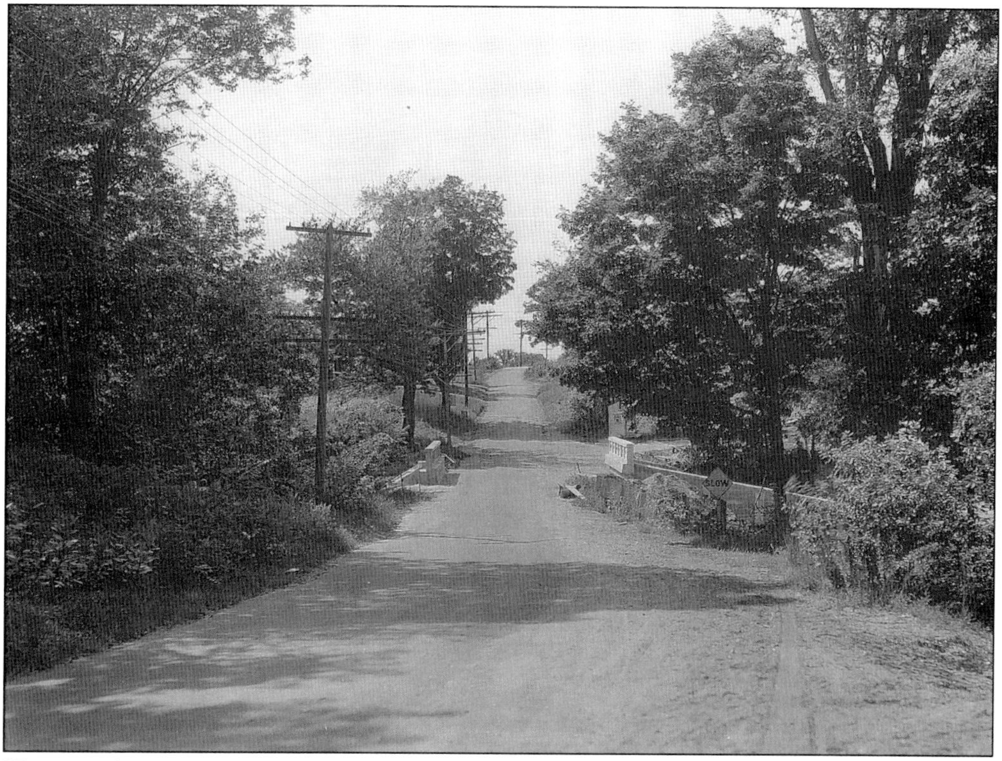

Holyoke Street at Harris Pond, 1930s. Looking west, up the hill towards West Street, one gets a sense of open space, quiet country air, and cool summer breezes. Much of Ludlow's landscape has changed over the last 100 years, some of it dramatically. This picture is immediately recognizable, yet somehow seems to be very far away.

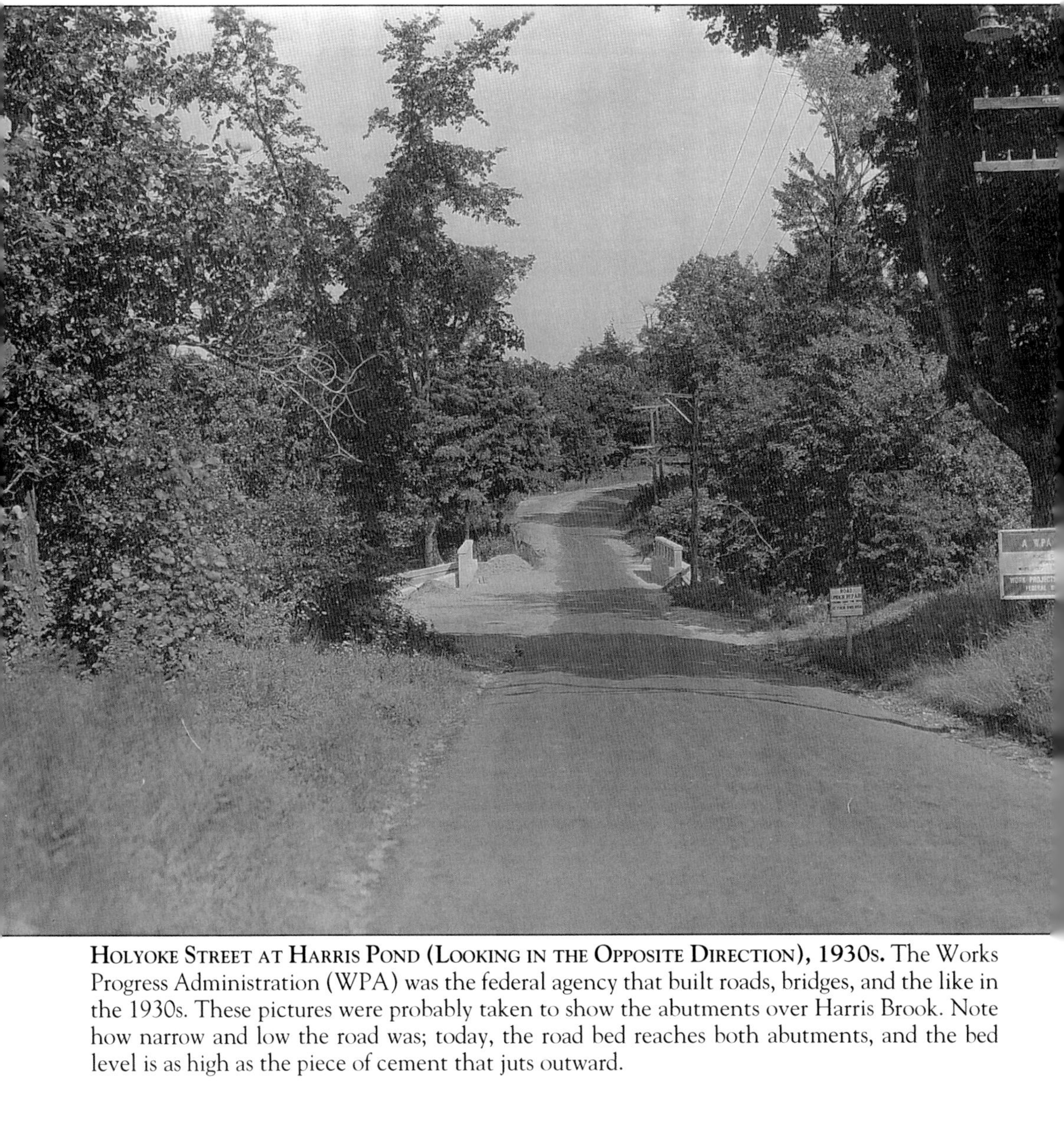

HOLYOKE STREET AT HARRIS POND (LOOKING IN THE OPPOSITE DIRECTION), 1930s. The Works Progress Administration (WPA) was the federal agency that built roads, bridges, and the like in the 1930s. These pictures were probably taken to show the abutments over Harris Brook. Note how narrow and low the road was; today, the road bed reaches both abutments, and the bed level is as high as the piece of cement that juts outward.

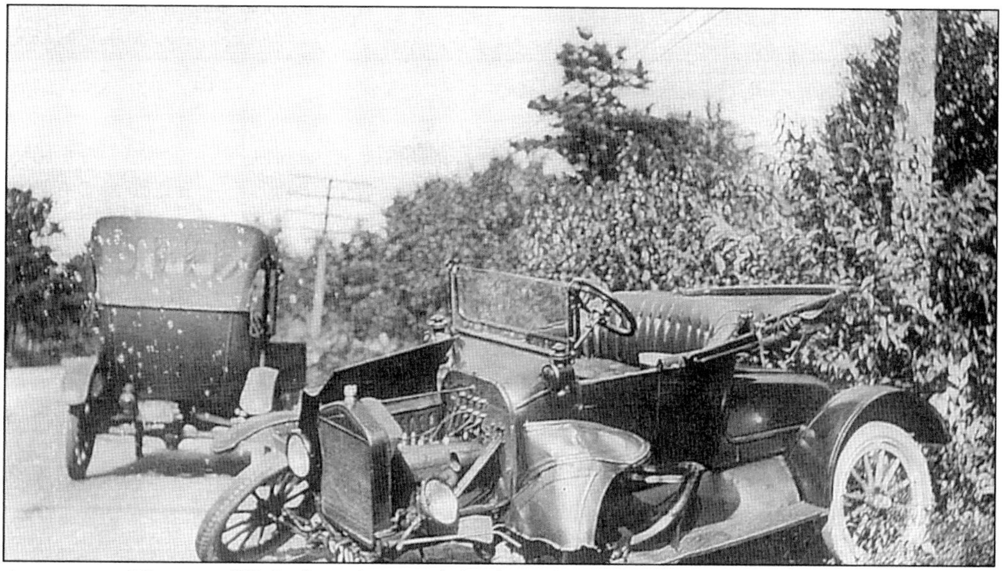

ACCIDENTS HAPPEN. With the advent of the horseless carriage came all the problems of car ownership. Fortunately, accidents such as this did not happen very often.

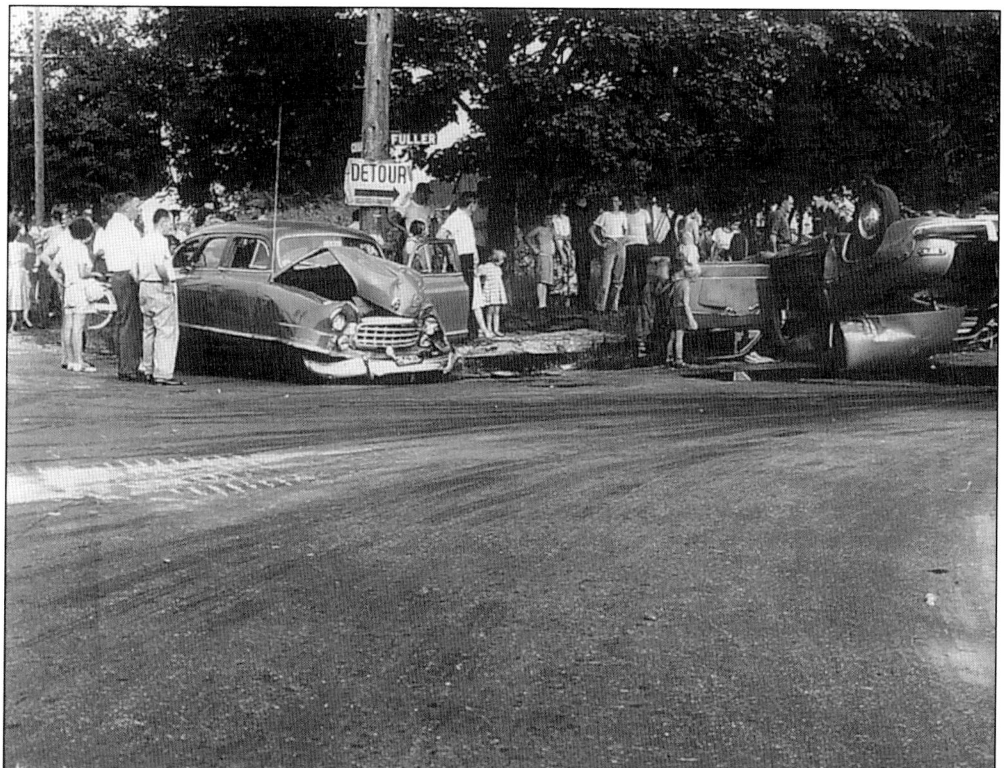

MORE TRAFFIC WOES, AUGUST 14, 1951. Chapin and Fuller Streets were the scene of this serious accident. There are two boys standing near the overturned car, anxious to get a look inside.

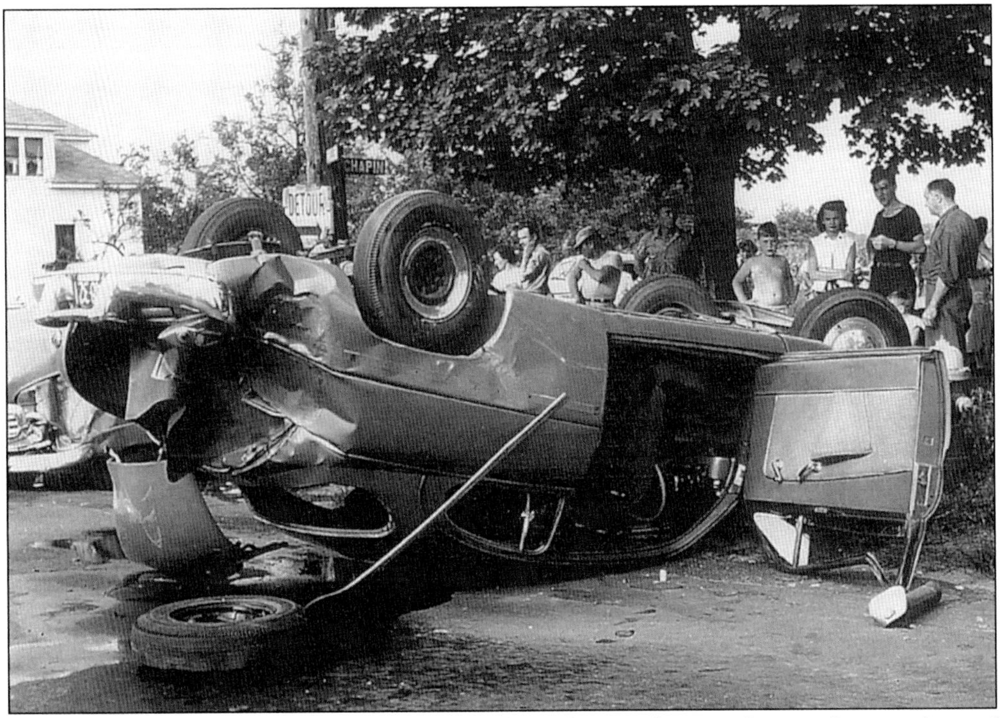

TWO CAR ACCIDENT, AUGUST 14, 1951. For all the damage that was done to this car, the roof seemed not to have budged.

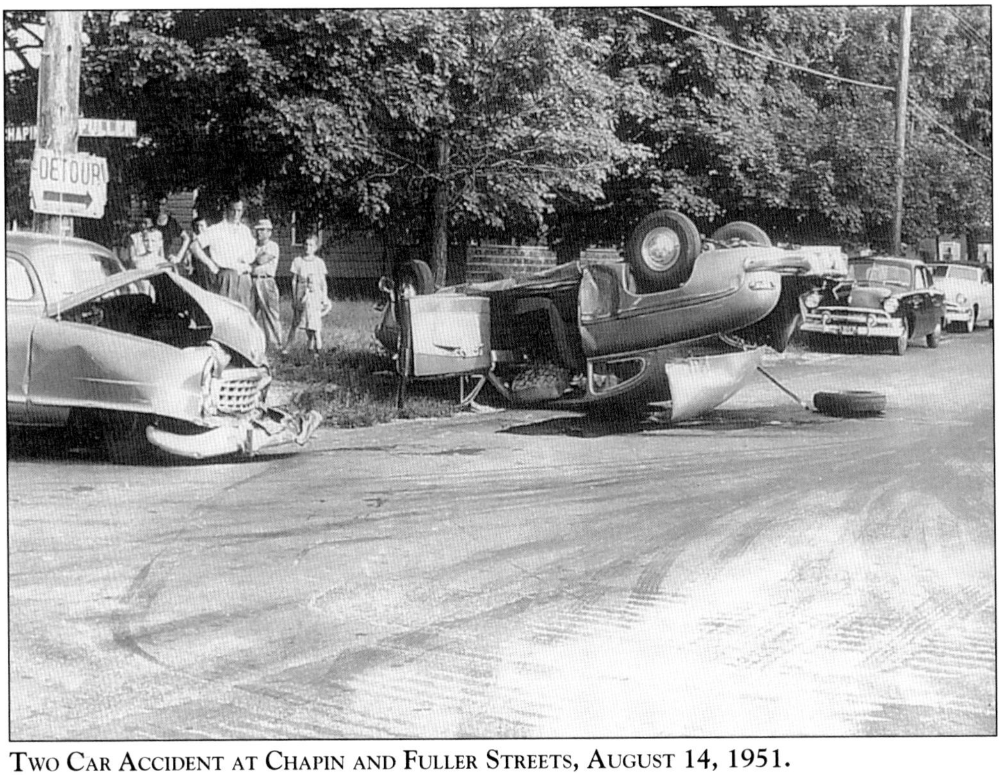

TWO CAR ACCIDENT AT CHAPIN AND FULLER STREETS, AUGUST 14, 1951.

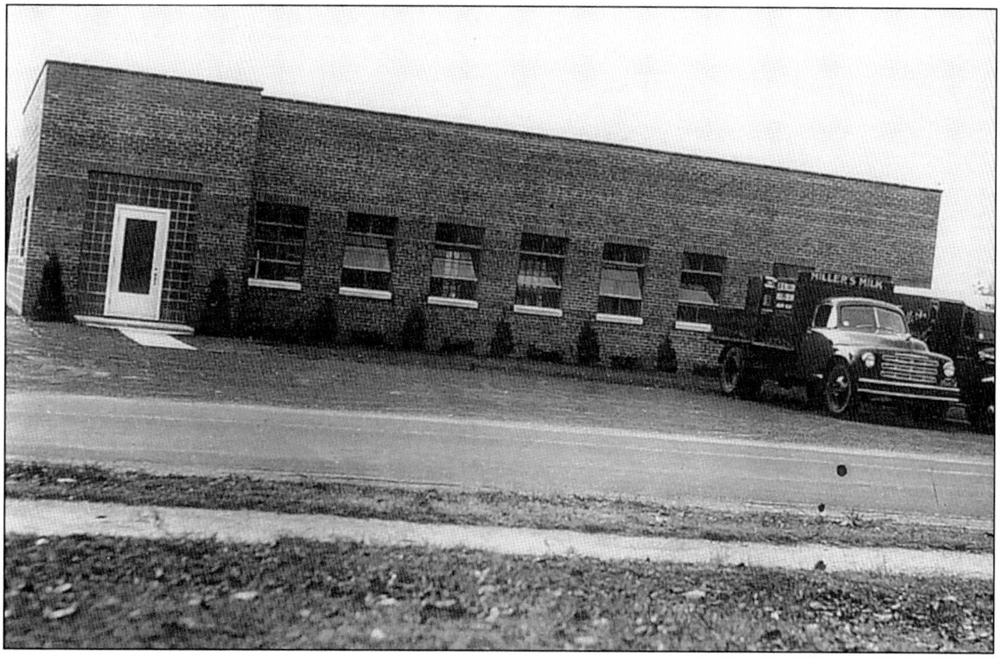

MILLER'S DAIRY, CENTER STREET, C. 1950.

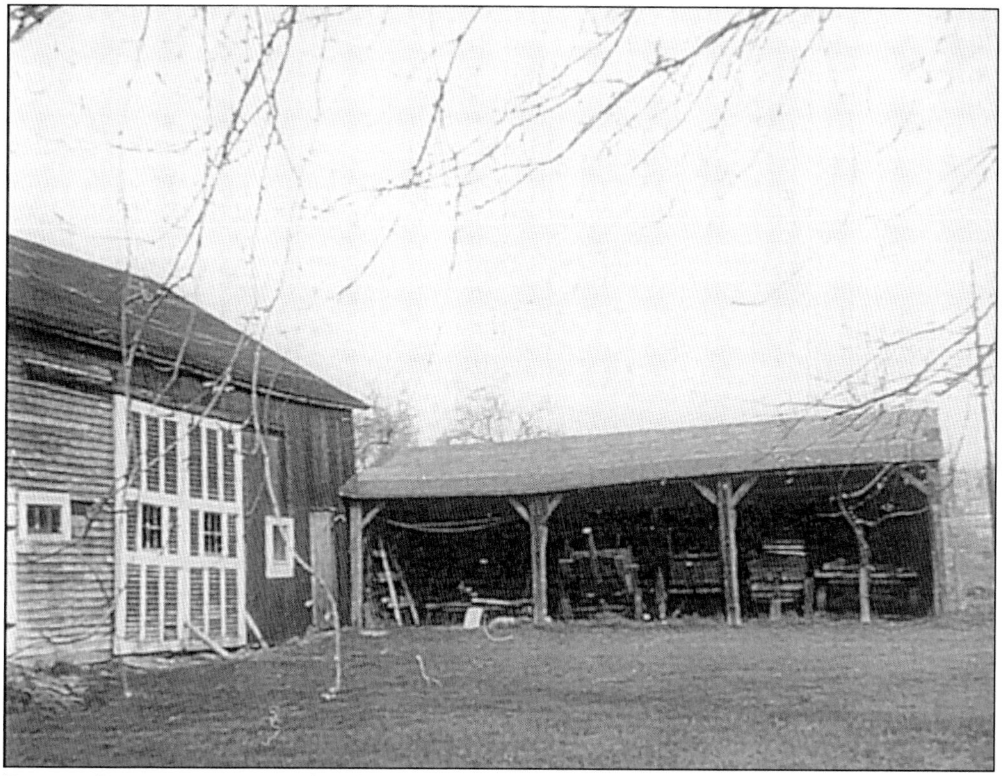

RHODES BARN, C. 1967. Ned and Girlie Rhodes's barn and carriage shed at 529 Fuller Street was torn down shortly after this picture was taken. Several old wagons are visible inside the shed. (Photo courtesy Ruth Gilman.)

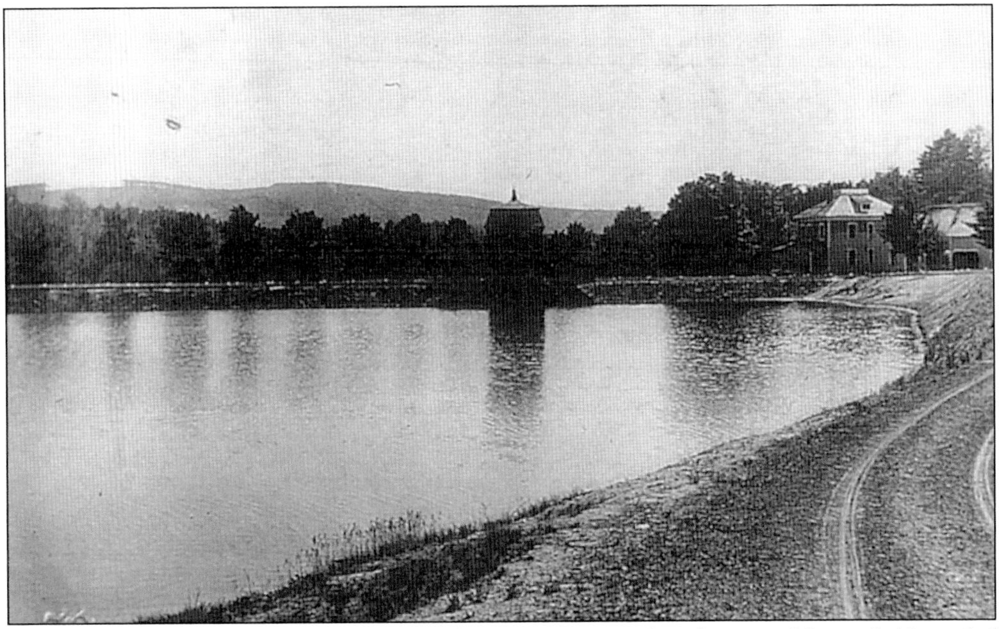

SPRINGFIELD RESERVOIR, c. 1920. When it became apparent that the city of Springfield needed a reservoir to serve its growing metropolis, land was taken from Ludlow, much to the dismay and shock of townspeople. Granted by the Commonwealth of Massachusetts legislature, construction began in 1873 in a northeast section of town called Cherry Valley. Work was completed in 1875. Its capacity is 2 billion gallons, and it has 7 miles of shoreline. Until December 1909, the reservoir provided the only water storage for the entire Springfield water system.

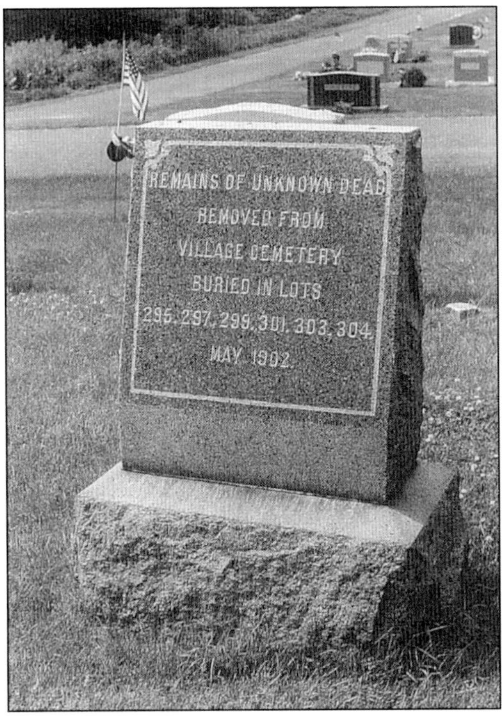

TOMBSTONE OF THE UNKNOWN DEAD. This stone marks the remains of the unknown bodies that were moved from the Village Cemetery to Island Pond Cemetery in May 1902.

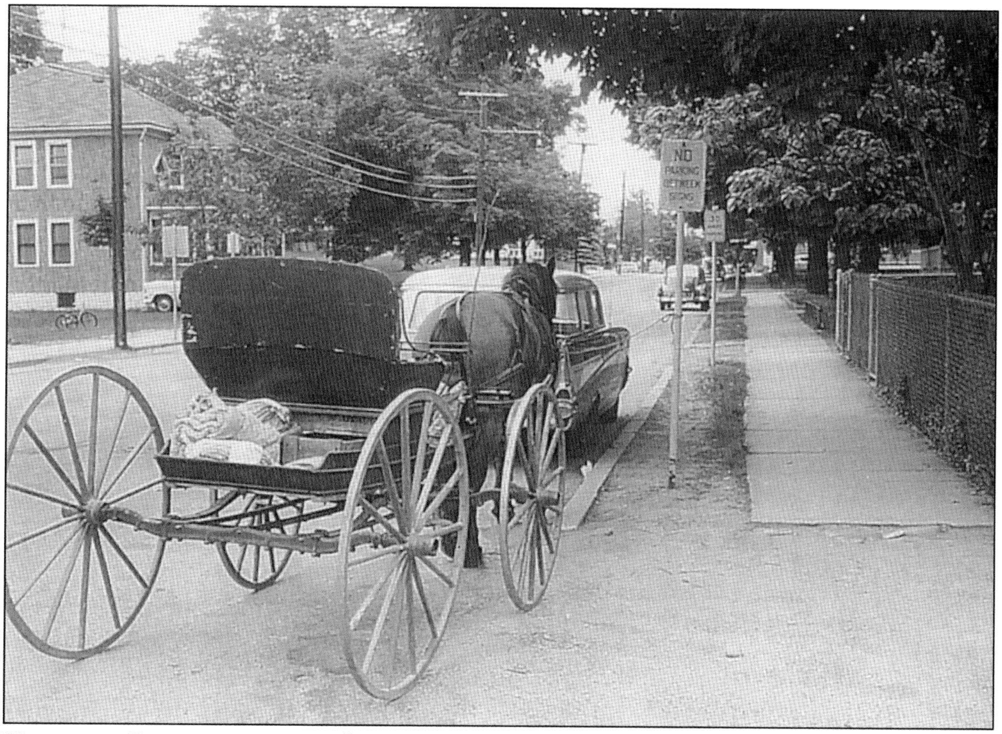

Horse and Buggy, c. 1950s. Those were the days when horses and cars could almost co-exist harmoniously.

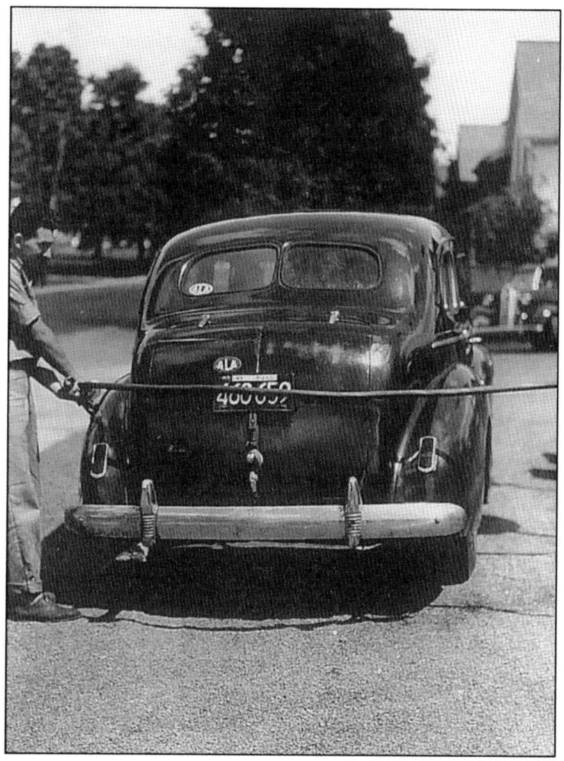

Gassing up on East Street. This photograph was possibly taken at Mario's, c. 1950.

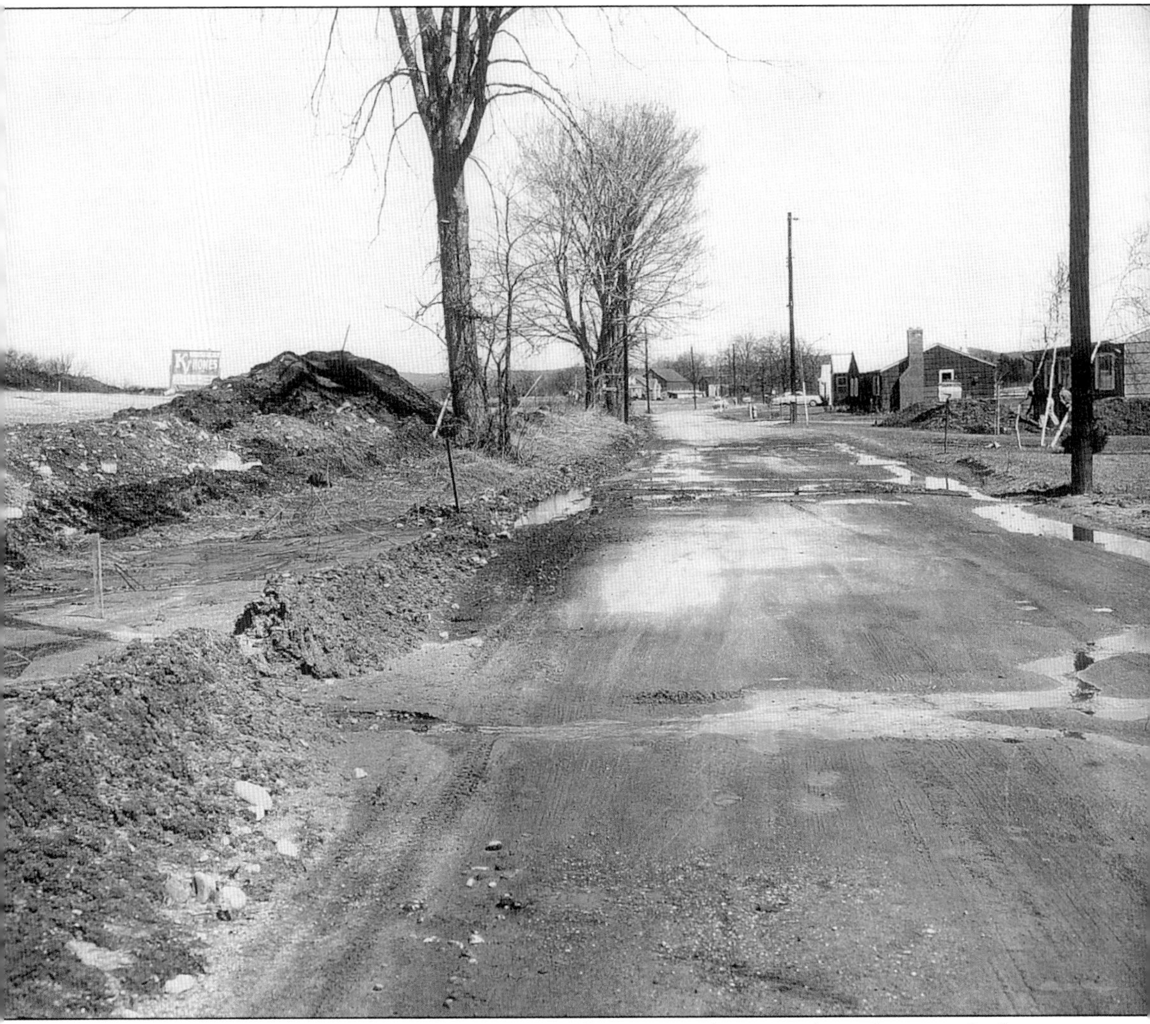

KENDALL STREET, 1950S. Looking towards Fuller Street, this view shows how much the non-paved Kendall Street closely resembles the Kendall Street of today. One stark difference is the absence of houses to the left. Construction would soon begin.

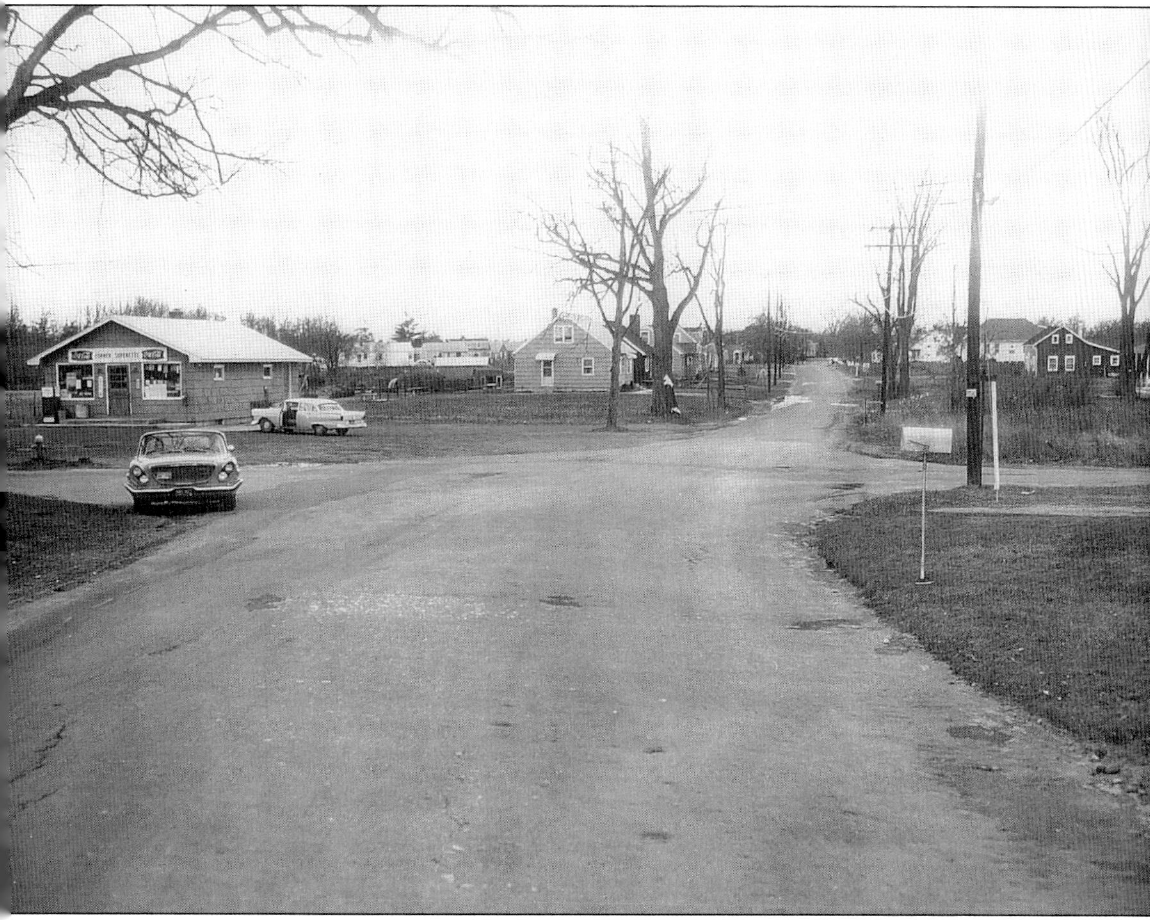

HOLYOKE AND WEST STREETS, 1950S. This is an eye-opening look at what has become of Ludlow. This quiet, country intersection is now a bustling snarl of traffic, lights, and noise, especially at commuter time. The Corner Superette (upper left) was, in more recent years, a Jane Alden convenience store.

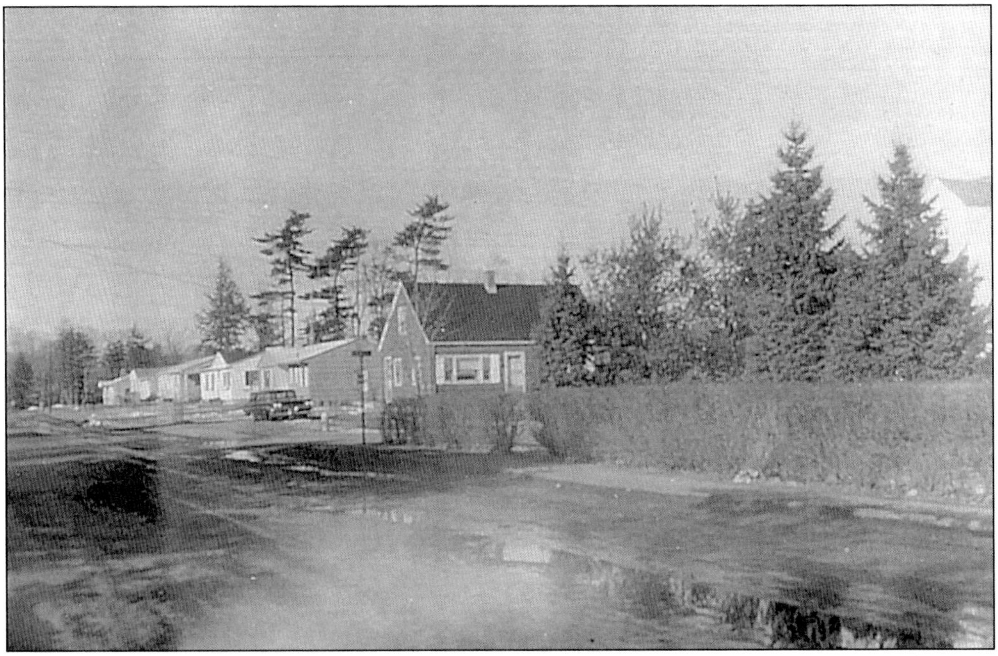

Haswell Circle at Holyoke Street, c. 1950. The baby boom years following World War II saw the town's population double; housing construction nearly tripled. The number of houses in 1947 reached 1,507, and in 1968 had increased to 4,265. Haswell Circle was one of many new developments.

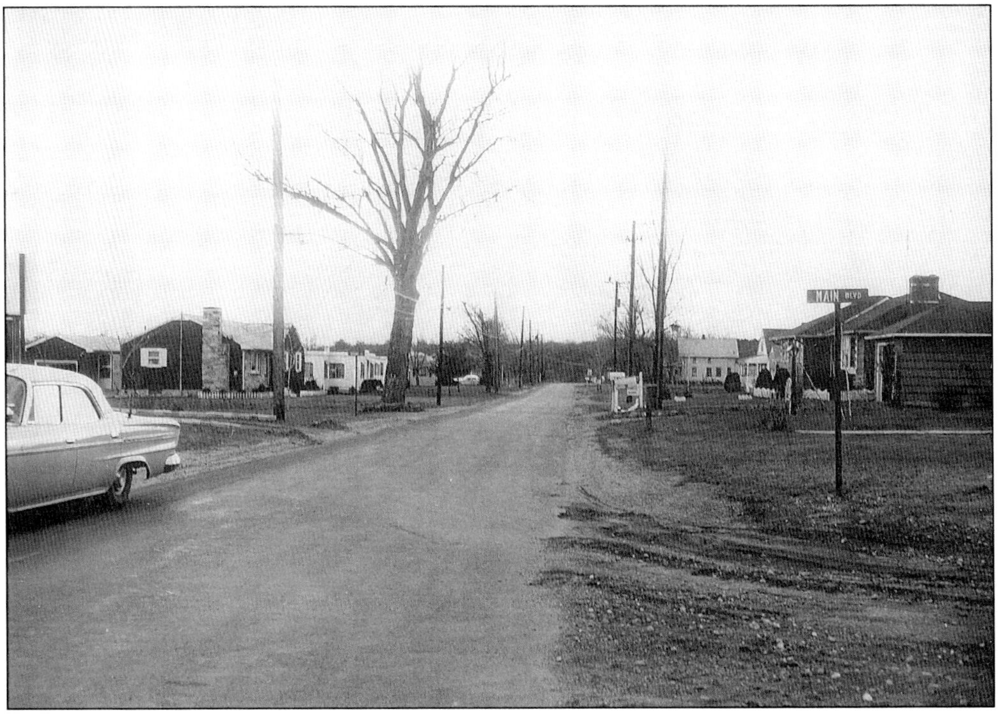

West Street at Main Boulevard, Looking towards Cady Street, 1950s. The once-dirt country roads are now ribbons of asphalt.

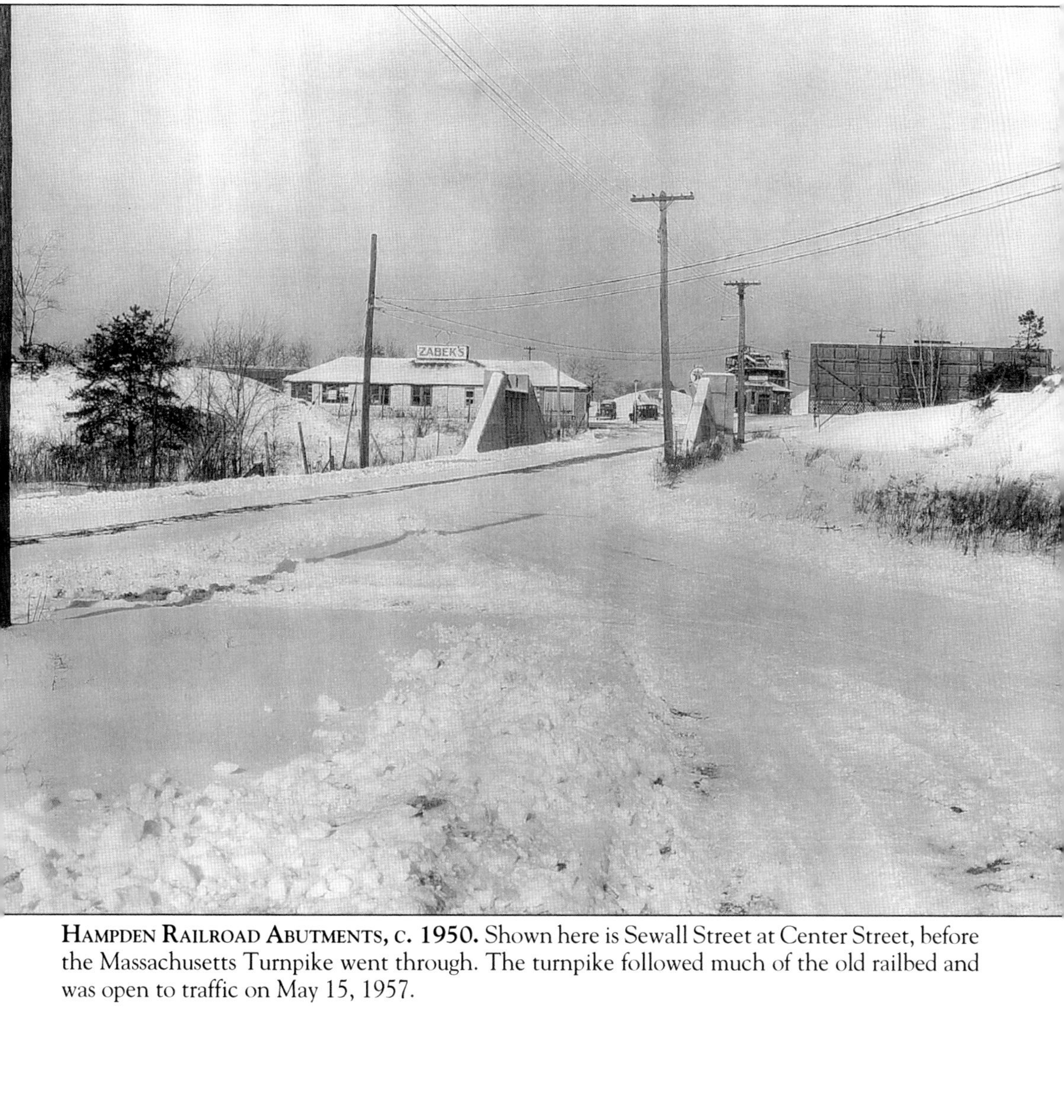

HAMPDEN RAILROAD ABUTMENTS, C. 1950. Shown here is Sewall Street at Center Street, before the Massachusetts Turnpike went through. The turnpike followed much of the old railbed and was open to traffic on May 15, 1957.

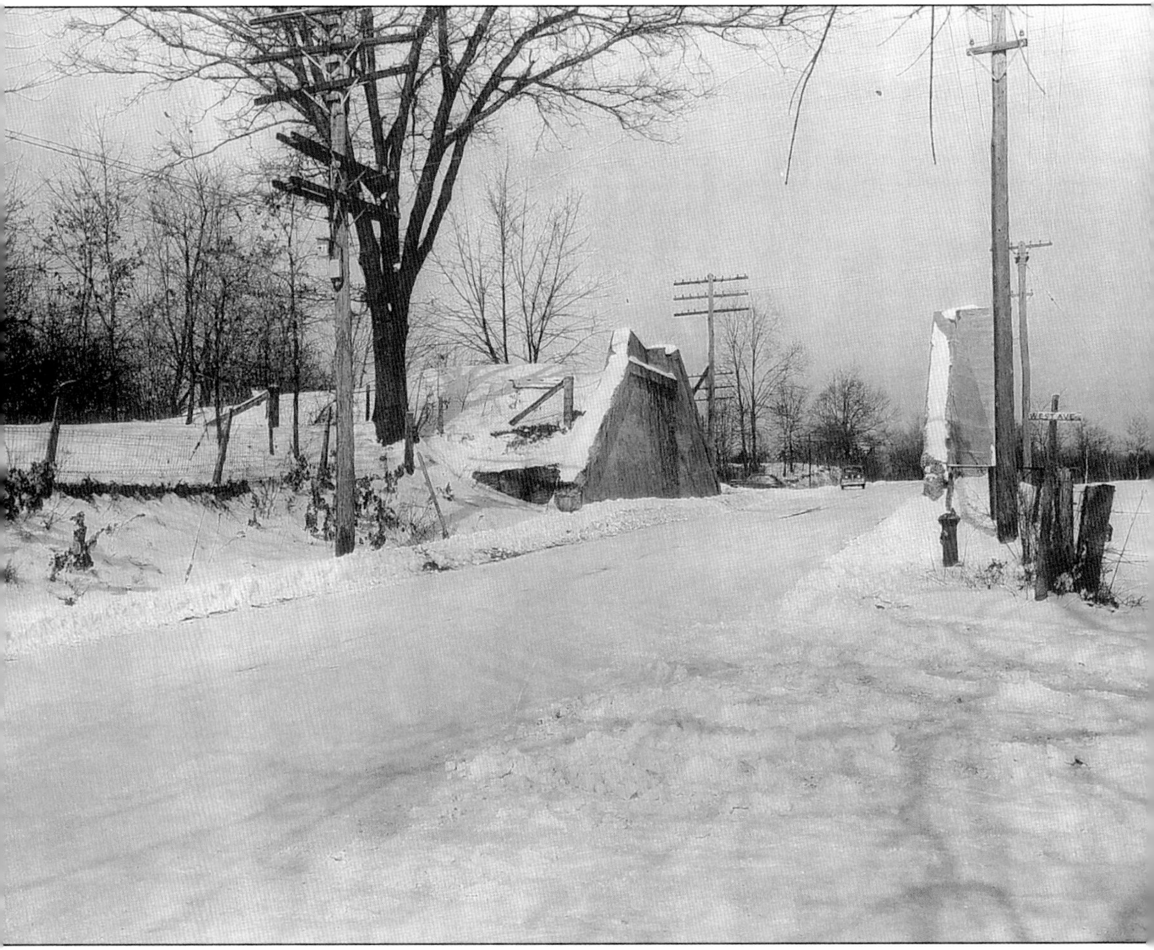

HAMPDEN RAILROAD ABUTMENTS AT WEST STREET AND WEST AVENUE, C. 1950.

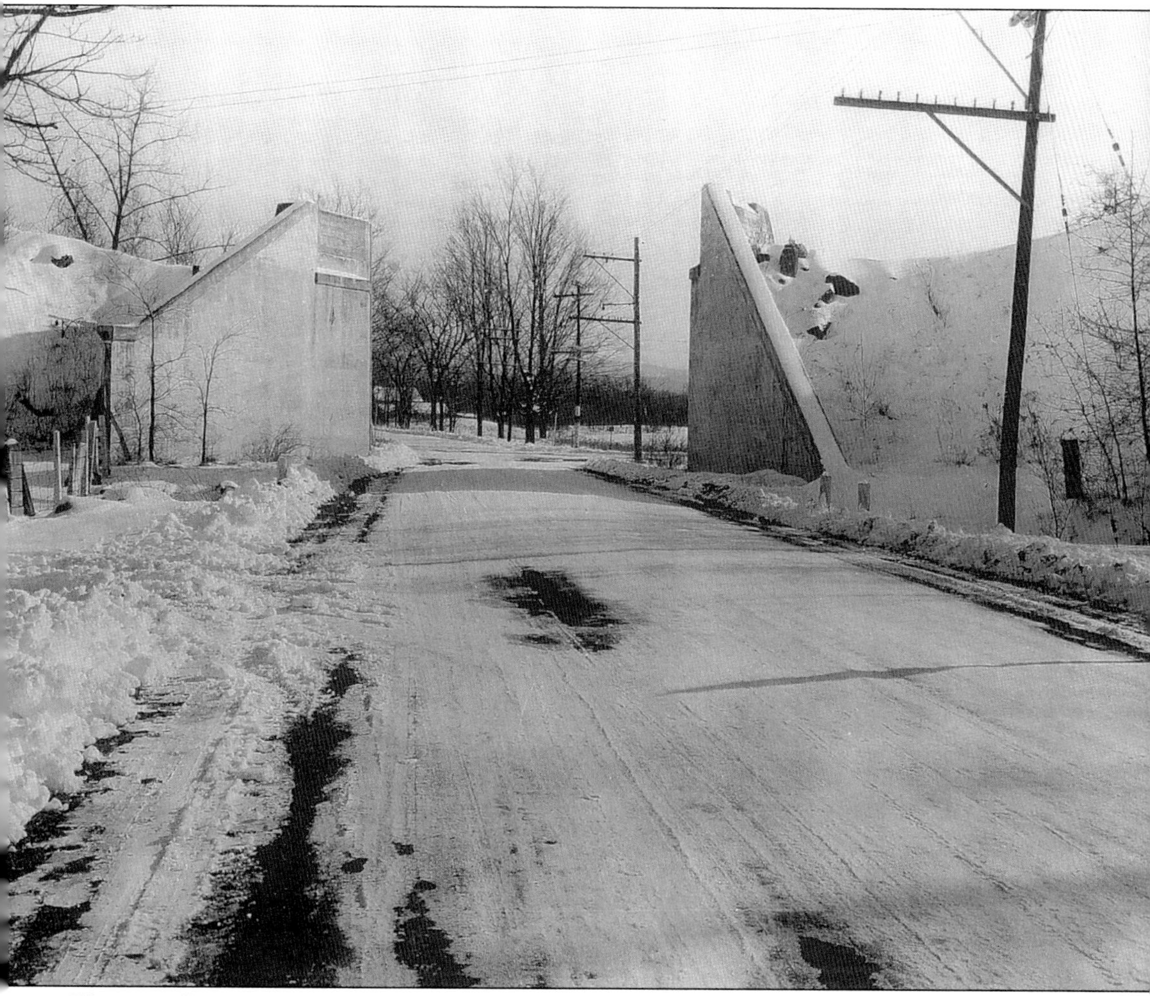

HAMPDEN RAILROAD ABUTMENTS, C. 1950. This is a view of Miller Street, looking north.

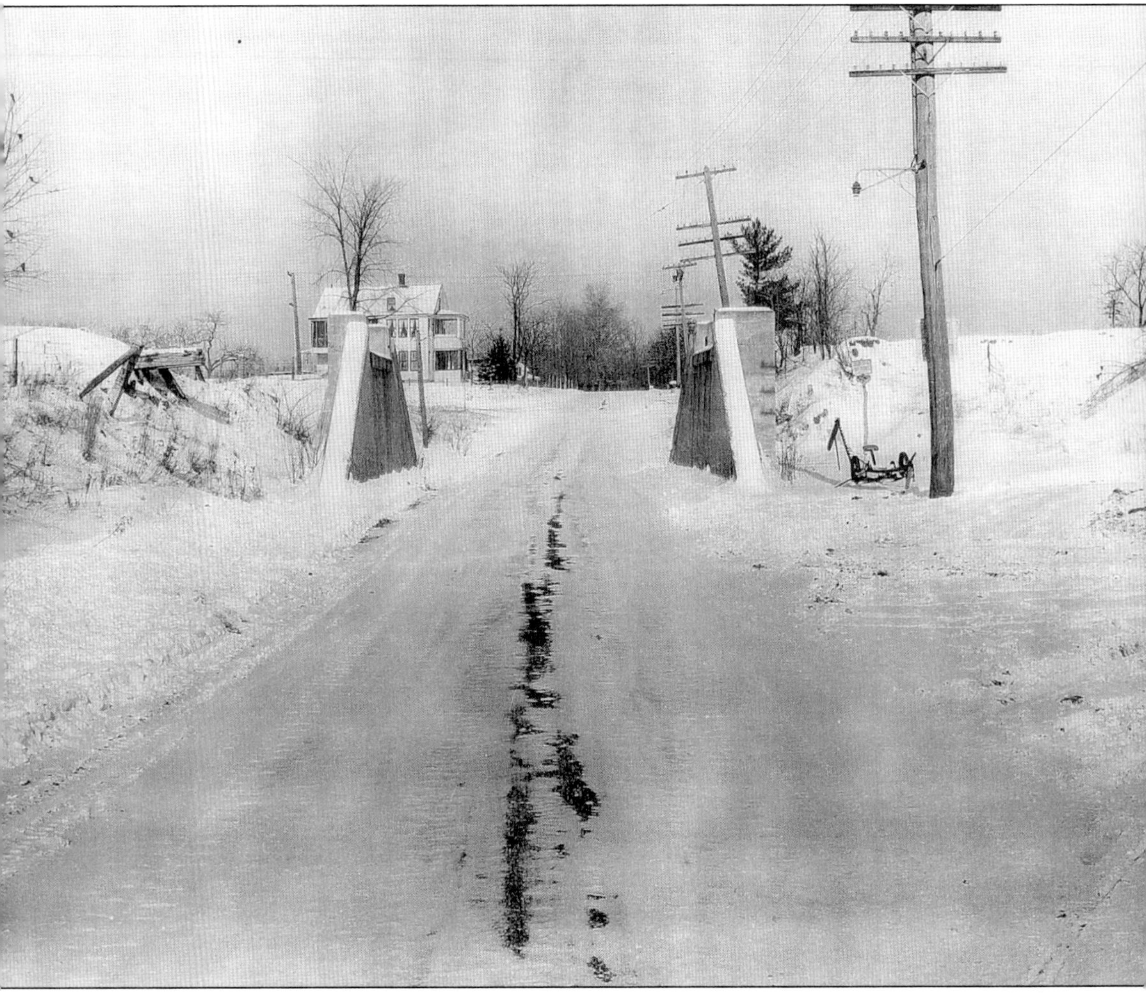

HAMPDEN RAILROAD ABUTMENTS, C. 1950. Shown here is a view of Fuller Street, looking north.

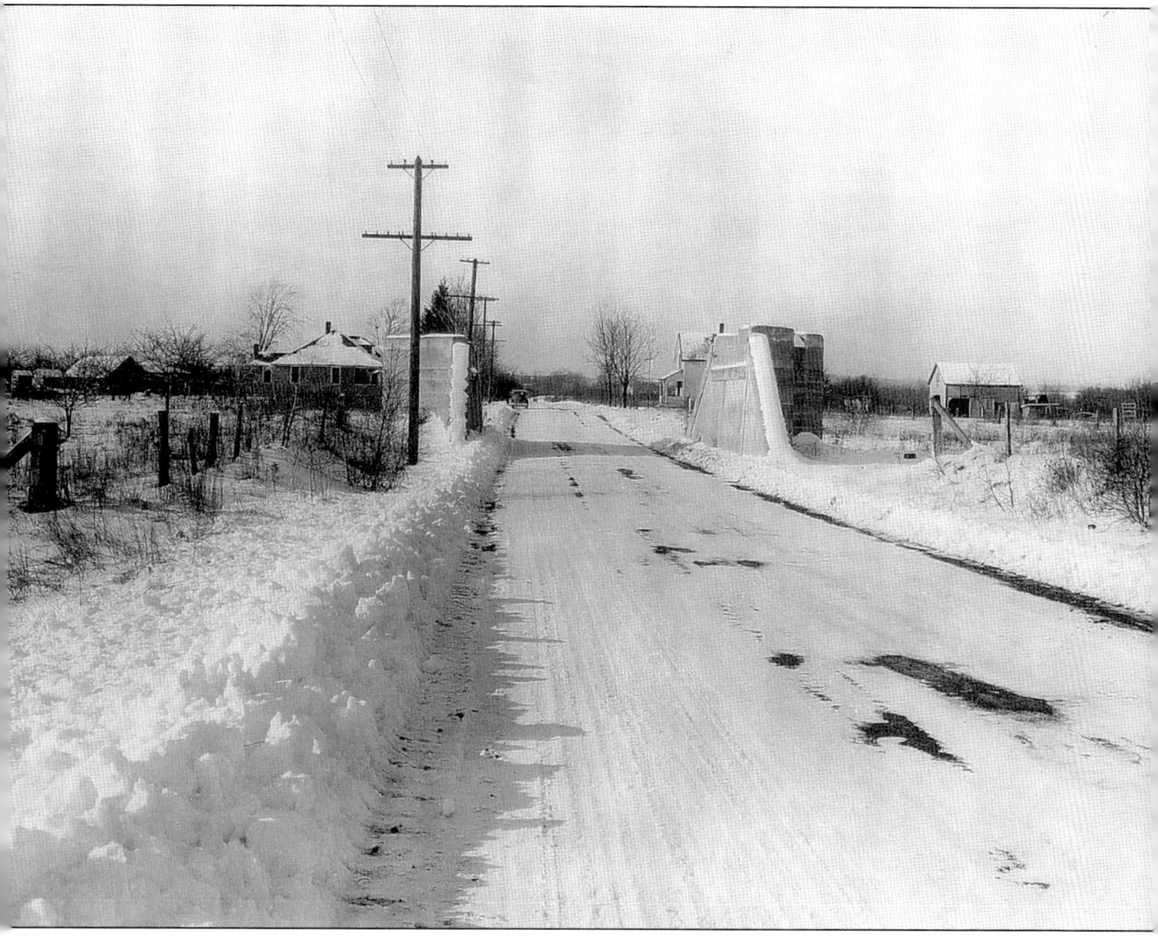

HAMPDEN RAILROAD ABUTMENTS, C. 1950. This is a view of Chapin Street, looking northwest.

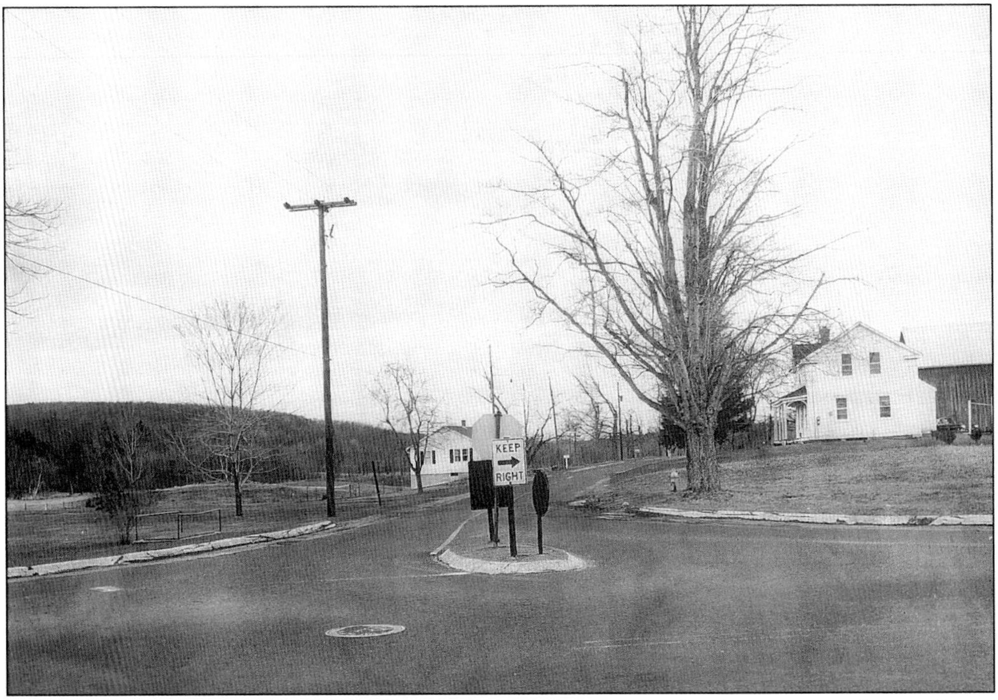

JUNCTION OF MILLER, LYON, AND CENTER STREETS, C. 1950. Looking across Center Street toward Miller Street, much of this remains the same (with the omission of the island).

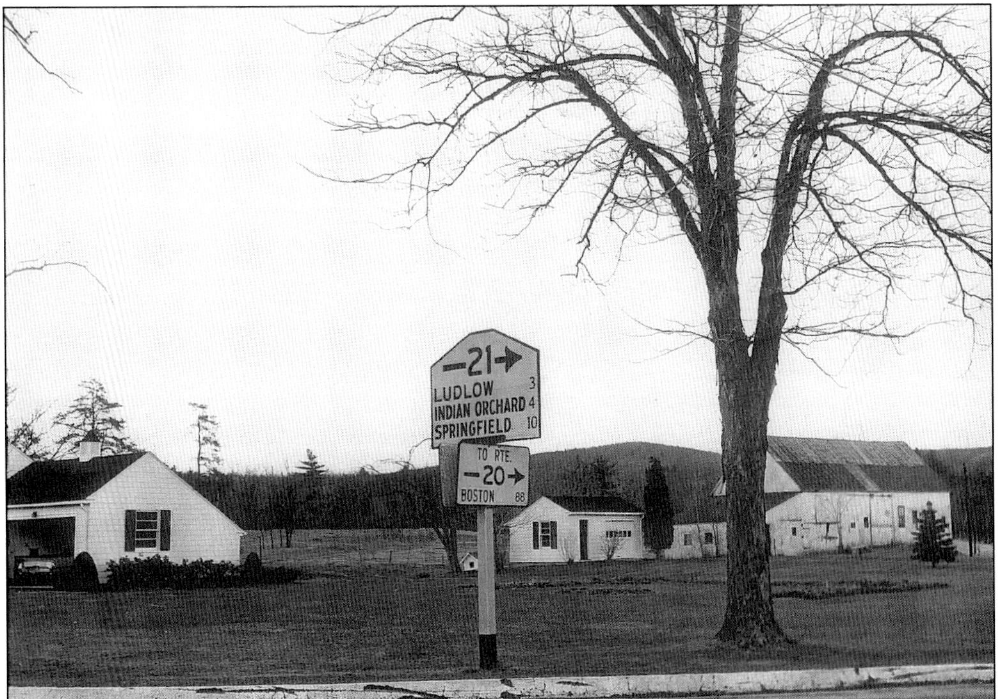

MILLER AND CENTER STREETS, C. 1950S. The route signs in this view show that Ludlow (Village) is 3 miles away.

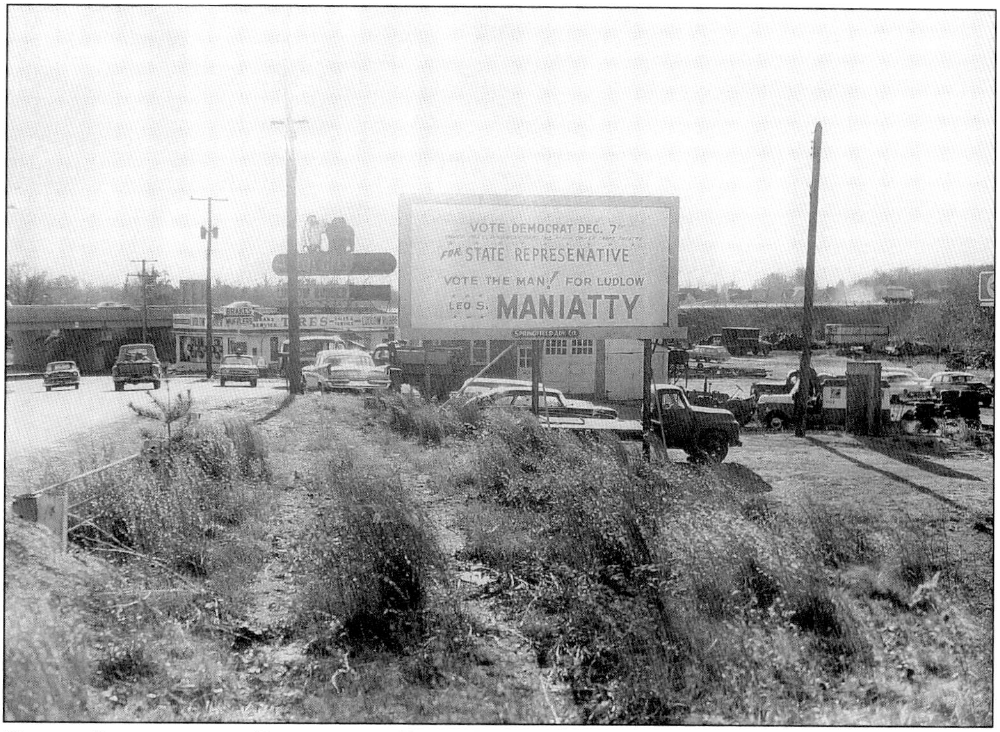

CENTER STREET AT THE PRESENT-DAY BIG Y PLAZA, LATE 1950S. The Massachusetts Turnpike is already in use; Ludlow Rubber is shown where Burger King is today.

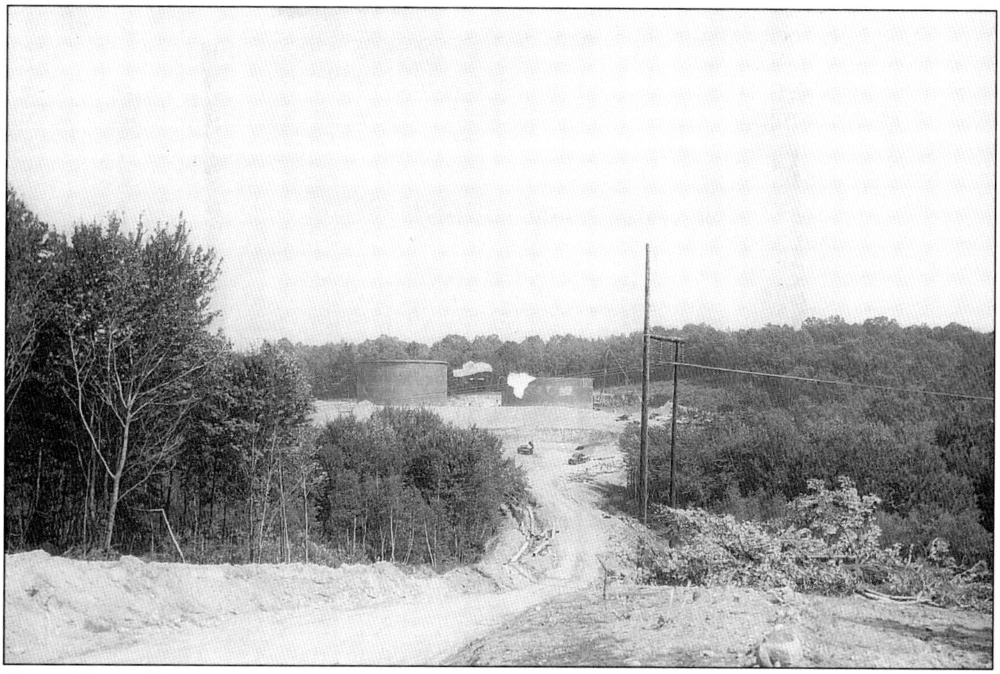

TANK FARM ROAD. Construction of a transmission line and two large storage tanks was completed in the 1950s. The jet fuel tanks, which service Westover Air Reserve Base, were an investment of thousands of dollars at the time .

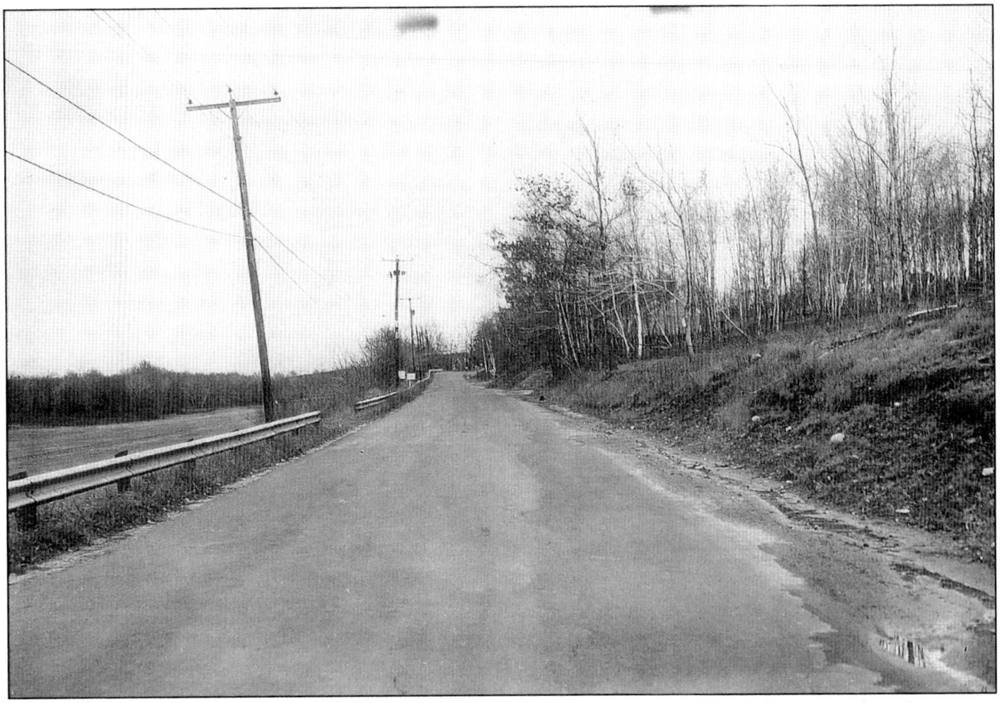

WEST STREET, LOOKING NORTH, C. 1950S. The open fields on the left are, today, home to businesses, construction companies, and, beyond the trees, an industrial park.

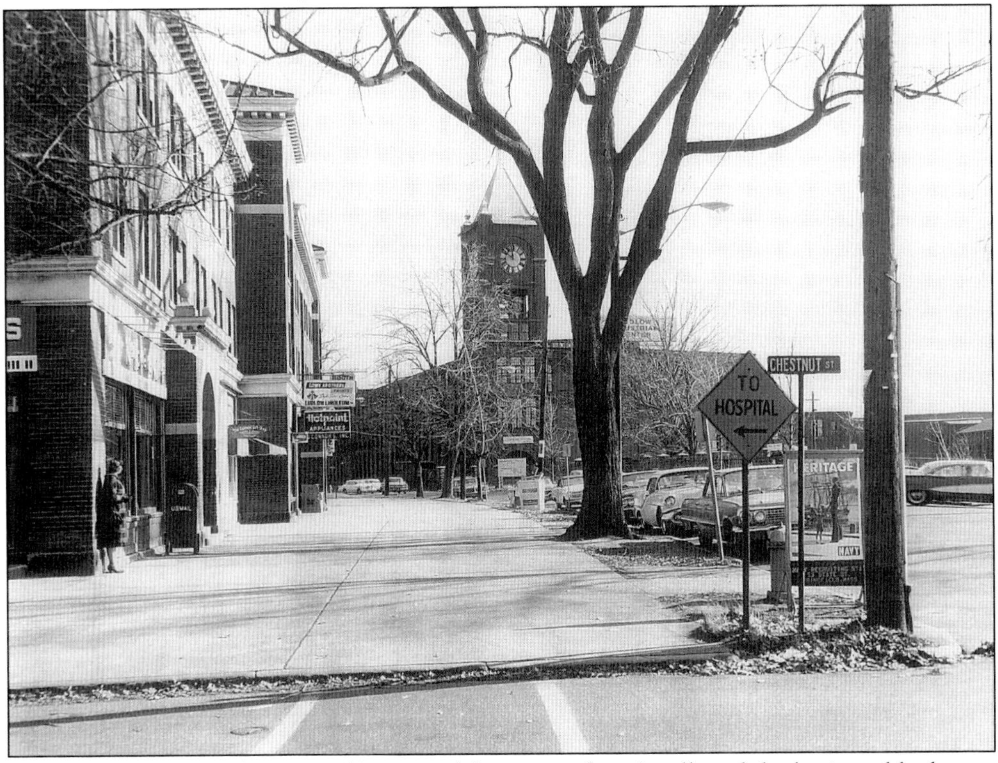

THE CLOCK TOWER. This is a 1950s view of the tower, the #8 mill, and the business block.

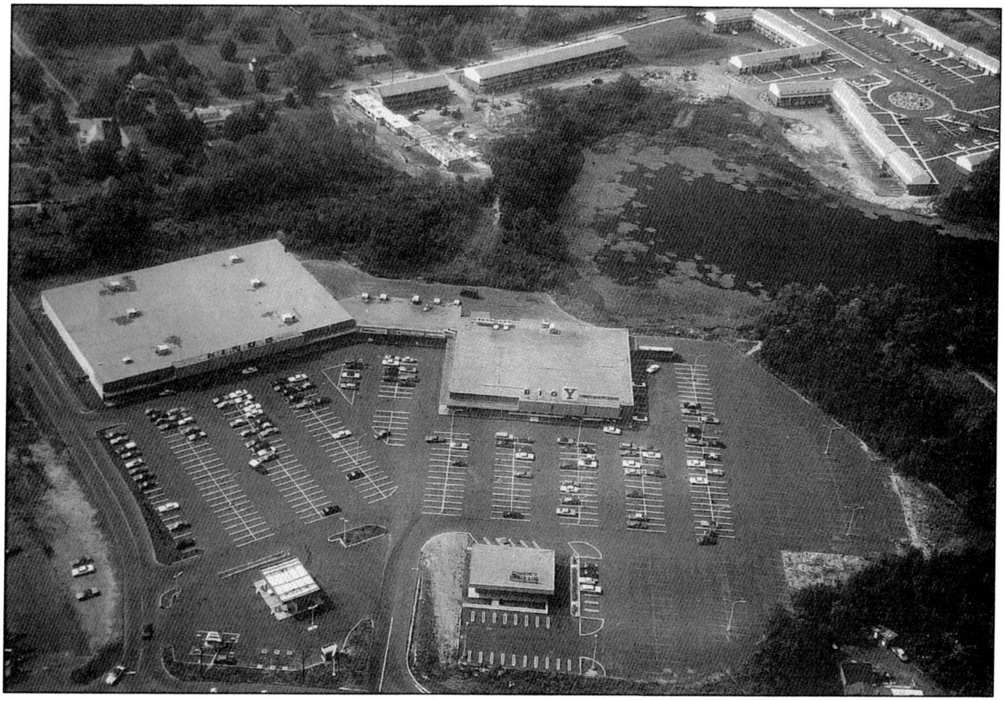

Aerial View, c. 1960s. Shown here is the Big Y shopping plaza with Kings Department Store, Big Y Supermarket, Community Savings Bank, Fill 'Em Fast, and Blisswood Village apartments in the upper right corner. Princess Parlor, located in this plaza, was a favorite school hangout for several years. Note that there is no traffic light at the intersection of Cherry and Center Streets.

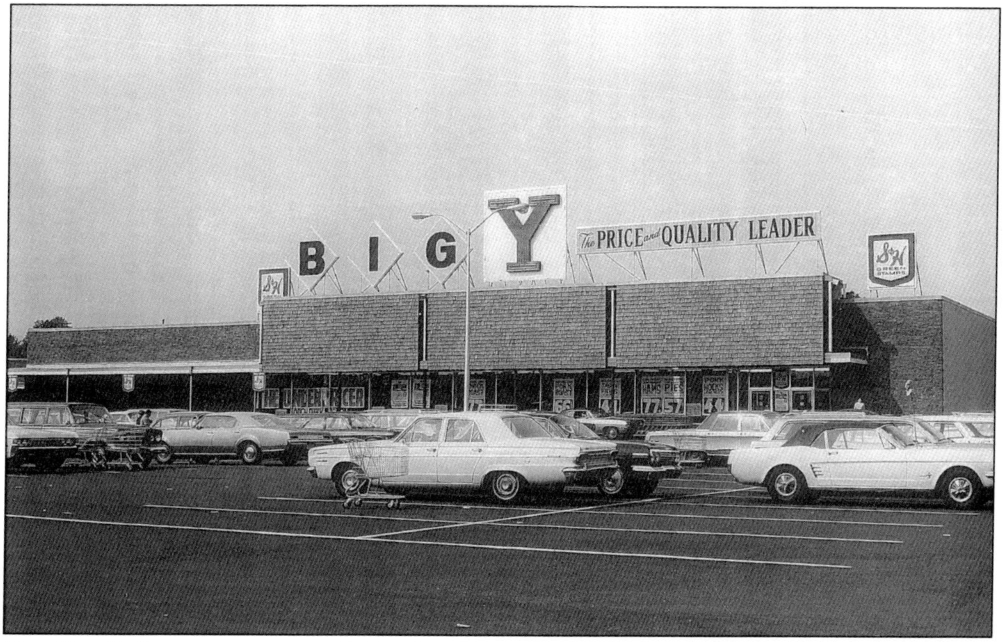

The Big Y Supermarket, c. 1960s. In this view of Ludlow's only grocery store (then and now), one can not help notice the S&H green stamps and prices of the day: pies 57¢; pork roast 66¢ per pound; and chuck roast 77¢ per pound.

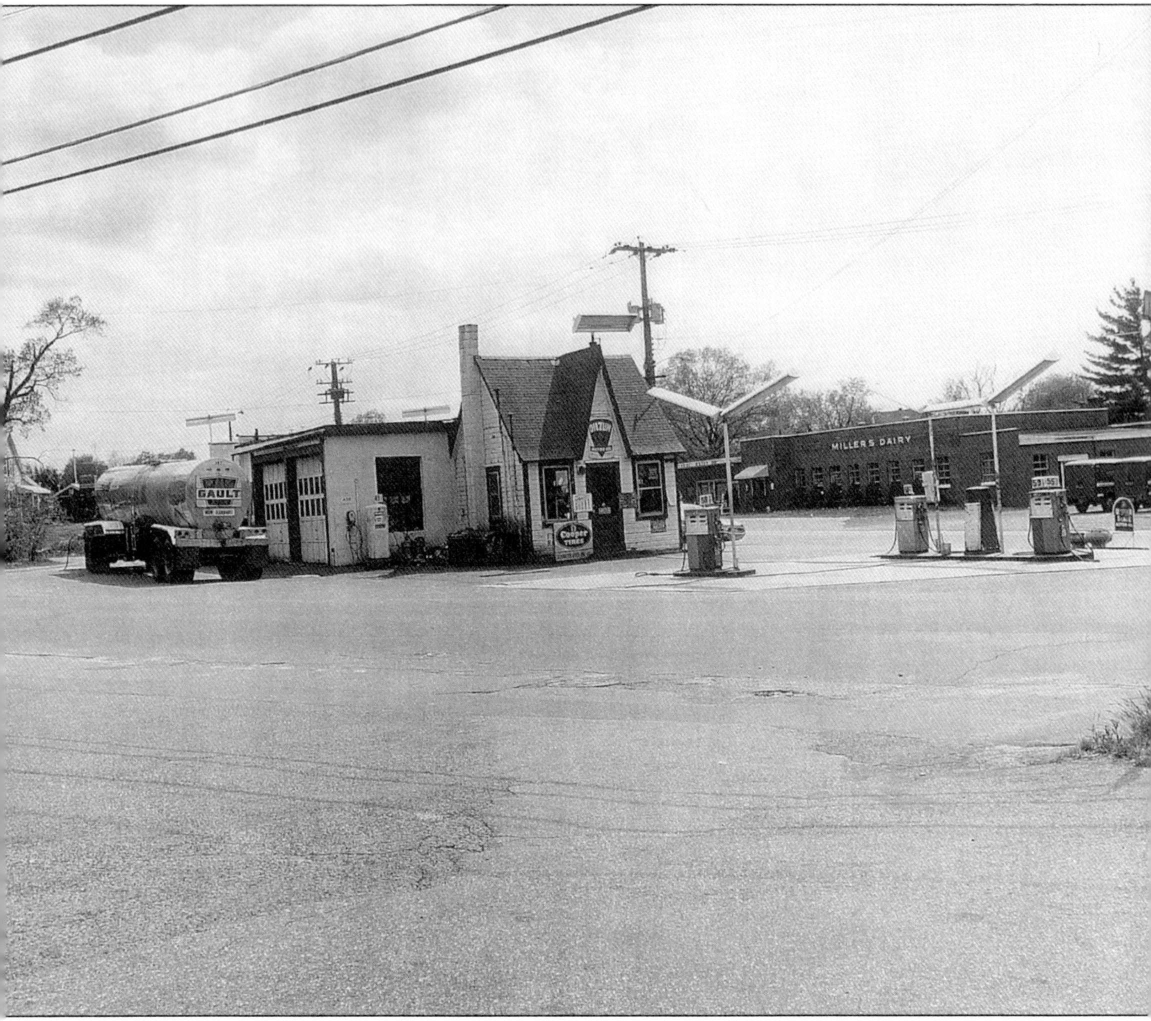

Langevin's Gas Station, c. 1960s. Miller's Dairy is in the background, on Center Street. Both businesses are now defunct.